March 1977

PSYCHOANALYTIC EDUCATION
AND RESEARCH

PSYCHOANALYTIC EDUCATION AND RESEARCH

The Current Situation and Future Possibilities

STANLEY GOODMAN, M.D., Editor

INTERNATIONAL UNIVERSITIES PRESS, INC.
New York

Library of Congress Cataloging in Publication Data

Main entry under title:

Psychoanalytic education and research.

Summary of proceedings of the Conference on Psychoanalytic Education and Research, organized by the American Psychoanalytic Association and held in Hot Springs, Va., from Sept. 30 to Oct. 4, 1974.
        Bibliography: p.
        Includes index.
        1. Psychoanalysis—Study and teaching—Congresses. 2. Psychiatric research—Congresses. I. Goodman, Stanley. II. Conference on Psychoanalytic Education and Research, Hot Springs, Va., 1974.

RC502.P74   616.8'917'0711   76-44638
ISBN 0-8236-4410-3

Manufactured in the United States of America

CONTENTS

Foreword

At the midwinter meeting of the American Psycho-
analytic Association in December, 1970, Dr. Bernard
Bandler, a former Association president who had recently
assumed the position of Director of the Psychiatric
Training Branch of NIMH, suggested to Dr. Albert
Solnit, President of the Association, and Dr. Francis
McLaughlin, Chairman of the Board on Professional
Standards, that NIMH might be interested in funding a
Conference on Psychoanalytic Education and Research
updating the survey and report made to the Association
over a decade earlier by Bertram Lewin and Helen Ross
(1960). After careful consideration, including consultation with the Coordinating and Executive Committees,
it was decided that the Association should sponsor such a
conference. Drs. Solnit and McLaughlin appointed a
Planning Committee for the conference, a joint committee of both Board and Council, consisting of Drs.
Kenneth T. Calder, Herbert S. Gaskill, Francis
McLaughlin, Albert J. Solnit, and Robert S. Wallerstein.
Drs. Wallerstein and Gaskill were designated co-chairmen of the committee, which was subsequently enlarged
by the addition of Drs. Edward D. Joseph, Burness E.
Moore, George H. Pollock, and Edward M. Weinshel.

Drs. Solnit and McLaughlin charged the new committee with organizing a conference to review the current status of psychoanalytic education and research and develop a systematic critique and recommendations for change. They also wished to gain a perspective on the future of psychoanalysis in the light of pressing societal concerns and the significant changes occurring in all aspects of education, including medical and psychiatric education.

During the next eighteen months the Planning Committee members met many times and were in constant communication as they gradually refined the objectives of the conference, evolved its organizational plan, invited the participants, and submitted a series of grant proposals to underwrite the conference financially.

Our society is in a period of rapid transition producing major social and cultural changes. Fundamental questions are being raised about cherished traditions and assumptions, with an emphasis on new approaches and solutions. If psychoanalysis wishes to participate in this evolutionary process in a planned and knowledgeable way, it seems wise to rescrutinize our objectives and attempt to make reasoned choices about future directions. A major challenge confronting society is the need to improve significantly the delivery of health care, particularly for the socially and economically disadvantaged. Psychoanalysis, as one of the treatment modalities in the spectrum of current therapeutic interventions, must consider its proper contribution to possible social solutions in this area.

Many of the issues involved in psychoanalytic education noted by Lewin and Ross still confront psychoanalytic education today. The Association recognized this in the founding of the Committee on Psychoanalytic Education of the Board on Professional Standards (COPE), which has in turn created a number of research and study groups to clarify a variety of unresolved questions in psychoanalytic education. Recent panel reports by past and present members of COPE have summarized the work of COPE and have outlined the areas requiring further investigation (Calder, 1972; Fleming, 1972; Arlow, 1972; Pollock, 1972; Wallerstein, 1972). Over the years the work of COPE has been an instrument for change in our educational enterprise.

With all of this, psychoanalytic education has achieved considerable sophistication in training for therapeutic competence. However, the issues more specifically relevant to psychoanalytic scholarship and research were not dealt with systematically in the Lewin and Ross report and clearly deserved careful consideration. It was hoped that the conference would consider not only how to work toward the resolution of these educational and research issues, but equally how to broaden our horizon in order to be more effective in shaping the future of psychoanalysis.

With all these considerations in mind, the Planning Committee decided that the conference should address at least three general areas: (1) philosophy, objectives, and practices of psychoanalytic education; (2) the relation of psychoanalysis to social issues as well as its interface with other behavioral sciences; and (3) psychoanalysis as a science, in particular psychoanalytic research. Later these general objectives were subdivided and assigned to nine preparatory commissions: I. The Tripartite System of Psychoanalytic Education, II. The Ideal Institute, III. Age and the Psychoanalytic Career, IV. Relationship of

Psychoanalysis to Universities, V. Relationship of Psychoanalysis to Current Changes in Medical and Psychiatric Education, VI. Psychoanalytic Education and the Allied Disciplines, VII. Psychoanalytic Research, VIII. Relationship of Psychoanalysis to Social and Community Issues, IX. Child Analysis.

Finally, a special subcommittee was appointed to update the survey data. Although the Planning Committee had attempted to explicate the relevant issues and dimensions of survey data to be elicited, the preparatory commissions were invited to further delineate their objectives and to request additional relevant data. From the beginning it was clear that the charges to the individual commissions often included areas of overlap between two or more commissions; however, it was thought that this would only add to the depth and richness of the conference discussion.

In selecting the conference participants an attempt was made to include not only the Association leadership, but also both older and younger individuals from every psychoanalytic society and institute, including several candidates, and a few selected individuals representing areas of expertise outside of psychoanalysis. The final list of 168 participants involved slightly more than ten per cent of the Association's total membership. In addition to a chairperson and recorder, each of the nine preparatory commissions had fifteen members.

Outside funding was difficult to obtain despite initial encouragement from NIMH. In part, this was an expression of governmental reassessment of national priorities and increased financial constraints upon NIMH grants at the time of our application. Fortunately, the enthusiastic endorsement of our Association, three grants from the Grant Foundation, and contributions from Dr. Bettina Warburg and an anonymous donor enabled us to defray all the administrative and planning costs of the conference. The major brunt of the financial burden, however, was borne by the individual participants. No reimbursement for expenses was available for participation in either the conference itself or the several prior meetings of each preparatory commission. This very large voluntary contribution to the conference by the many participants is one of which our Association may feel proud indeed.

The conference timetable was divided into four stages: the planning phase (January 1, 1971 to June 30, 1972); preparatory phase (July 1, 1972 to March 31, 1974); conference phase (April 1, 1974 to October 30, 1974); and report phase (November 1, 1974 to December 31, 1975). The activities of the Planning Committee during the planning phase have already been discussed. The preparatory phase involved: (1) the invitation of participants to membership on the commissions, (2) the organization of the commissions by the chairpersons, (3) the data-gathering through the survey, and (4) the organization of two major meetings of all the preparatory commissions.

Initially, commission subcommittees were assigned specific aspects of each commission's charge on which to prepare working papers for the first meeting of each commission. Each commission met in December, 1972 for one or two days to discuss the preliminary working paper and to consider its assigned charge in greater depth. These commission meetings were high points in the conference's development and provided challenging interchanges among participants. The Planning Committee members rotated among the commissions, which were all meeting simultaneously, and thus provided liaison between them. During the next year the commissions developed additional working papers through interim meetings of their subcommittees or by individual assignment. Each chairperson and recorder subsequently wrote an over-all position paper for their commission which was subjected to critical discussion by the commission members at their second full-day meeting in December, 1973. Following this meeting the position paper of each commission was rewritten and circulated among its members for further review and comment. The final versions, written by the commission chairpersons and recorders, were circulated in May, 1974 to every participant of the forthcoming conference, as well as to all the societies and institutes. In this brief summary it is impossible to convey the dedication and hard work of each participant in producing these thoughtful explorations of the substantive topics of the conference. The questionnaire survey was well conceptualized by the subcommittee assigned to this task and elicited significant current data of special relevance to our educational activities.

The conference itself took place from September 30 to October 4, 1974 at The Homestead in Hot Springs, Virginia — an ideal setting for sustained and unhurried intellectual and social interchange. The conference format involved a series of plenary sessions followed by group discussions on the report of each commission. Each plenary session was devoted to the report of one commission's position paper and was opened with a formal discussion by a person who had not been a member of that particular commission. The discussants thus took a fresh look at the work of each commission and often provided additional responses to a particular area of inquiry. The chairpersons and reporters of the different commissions then responded to the discussant's presentation, beginning a vigorous dialogue. The conference discussion groups were constituted in such a manner as to cut across the original preparatory commission memberships; each discussion group was composed of one or two participants from each of the original commissions. The discussion groups included recorders who summarized the opinions and attitudes expressed within the group during the week.

The Planning Committee members are deeply grateful to Dr. Stanley Goodman, a conference participant and preparatory commission chairman, for undertaking the editorial task of creating this condensed conference report. His lucid and faithful editing has synthesized the massive amount of material relating to the conference, and in a concluding chapter he has presented his own view of the challenges and tasks ahead.

We believe that the conference has realized the initial goals and expectations of Drs. Solnit and McLaughlin. In a most important sense, however, the objectives of the conference are necessarily only partially achieved to date. This critique of psychoanalytic education and research has identified many of the ambiguities and uncertainties involved in our professional activities; it has also more accurately defined those topics about which we are in agreement. The task ahead obviously requires ongoing collective discussion to allow us to respond effectively to the challenges and opportunities confronting psychoanalysis. It is hoped that this volume will serve in some measure as a catalyst in that essential organizational process of constructive change.

In bringing to a close the formal aspects of the conference, the Planning Committee wishes to express its appreciation to all members of the American Psychoanalytic Association, to the conference participants, in particular the chairpersons and recorders of the preparatory commissions and to the individual contributors and the Grant Foundation for their support of this endeavor. Mrs. Helen Fischer, Administrative Director of the Association, and her staff at the Central Office deserve our special gratitude. Their contribution was essential to the conference's success. They were untiring in their efforts to carry through the many administrative tasks connected with the various meetings, the voluminous correspondence, and the duplicating and distributing of the various preparatory commissions' documents during the past four years.

Herbert S. Gaskill, M.D.
Robert S. Wallerstein, M.D.
Co-Chairmen, COPER Planning Committee

Editor's Introduction

This volume presents the substance of the 1974 Conference on Psychoanalytic Education and Research (COPER) organized by the American Psychoanalytic Association. The conference was attended by a representative group of psychoanalytic teachers, a number of recent graduates and analytic students, all interested in the future development of the science and profession of psychoanalysis.

It is hoped that the reader will be afforded a clear sense of the fundamental issues currently confronting psychoanalysis and a useful awareness of the present views and proposals of the participants. The book is addressed to several audiences: the psychoanalytic educators who did not attend the conference; all psychoanalysts who, although not actively occupied with psychoanalytic education per se, are nevertheless understandably interested in matters that may directly or indirectly affect the development of their profession; students and potential students of analysis whose studies and career choices may be helpfully informed by this report; other behavioral scientists who may be interested in this current systematic self-assessment by psychoanalysis, particularly in what it may portend for future informational exchanges and

1

scientific collaboration; interested members of the general public who may learn both more and less than they wish to know about psychoanalysis from this account, but may at least receive some assistance in deciding for themselves whether it is indeed alive and reasonably well.

The conference represents an organizational response to a number of internal and external issues demanding special attention, study, and deliberation not permitted by the usual pressing schedule of local and national educational or administrative meetings. Even though every topic discussed at the conference has long been under serious and repeated scrutiny by various committees of the Association's Board on Professional Standards, a focused effort to clearly identify basic problems, their probable sources, and possible solutions was seen as necessary and potentially extremely valuable.

The last conference of comparable intention and scope was held in December, 1955 to review the problems and prospects of psychoanalytic education in the wake of the extremely rapid growth of training following World War II. That conference produced the Rainbow Report (1956) (so-called for no other reason than that each of the six preparatory commission reports was reproduced on different colored paper). Rereading that report now is an experience at once sobering and encouraging. On the one hand, many of the problems in psychoanalytic education and research today were already recognized quite clearly twenty years ago, but have not yet been resolved satisfactorily; on the other hand, it is reassuring to know that collectively we haven't just now arrived at a sudden belated realization of many long-existing problems, but rather that the lengthy struggle toward adequate solutions may be due, at least in part, to the inherent difficulty and complexity of the problems themselves.

The 1955 conference led to the appointment of Bertram Lewin and Helen Ross to conduct a thorough survey of analytic training, and in 1960 they published the results in *Psychoanalytic Education in the United States*. The Rainbow Conference, the survey, and the book itself all led to intensive review and re-evaluation of educational policies and practices. It is hoped that the more recent conference and the many postconference projects already underway will result in a similar process of continuing stimulation and constructive progress.

Those who actually participated in the 1974 conference were certainly stimulated by the opportunity and the challenge to question, re-assess, and possibly revise basic assumptions and particular views regarding the objectives of psychoanalytic education and research. There was a general readiness for self-criticism and little apparent inclination toward self-congratulation. Although there was good recognition of the reality of many social and economic factors not within our control, the discussions primarily stressed our own responsibilities for problems and the internal obstacles to change — not altogether surprising in a group of psychoanalysts. The sometimes strong, even occasionally excessive criticism expressed in regard to this or that aspect of our work as educators or scientists is thus consistent with our usual professional emphasis on that which impedes healthy functioning and developmental progress rather than on a reassuring inventory of past accomplishments.

The nine preparatory commissions were each explicitly charged with the responsibility of generating extensive conference and postconference discussion; declared positions and recommendations had the purpose of stimulating, not foreclosing, further thoughtful consideration and debate. Happily, the commission reports had precisely the intended effect.

The conference itself produced a range of direct, complex, and subtle effects on the individual conferees. Convictions were sometimes confirmed, occasionally modified; questions were raised about almost everything, and confidently answered in a few instances; solutions were proposed that seemed eminently practical to some and vainly utopian to others. It does not seem unreasonable to suppose that many who attended the conference were constructively unsettled, to the extent that their subsequent consideration of certain issues has surely been affected. Individual papers on various conference issues have already been contributed to the literature and will undoubtedly continue to appear in the future.

By this time there have already been extensive and continuing discussions at the local institute level of the conference topics and their implications. The Association has been actively encouraging such discussion in the 31 Affiliate Societies as well as in the 23 Approved Institutes since our professional and scientific evolution obviously depends so critically on the direction and adequacy of our educational effort. Members of the conference Planning Committee participated in a panel reviewing the conference at the national forum provided by the December, 1974 meeting of the Association (Panel, 1975).

The positive consequences of the conference can also be seen in the ongoing deliberations of the Board on

Professional Standards as it acts to maintain standards through its review of educational policies, procedures, and practices. Various Board standing committees have re-addressed themselves to the study of particular questions within their purview. Thus, the Committee on Psychoanalytic Education (COPE) is continuing its study project on the training analysis. It has already completed a long-term project on supervision, and is considering new study projects on selection and curriculum. The Child Analysis Committee is sponsoring a developmental core curriculum study project to elaborate on the suggestions of the preparatory commision report on child analysis. The ad hoc committee to follow up the conference (Post-COPER) had already been appointed at the time of the conference and has since been occupied in efforts to stimulate and facilitate local and national study and discussion of conference issues. Eventually it will initiate specific recommendations for the Board's consideration. An ad hoc committee of the Board to study prerequisites for training (CPT) was appointed in December, 1974. The committee was created in direct response to the discussion of an institute's proposal to accept a group of nonmedical, but otherwise personally and educationally qualified students for clinical training on an experimental basis; indirectly, however, the committee's charge resulted from the renewed impetus toward exploration of desirable change provided by the conference.

This book attempts to group the preparatory commission position papers and their specifically elicited responses according to whether their primary emphasis is on particular aspects of psychoanalytic educational methods and content, issues related to psychoanalytic research, or the relation of the psychoanalytic educational structure to other educational or social structures and the implications for psychoanalysis as a profession and science. It will soon be clear that this plan is easier to describe than to accomplish in fact. Most of the reports and discussions, whatever their nominal and formal point of departure, soon became involved in following the many threads of considerations and implications, arriving at common themes of ways and means, priorities and objectives, and speculative consequences. Whatever the resulting difficulty in arranging the book's contents in a systematic sequence, the unavoidable overlap and repetition in the reports and their discussion was useful in illuminating the connections between various assumptions and gradually clarifying the rationale for certain conclusions that might otherwise have remained unclear.

The original commission reports, the full comments of each plenary discussant, the recorders' summaries of the conference discussion groups, and the survey are available (at cost) on request to the Association's Central Office. Therefore, in an attempt to produce a readable book of manageable length, the reports themselves and the comments of the plenary discussants are presented in somewhat condensed versions. The accounts of the discussion groups have been rendered into even briefer general summaries, primarily to indicate the nature and variety of responses and attitudes expressed by the participants and the general trends of agreement or disagreement with particular recommendations. No effort was made either at the conference or later to conduct a statistical survey of opinions or bring particular recommendations to a vote. This policy was consistent with the wish to minimize any tendency toward the polarization of discussion or an atmosphere of legislative advocacy, and to maximize the candid mutual exchange of thought and speculation without premature closure.

The central section of the book concludes, as did the conference itself, with individual summations of the conference by two members of the COPER Planning Committee. Both Albert Solnit and Robert Wallerstein had the opportunity to attend all the discussion groups during the course of the conference, and they provided the final plenary session with their immediate individual impressions of the conference's work and speculations on its potential achievement.

A survey of psychoanalytic education in the United States as of 1971 was undertaken to update certain aspects of the 1958 data included in *Psychoanalytic Education in the United States* (Lewin and Ross, 1960). It was distributed to all participants before the conference, and a summary of its findings is included.

In a final chapter, the editor responds to the generous invitation extended to him by the conference Planning Committee and offers a personal contribution to the ongoing postconference discussion of the problems and prospects of psychoanalytic education and research.

The Tripartite System
of Psychoanalytic Education

Joan Fleming, M.D., Chairman
Stanley S. Weiss, M.D., Recorder
Charlotte G. Babcock, M.D.
Victor Calef, M.D.
Jacob Christ, M.D.
Paul A. Dewald, M.D.
Alan J. Eisnitz, M.D.
Leon Ferber, M.D.
Sanford M. Izner, M.D.
Daniel S. Jaffe, M.D.
Aaron Karush, M.D.
John F. Kelly, M.D.
James Mann, M.D.
Paul H. Ornstein, M.D.
Arnold Z. Pfeffer, M.D.
Daniel Shapiro, M.D.
Troy Thompson, M.D.
Ralph W. Tyler, Ph.D.
Edward M. Weinshel, M.D.

The Tripartite System
of Psychoanalytic Education

ORIGINAL CHARGE

Re-evaluation of the roles and the relation to one another
of the training analysis, formal seminar curriculum, and
supervised clinical experience. What is the appropriate
place of each in analytic education? How seriously do we
take each of them? How adequate is each as a learning
experience and as a contribution to analytic education?
How interdependent or separate should these training
components be? How much influence, if any, should the
student's training analyst have upon the student's training progression? Should there be alternatives to uniform
rates of progression through training? What do we mean
by "an analyst"?

PREPARATORY COMMISSION REPORT

The commission was confronted with the task of exploring the present system of psychoanalytic education to
evaluate its goals and its methods, identify its strong and
weak points, and recommend indicated changes. The

first step in approaching this assignment was to review the present system in broad perspective. From a historical point of view, the educational process has evolved into three phases. Each phase provides different kinds of learning experiences, all of which contribute to the education of an analyst. The first phase, the training analysis, lays the foundation for the development of sensitive, empathic understanding, which is then linked with cognitive, explanatory understanding through the course and seminar sequence, the second phase of the learning program. In the third phase, the conducting of analyses under supervision, both of these learning experiences are further developed and integrated with clinical skills that lead to therapeutic effectiveness and psychoanalytic scholarship.

To put more substance on this outline, we looked carefully at each of the three phases and tried to define the educational objectives of each; we then evaluated our success in attaining these objectives. We attempted to spell out the common denominators in each phase and the bridges from one kind of learning experience to the next.

In our present program, we assume that the training analysis should be the first experience in the educational process and that for the student its initial objective is relative freedom from neurotic symptoms and other pathology that would interfere with analytic competence. In addition to therapeutic change, we place high value on the learning experiences of introspection, self-observation, resistance, and transference regression that lead to this therapeutic goal. These experiences are part of the therapeutic process with every analytic patient, but they also contribute to the professional goal of an analytic student. We believe that this kind of experiential learning is a fundamental step in the total educational process.

What is experienced in the training analysis needs to be placed in a cognitive frame of reference. The second and third phases of the tripartite design, the seminar program and the supervised psychoanalytic work, contribute to this objective. In the supervisory situation, where the introspective skills learned in the experience of being a patient are combined with the explanatory concepts acquired in cognitive learning situations, the analytic student develops a therapeutic instrument, learning to move flexibly between experiencing and observing the clinical situation and to combine empathic understanding with insightful, technical response.

We surveyed the history of the tripartite system in psychoanalytic education. A number of authors have written on the subject, either from the point of view of personal experience in the early twentieth century (E. Jones, 1959; Bernfeld, 1962; Benedek, 1969) or from a retrospective account of the efforts to organize psychoanalytic education to achieve group responsibility for the competence of graduates (Eitingon, 1926; Sachs, 1947; Knight, 1953; Balint, 1954; Lewin and Ross, 1960; Fleming and Benedek, 1966). These historical perspectives stress how the beginnings of the educational effort focused on understanding Freud's new ideas. At that time students were usually practicing psychiatrists who wanted to apply the new ideas in their work with patients. In a relatively short time, the technique of free association and the interpretation of resistances and transference phenomena became the primary principles of the treatment process. The first teacher, of course, was Freud whose teaching methods involved small group discussions and consultations about cases. The first generation of students rapidly became the teachers of the next generation, and for a long time the method of education was that of an apprentice system in which the teaching analyst performed the functions of analyst, teacher of theory, and clinical consultant, sometimes in sequence, sometimes almost simultaneously (Benedek, 1969).

The psychoanalytic method of treatment is an effective research method for collecting data on the functioning of the human mind. It is not the only situation or method of observation providing such data, but it does offer a unique means for contact with unconscious levels that simple observation of behavior, individually or in groups, does not provide. Learning the psychoanalytic method in order to become a competent psychoanalyst is an essential goal of psychoanalytic education, whether that competence is used primarily for therapeutic purposes, for extending the area of our understanding of behavior, or for the application of psychoanalytic theory to such fields as education, law, medicine, social work, nursing, religion, and government.

With the current expansion and extension of psychoanalytic knowledge and increase in the number of competent psychoanalytic practitioners, analytic educators are faced with important questions. Should we remain primarily educators of professional therapists? What is needed to educate a psychoanalyst who can continue to recognize unanswered questions about behavior and is motivated to try to find answers? Can such learning goals be built into the program for psychoanalytic education? Can we construct an educational track that provides basic learning experiences, as well as continuing educational opportunities and support for scientific exploration?

This commission studied the question of evaluation and strongly affirms that evaluation is an essential ongoing process in education. We must assess the student's achievement of the program's over-all objectives before graduation and certification; we must also periodically determine the learning achievement necessary for progression within the program. Evaluation must be done by both teacher and student. The teacher assesses the student's learning and progress in relation to the program's various objectives as well as the student's correction of any learning deficiencies. The student assesses his own educational progress in relation to what he needs to learn and his learning problems, as defined by his teachers.

The process of evaluation can be developed into a useful tool for facilitating education, but it may be that neither the teacher nor the student fully recognizes its value. There is some objection to evaluating and being evaluated, on the part of both teachers and students, which may have its source in the wish to maintain "neutrality," "objectivity," and a "nonjudgmental position." While each of these attitudes is important in the work of analyzing, they should not hinder appropriate evaluation. Neutrality, objectivity, and a nonjudgmental attitude refer not so much to the act of evaluating, but rather to what may be done with the evaluation. Of course, the misuse of evaluation will certainly interfere with the educational process.

This report describes our re-evaluation of each phase of the educational program, emphasizing our sense of its basic validity and recommending changes in certain areas. As a result of our own demand for clarification of certain issues, a number of papers have been produced for future publication.

The Training Analysis

A subcommittee of the commission focused its attention on the role of the training analysis in the education of an analyst. The following ten points present the subcommittee's position on the most significant issues.

1. We recognize the training analysis as the keystone of psychoanalytic education and strongly recommend that it continue to be a primary requirement for psychoanalytic training. To many psychoanalysts such a recommendation might seem unnecessary. Nevertheless, statements have recently been made recommending that the requirement of a personal analysis be dropped or isolated from the other parts of the tripartite system and no longer remain a prerequisite for theoretical and clinical learning (Lipton, 1972). Little hard data have been offered to support the contention that the training analysis is nonessential. In fact, there is increasing evidence of the value and necessity of the personal experiences of the training analysis for the future analyst. We do not subscribe to the contention that the training analysis cannot be conducted effectively within the psychoanalytic institute. It is true that a "required" training analysis represents, in some respects, an apparent contradiction to the more general philosophy of analytic therapy and inevitably must mobilize certain conflicts in the analysand. Although we may wish to reduce the burdens of the requirement, we are convinced that we should not abandon the training analysis and its benefits.

2. Arguments as to whether the training analysis is a therapeutic or an educational experience are essentially fruitless. Unless education and therapy are defined very narrowly, any analysis has both educational elements and therapeutic goals.

3. We very much need a more specific understanding of the ways in which the analytic work and techniques are used by the analytic teacher and student for educational purposes.

4. Our knowledge of the prerequisite aptitudes, skills, and abilities essential for psychoanalytic work with patients is still insufficiently refined. The expansion and extension of such knowledge will help us accomplish our student-selection procedures in a more effective and economic manner, and will also aid in further clarification of the goals of the training analysis as well as the training in general.

5. While the principle and practice of confidentiality in the training analysis should by no means be relinquished, it is around this issue that much of the opposition to evaluating and being evaluated revolves. The controversy has centered around the question of reporting to an educational committee concerning assessment of progress in the training analysis. It is the commission's position that the content of a training analyst's report need not involve secrets or confidential material. Information including deductions and judgments about functions necessary for doing analytic work is much more valuable. Instead of an endless search for absolute confidentiality, we need to develop adequate modes of communicating with each other in the service of our objectives.

The problem of reporting or nonreporting by training analysts does not seem to be the basic issue, provided the relevant evaluations of progress are made (McLaughlin, 1973; Calef and Weinshel, 1973; Fleming, 1973). The student in analysis will certainly feel more anxious about being evaluated if these anxieties and their infantile roots are not adequately analyzed. If the student is actively involved in this area of analytic work and in a self-evaluation of progress in relation to professional development, a resolution of old conflicts and a new integration of development toward individuation can be better achieved. The crucial issue is in the analysis of the qualifications for our particular professional education; this is so whether or not the training analyst reports.

Another value to reporting lies in the opportunity for collective assessment of structural change resulting from analysis. This conceptualization of developmental change and maturation, whether we call it therapeutic or educational, provides additional knowledge about. ego development and the effectiveness of psychoanalysis. It provides valuable follow-up data on the analytic therapeutic process, various factors in personality development, and the stresses that hamper or facilitate the work of adaptation. A vast reservoir of scientific information will remain on an intuitive, uncommunicable level if we neglect the opportunities our educational data offer us.

A brief review may be in order on the changes in attitude toward the training analysis and its objectives. Sixty years ago the purpose of the personal analysis was essentially didactic and of short duration. Often the student was analyzing patients without supervision prior to an encounter with his or her own unconscious through analytic therapy (E. Jones, 1959). As early as 1911, when countertransference phenomena began to be recognized, the aims of analysis for a beginning analyst shifted toward a therapeutic goal that would at least relieve some conflicts, achieve some insight, and reduce the interference of defensive "blind spots." Thus, although the training analysis continued to be a prerequisite for courses and clinical work, its contribution to the professional education was made less explicit.

If the training analysis is considered as quite separate from the other educational experiences, criteria for appropriate progression to courses and cases cannot be properly formulated from an educational viewpoint and may just consist of standardized time intervals, such as six months or one year in analysis. Such an approach is not adequately based on an appreciation of each student's individual talent, ability, and rate of development, something that analysts certainly know about. While the analysis is perceived as preparatory and corrective, its specific objectives often are not made explicit.

Recent attitudes toward the training analysis and student progression from patient to analyst have evolved two somewhat different models: the therapeutic and the more comprehensive professional preparatory model. In those institutes that see the therapeutic goal as the predominant one, the training analysis has lengthened and has tended to become more separate from the rest of the program. In other institutes, where a professional preparatory model has been accepted, attempts have been made to diminish the isolation of the analytic experience. Student deficiencies in academic or clinical work made the training analysts in these institutes aware that premature progression from patient to student to student analyst could cause the analytic work, both as patient and as student analyst, to become unproductive and resistively intellectualized, and transference development to be interfered with by displaced transferences onto teachers, supervisors, and classmates, sometimes bringing the personal analysis to a standstill.

From our evaluation of the first phase of the tri-partite program, it seems that our primary problem is the integration of the training analysis with the other phases of the total educational process, rather than its separation from them. The Committee on Psychoanalytic Education (COPE) is involved in a relevant study and the Pre-Congress Conferences on Training of the International Psycho-Analytical Association have stimulated active discussion about this issue.

A study was conducted by sending a questionnaire to all of the graduates of the Columbia Psychoanalytic Institute (Shapiro, 1973). The original questionnaire was sent to 198 graduates with 122 (63 per cent) responding. It focused primarily on the graduate's feeling as to whether the training analysis had produced "satisfactory" results. One hundred four (85 per cent) of those respond-ing "viewed their own therapeutic gains as satisfactory" and 39 (32 per cent) "gave a highly favorable view of their analytic gains." Along with this estimate of therapeutic change, various factors interfering with a satisfactory result were identified and discussed.

The three important factors named by the respon-dents as contributing to the success or failure of their training analysis are, in order, the student's character-ological problems, the fact of the training analyst's evaluative and reporting function, and an overestimation and excessive identification with the training analyst. The question is why these factors seem so prominent to the respondents as the presumed causes of difficulties in their personal analytic experience. Why do these defenses

against neurotic conflicts become such a prevailing transference resistance and why are they so hard to analyze?
Several of these problems clearly require continued
exploration and discussion. We believe that the increased
individualization of the training experience on the basis
of better data for the evaluation of progress constitutes a
worthy goal of psychoanalytic education despite the time
and energy demanded of both students and teachers.

Shapiro (1973) states that "three-fourths of the re-
spondent analysts reported a favorable impact from the
training setting." "For half of this group it facilitated,
through recognizing and dealing with blind spots,
countertransferences, and defensive reactions to supervisors and patients," and in this process, increased access
to emotional states and conflicts. Shapiro's study con-
firms how important it is for a student to be in analysis
while in supervision and how important it may be to
consider return to analysis when self-analysis, developed
in the training analysis, proves inadequate for conflicts
revived during clinical work. He concludes that there is a
reciprocity between the personal analysis and the acquisition of analytic skills: learning was facilitated by the
expansion of the future analyst's empathic, introspective,
and interpretive capacities through the training analysis;
and the training analysis, in turn, was usually enriched by
the emotional experiences of the other aspects of the
training situation.

6. We recognize that the training analysts may
contribute to the difficulties of the training analysis.
However, while acknowledging their transferences,
countertransferences, narcissistic tendencies, and other
potential psychological defects and deficiencies, we also
suggest that there may be a tendency to overemphasize

the relative importance of these factors for the training analysis. These problems may exist in all analyses.

7. An analysis conducted within the framework of the psychoanalytic institute carries the potential for certain problems, but these are neither absolute nor insurmountable, and in most cases they can be utilized constructively in the analysis. With all its imperfections, the institute offers the best setting currently available for psychoanalytic education. We must remain aware, however, of the psychological impact of the institution. The training analyst must be able to function with some degree of comfort in the fish-bowl atmosphere of the institute, and the student must have the capacity to understand and accept both the reality of the training situation and the specific requirements of that reality.

8. The recurrent debate on reporting or nonreporting by the training analyst revolves around an essentially spurious issue. The real issue is not the analyst's prerogative to report, but rather the obligation to assess in an ongoing way the progress of the student's analysis. While such assessments are an integral part of any analysis, they take on special significance in those who are to do analytic work with patients.

9. A most important cluster of assessments with which the training analyst must deal relates to the student's progression within the institute's training sequence. In this respect we must continue to sharpen our observations and formulations of the criteria for such progression and to articulate them as precisely as possible. It is necessary, of course, to recognize the pitfalls of overschematizing and oversimplifying these matters.

10. The training analysis component of psychoanalytic education demands continued observation and

study, detailed analytic data, and the opportunity to exchange pertinent information and experience. Much current sentiment argues that there is not and should not be any difference between analysis done under the aegis of training and analysis with only therapeutic goals. From this viewpoint the analyst should simply analyze and not be concerned with anything else. It should be stressed, however, that the student in training analysis enters into that experience with quite special motivations, goals, and identifications, which must then become part of the analysis.

The commission believes our educational program would be strengthened by the integration of its three phases. So far, we have opposed the tendency to isolate the training analysis from its place as a prerequisite and preparatory educational experience. In light of this, we wish to recommend the use of evaluation by faculty interviewers for the several necessary progression decisions within the tripartite program. The rationale for such a procedure is based on the assumption that a student must have shown potential for development as an analyst when evaluated in admission interviews; a subsequent interview before admission to the academic program would provide further information about the student's aptitude for analytic work and indicate what has been gained so far from the personal analytic experience.

The following are suggested criteria for evaluating a student's readiness for educational progression:

1. The development of the student's ability for empathic communication with self and others through introspection, association, and interpretation.

2. Evidence of adequate experience in learning directly and personally about the "feel" of conflict, anxiety, resistance, defense, symptomatic behavior (such as learning blocks), dreams, regression, transference, and the discovery of genetic determinants.

3. The degree of insight into the conflicts that have played a major role in determining the student's character structure and neurotic symptoms, in particular the Oedipus conflict and its resolution.

The tripartite commission opposes automatic progression from analysis to courses and cases; it emphasizes the need for active analysis of these steps; it recommends informed assessment by evaluators outside of the analytic situation, as well as an evaluation by the training analyst and the student patient within the analytic situation.

THE THEORETICAL PHASE

A subcommittee of the commission studied the second phase of the tripartite program, i.e., the series of courses on psychoanalytic theory and method of treatment. This phase of the program is commonly referred to as the curriculum, and the learning objectives require more traditionally cognitive approaches. It is during this phase that students learn the explanatory concepts derived from clinical and direct observations of behavior, follow the development of psychoanalytic psychology, and come to understand cognitively their own experiences as a patient in analysis and their observations in clinical situations.

The question has long been discussed about the effect of the personal analysis on learning in the seminar. Students tend to identify with their training analysts and transference reactions are always present. Regression as a consequence of the analysis may not only influence the capacity to learn but may also be manifest in feelings of rebellion against being a student once more. Teachers should be able to manage such situations without resorting prematurely to the conclusion that the student is acting out. Some institute teachers tend to maintain an "analytic" stance and overlook such teaching devices as encouragement and immediate reinforcement of learning in the seminar room.

A faculty dedicated to its mission and working collectively cannot learn for the student, but it can make it possible for an optimal learning situation to exist. The kind of curriculum we design and offer may significantly help or hinder the student's continuing education after graduation. Teaching is properly understood as guided learning and not simply as the presentation of information. Part of the teacher's job is to know how to plan a course, define its objectives, and devise methods of teaching them. A faculty working collaboratively on these tasks may achieve a harmonious program, of benefit to both students and instructors.

A primary concern of the curriculum committees of all institutes is to provide the core of knowledge that a student should learn. We expect a student to gain an understanding of the mind, how it is organized and how it functions, both in health and in disease. The student should become familiar with Freud's major concepts and the ways in which those concepts have been reinterpreted or expanded and extended by others. The student should also become familiar with the unresolved or incompletely answered issues in Freud's concepts. We recognize the importance of teaching the historical development of psychoanalytic theory and practice, including present-day conceptual models.

The integration of the theoretical phase with the personal analysis and supervision is wholly dependent upon the extent to which the theoretical phase becomes a genuine teaching and learning experience. Here again the close integration between theoretical and clinical work is apropos. The richest opportunity for such integration occurs in the supervisory process, but in both the seminar program and in supervision, integration obviously may be enhanced by the knowledge and skill of the teachers.

Institutes may tend to gravitate into a "lock-step" curriculum, where despite an awareness of individual differences, group instruction is so organized that all members of the group are expected to proceed at the same tempo. There should be some flexibility since a rigid system tends to be deadening and boring to some of the students and overwhelming to others. This does not mean that the student should pursue all learning at a completely self-determined speed. Even for adults, it is easier to conform to a reasonable schedule. Furthermore, learning can be a social process; some subjects and ideas are clarified more easily in a group.

Methods of assessment of learning are the responsibility of both teacher and student. Institutes should maintain a reliable "feedback" system. Under such a system the student gains information quickly about the adequacy of his or her learning performance. If it is not satisfactory, there should be an assessment suggesting the nature of the inadequacy and appropriate corrective measures. Without feedback, learning may be too slow and certain students may become needlessly discouraged.

An important educational function is the evaluation of teacher effectiveness. Whatever means is chosen for teacher evaluation, it is important to learn from the instructor what the course was intended to accomplish. The students may then be approached, individually and collectively, to determine what they thought they were expected to learn, as well as what they felt they should have learned. The information thus obtained can be transmitted to the instructor who may then be able to modify the learning experience in a useful manner. Obviously, the instructor must be able to accept the student evaluations and use them constructively.

Our commission suggests to the Board of Professional Standards that a new series of workshops be offered to analytic faculty members on evaluation and methods of assessment of teaching and learning in the curriculum.

There was a general agreement among the subcommittee that up to the present time selection of faculty has been more or less on the basis of personal impression, professional reputation, or other factors not necessarily related to the individual's interest in or capacity for teaching. In some institutes the evaluation of a potential teacher is made by individuals who know him and who then recommend him. The potential teacher is then invited to participate at an assistant level and is observed on the basis of his interactions with the class, as well as his knowledge of the subject. Other institutes have a nominating committee to pick the faculty. And, in some institutes, faculty selection is occasionally made on the recommendation of a single person.

It was generally agreed that two of the essentials in the selection of teachers should be the individual's deep interest and personal commitment to the role of teaching along with some past experience of teaching, as well as general intelligence and willingness to learn the process of teaching. The factors of motivation and intelligence, for example, might be demonstrated by a potential teacher by his or her developing a course, including course objectives, methods of reaching them, conceptions of learning, and methods of assessment of learning. The initial selection of a teacher would be based on the individual's expressed interest in teaching, reputation in other settings as an effective teacher, demonstrated capacity for communication of ideas, general knowledge of the principles of pedagogy, etc. In a sense, the demonstration of these qualities and capacities is the responsibility of the person desiring to be considered for the role of teacher. The subsequent development and education of the individual as a faculty member and improvement as a teacher becomes, in part, the institute's responsibility.

There are a number of other characteristics of good teaching and teachers that should be considered, both in terms of initial faculty selection and subsequent faculty development. An obvious but important attribute of a good teacher is a willingness to instruct rather than to express or pursue personal intellectual interests. The teacher can always supply additional material, but there must be a willingness to delineate those things that are truly essential. The individual instructor must also be able to accept a role as only one part of the total educational enterprise of the student and must be able to work as a member of a faculty. Individual teachers should be willing to participate in shared faculty tasks, such as the development of an institute teaching syllabus outlining what students should learn, listing the courses in which the topics would be dealt with, detailing the plan of student learning in each course, describing in detail what areas would be covered and from what points of view, and including carefully selected assigned reading. Obviously, this type of group enterprise takes considerable time, effort, and thought.

The effective teacher is capable of patience during the phase of internalization of material by the student. Many professional curricula undertake too much and do not recognize the amount of time required to internalize certain concepts and to be able to apply them to real situations. There is a vast difference in the time required to present a concept and the time required for the student to make it a part of his or her own mode of operation.

Another criterion in the selection and development of faculty is the pedagogic capacity to link theory and practice in an effective manner. It is important that the instructor should be a model for such a synthesis of theory and practice.

An important aspect of learning for students (and thus for the selection of appropriate teachers) is the need to have reassurance that appropriate progress is being made in the learning process. Implicit in this requirement is the capacity of the teacher for empathy with the student and a willingness to interact with the student at the level of the task upon which they are both focused.

It may be useful to put into the form of a series of questions those issues we consider relevant to the theoretical phase. We hope such questions will prove useful for stimulating continuing thought, discussion, and improvement of this important aspect of psychoanalytic education.

1. How may the faculty understand the relative value placed by the student on learning the theory of psychoanalysis? How does the students' evaluation of the relative importance of theory reflect, or not reflect, the relative value placed by the particular faculty on theory?

2. Which factors relevant to possible resistance to the learning of theory are most significant for a particular institute at a particular time—(a) disinclination of students based on previous academic background or individual temperament, (b) inadequate curriculum planning for effective learning sequences, (c) teaching that does not fully integrate theoretical and clinical considerations, (d) insufficient attention to faculty development and coordination of collaborative efforts to reach the institute's objectives?

3. Should not as much attention be given to the selection of faculty as to the selection of students?

4. What are the criteria used for assessing learning and deciding on progression in the theoretical phase? Are students regularly requested to repeat courses in which they have not been able to demonstrate adequate mastery of the material? What are the implications of an absence of such a policy?

5. What is the usual and accepted practice regarding the teaching of theory in the supervisory situation?

The Clinical Phase

The attainment of clinical competence is a universally accepted aim of psychoanalytic training, the only exceptions being certain students who undertake the training for the application of analysis in other fields. Basically clinical competence means the ability to use the process of psychoanalysis as an instrument for understanding the patient and, mainly by interpretation, enlarging his insights with resultant therapeutic benefit. Several ideas are implicit in this rather general definition:

1. The recognition of the psychoanalytic treatment situation as an evolving process. Therapeutic intervention is then understood to require the awareness of the dynamic forces contributing to this process.

2. The development of the capacity to apply theoretical learning to the clinical situation. Although intuitive understanding and natural therapeutic ability are much admired and desirable, their reliability and dependability are enhanced by a conceptual foundation.

3. The capability of independent use of the analytic method as a therapeutic and investigative tool. While it is recognized that not every student actually uses psychoanalysis as an investigative research method, it is expected that it may be used independently as an investigative therapeutic method with patients.

The universal method for teaching clinical competence and assessing its attainment is supervision of the student's analytic casework. In fact, the evaluations by a student's supervisors are the most important basis for graduation decisions, and most of the time spent in teaching and close observation, outside of the personal analysis, is in supervision.

Another teaching-learning situation for learning clinical skills is the clinical conference. There are different kinds of conferences, such as the continuous case seminar (weekly or biweekly) in which students participate either as presenters or as auditors and discussants of a clinical presentation. Other forms include those in which several sessions are spent on a special problem presented in a case, first reviewing the development of the analysis up to the point to be presented, and then perhaps presenting in detail several consecutive sessions from the particular period in question. Still other clinical conferences may address specific issues such as evaluation or suitability for analysis, the beginning phase, the transference neurosis, and problems associated with termination, or comparisons of early sessions in analysis with those occurring much later. There are conferences in which a faculty member or a recent graduate presents material from one of his or her own analytic cases to enable candidates to see the development of an analytic process at a time when they themselves may still be relatively inexperienced.

Most institutes require some form of written case reports. These are used as an additional method of evaluating clinical learning, and they may also be used for instructional purposes, the report being reviewed in varying detail with the student.

There are, of course, specific courses that discuss the theory of technique at various levels. These courses aim to provide a general theoretical framework for the therapeutic approach, and are the learning situation in which the most systematic effort is made to correlate theoretical knowledge with technique.

The following considerations are relevant to clinical teaching and evaluation:

1. The phase of the student's training. The goals are different for students early in training than for those advanced in their training. Similarly, the evaluation of students depends upon their stage of training. Obviously,

we expect more from those who have had a longer opportunity to learn.

2. The relation of clinical training to the student's
personal analysis. For instance, a supervisor is often less
concerned about the student's countertransference problems if the student's analysis may be expected to address
the problem. Similarly, more blind spots are anticipated
in a student whose personal analysis is in its early phases.

3. Supervision is the best method of assessing the
capacity of the student to understand and manage a case,
with opportunity for major concentration upon minute
clinical detail if necessary. A case conference, in which a
case is presented for at least several sessions may be well
suited to evaluate the student's over-all understanding of
the clinical situation. Continuous case seminars, particularly for certain students who are not presenting, may
provide an opportunity to demonstrate their knowledge,
which may be masked by the anxiety stimulated by individual presentation.

It will be recalled that among the goals of clinical
teaching we stressed the desirability of development of
the capacity to recognize the analytic situation as part of
an evolving process. In terms of evaluation, it appears
that no single teaching and evaluating agent is sufficient
by itself for evaluating the development of the process
concept in the student. Clearly the mix of impressions
derived from the various teaching and evaluative situations is most reliable. It is also necessary to maintain some
kind of longitudinal frame of reference for viewing the
student's developing clinical competence. This can be
done in case presentations or reports covering the progress of an entire course of treatment, and can also be

observed in presentations that are part of a thesis or case-presentation requirement for graduation.

Evaluations by supervisors tend to emphasize the cross-sectional view, i.e., how the student is doing at a particular moment. Such evaluations should occasionally include a more longitudinal view. Performance with supervision does not, of course, completely reflect capacity to conduct analytic treatment independently.

4. A final consideration, and a very important one both in teaching and evaluation, is the suitability of the case material employed. All too often teaching, learning, and evaluation are handicapped when the clinical situation requires measures that grossly compromise the analytic method and result.

THE SUPERVISORY PROCESS

The educational purpose of supervision is to teach the nature of the psychoanalytic process and to aid in the development of skills necessary for its application. Specifically, an analyst's work involves perception, recognition, synthesis, and integration of the patient's verbal and nonverbal communications. This requires the ability to listen with free-floating attention, introspect, empathize, identify, and to have access to and control over a full range of affective and regressive processes in one's self and in the patient. Although the groundwork for such skills must necessarily be laid during the personal analysis and their cognitive organization carried forward by preparatory coursework, it is principally through the supervisory experience that an opportunity is provided for systematic application and working through with patients.

To function as an analytic instrument, the student must develop a sensitivity to the patient's anxieties and resistances, in order to maximize a therapeutic alliance in which the patient can permit regression and re-experiencing of the past in the transference as well as retain an observing ego function. The student must learn to judge the appropriate timing of interventions and interpretations, based on an understanding of the sequential developments and shifts in the analytic situation, with all of the dynamic contributions from transference and countertransference pressures. Genetic roots must be recognized through behavioral patterns and drive derivatives; and the effects of the analyst's own role in contributing to the patient's responses must be kept in sight through a constant self-analytic process. A familiarity with the manifestations of transference neurosis and its resolution must be acquired and a correlation between theoretical concepts and clinical practice must be achieved.

The supervisor, in the effort to bring these objectives to optimum fulfillment, encourages the learning alliance. A collaborative atmosphere, as free as possible from factors stimulating regression in the student, is desirable. Tendencies toward overconformity, submission, dependence, or oppositional attitudes in the student have to be watched for, as well as any evidence of authoritarianism on the part of the supervisor. The supervisor's accepting and understanding attitude should help to overcome discomforts that may to some degree be an inevitable accompaniment of the supervisory situation. Needless to say, respect for the clinical material, avoidance of competitiveness and arbitrariness, and tact are all essential in the development of the learning alliance.

Some difficulties do arise from the necessary evaluating function of the supervisor. An initial point to be evaluated is the student's rapport with the patient, which depends on an adequate degree of freedom from blind spots due to unresolved conflicts. An estimate of such freedom may be gained by observing the student's capacity for self-observation and access to preconscious motivations. A judgment has to be made about the student's understanding of the patient's material, as well as his level of insight, and the degree of effectiveness of his technique of communication with the patient. Further, the supervisor has to evaluate the student's conflicts and defenses within the supervisory situation, which can provide important clues to the problems still requiring personal resolution before optimal work with patients can be done. Not infrequently the student may subtly re-enact in the supervisory relationship the very tendency or defensive behavior with which the patient is confronting the student. For this reason, the student's style of reporting to the supervisor provides important information about the student's intrapsychic processes and contributions to the analytic as well as the supervisory interaction. The method of reporting presents a choice between verbatim process notes and retrospective summaries or extemporaneous descriptions. The dual requirements of precise content analysis and of nondefensive utilization of the material should be met in a flexible manner. The constant attuning of the analyst to the ego state and the analytic process, to determine the appropriate dosage of interpretations, etc., may be looked upon as a process parallel to the teaching relationship of the supervisor and student analyst, since the supervisor is attuned to the learning state or level of the student analyst and adapts the teaching technique accordingly.

A controversial question in supervision is that of the role of the supervisor in dealing with manifestations of learning blocks or conflicts in the student. The supervisor is called on to be helpful to the student while exercising an evaluating function; our earlier remarks about attitudes that can facilitate or hinder the learning alliance are relevant here. In the past some have advocated that the training analyst also carry out the supervision; others have suggested that the supervisor include therapeutic work as part of the supervision. The predominant view, however, holds that the supervisor should rely on confronting the student with the presence of a blind spot or defensive reaction to the patient rather than attempting transference or genetic interpretations of the student's countertransference problems, leaving management of such problems to the training analysis or self-analysis.

It is generally considered advisable that a significant part of the student's supervisory experience take place while still in training analysis so that conflictual reactions that come to the fore in clinical analytic work can be resolved in the training analysis. These two kinds of learning experiences have mutual goals and what happens in each situation can facilitate or interfere with optimal work in the other. This statement applies especially to the handling of countertransference problems as seen in supervision. Both training analysis and supervision aim to develop the student's analyzing functions.

The task of encouraging the student to do the thinking and the analyzing is not always easy, as there may be a tendency for the student to assume the role of an intermediary. The supervisor assists the student to self-confrontation rather than acting as an interpreter. The student may, indeed, demonstrate previous hidden resources during suspensions of supervision. Identification should occur with the supervisor's analyzing function rather than with the particular personality of the supervisor, who would then be used as an auxiliary observing ego or as a benevolent analytic superego.

ADMINISTRATIVE STRUCTURE

Psychoanalytic education evolved from a master-apprentice relationship to a system in which a group of educators, a faculty, is responsible for educating a group of students. The move toward group responsibility has made possible the teaching of an increased number of students by spreading the load over an increased number of teachers; it has provided not only for division of labor but also for exposure to the knowledge and skills of different individuals whose varying contributions enrich the experiential and cognitive learning available to the students. In addition, the emphasis on group responsibility has stimulated an appreciable increase in awareness of educational goals and the problems involved in achieving them.

Nevertheless, in spite of the advantages of group responsibility, it has presented problems inherent to groups that have complicated the implementation of educational policies in the institutes. Group activity requires leadership and coordinated work for efficient functioning. It requires definition of core functions and the establishment of administrative structures to see that they are carried out effectively. The faculty needs to be organized for the core functions it has agreed to perform, and the leadership must be given authority for planning and review of the policies and procedures, with clear lines of accountability. The faculty is expected to formulate the educational policies, and responsibility for their execution needs to be delegated. Certain decision-making powers may be delegated to committees but should be monitored by administrative officers.

A distinct advantage arises from an organizational structure where thorough debate about policies can take place. This requires planning by the leadership and the development of procedures for communication of information essential for clarification of the issues to be debated. It also requires definition of decision-making powers reserved for the faculty as a whole.

CONCLUSION

We have attempted to review the three phases of our present system of psychoanalytic education and to delineate educational objectives in each phase. We have emphasized the line of progression in the learning process from training analysis through theoretical and clinical learning and have stressed the importance of integrating this educational developmental process and the particular educational importance of continuing careful assessment of the quality of the teaching and learning. Various strengths and weaknesses in the conduct of the educational program have been indicated. We feel that further independent study and collective discussion of these issues will be useful in further improving the quality of psychoanalytic education.

It is necessary to look beyond the matters of content, desirable standards, and teaching methods to the administrative organization responsible for implementing the educational program. In spite of the great dedication and service given by an increasing number of faculty members, certain problem areas of our educational program can be attributed to inadequate administrative structure, avocational leadership, and difficulties in group functioning. We therefore strongly recommend that attention be given to these organizational matters as well as to the primarily educational policies and procedures.

PLENARY DISCUSSION — EDWARD JOSEPH, M.D.

We should consider precisely what we mean by psychoanalytic education. The concept of education is much broader than that of training. It may, of course, include learning to apply particular skills, but it emphasizes the acquisition of fundamental knowledge, the ability to extrapolate appropriately from that knowledge and to discover new knowledge. Our goal as psychoanalytic educators is to educate analysts whose education does not stop at graduation. The formal education period should be such as to encourage a lifelong self-educative process.

There are several specific elements to be acquired by the student through the tripartite psychoanalytic education. Most important in terms of the individual's future development is the ability to continue the preparatory personal analysis in self-analysis, not only for its therapeutic benefit but also for its enhancement of the ability to deal with the special analytic professional responsibilities and tasks. The continuing self-analysis maintains the analyst's sensitivity to the data obtained in the psychoanalytic clinical situation.

The report of the commission neglects one aspect of the educational sequence, namely, selection. Our educational goals have not been successfully achieved with every person admitted to our institutes. There should be further studies of the background, qualities, and capacities of both successful and unsuccessful students in order to improve selection criteria. It is even conceivable that with more sophisticated evaluation of applicants, certain individuals might be admitted with the recommendation that the personal preparatory analysis be delayed until the beginning of supervised work when its need might become more manifest.

An important corollary to the question of selection of students is the selection of teachers. We must continue to examine current practices and to compare them to desirable ideals. Particular teachers may be better qualified to function in one rather than another aspect of our three-part effort. We understand the importance of identification as an aspect of learning; we therefore hope our teachers will encourage identification with learning, with a scientific approach to our field, and with the analytic function of the analyst.

As the report indicates, there is a need to specify in greater detail the role of the supervisory analyst. There have been various responses to the issue of whether the supervisor should only point out blind spots and problem areas, or should go further and attempt to understand the personal implications of a particular technical difficulty with the student. Supervision should not be restricted to discussion of technique as applied to a particular patient, but rather should provide the opportunity for broader integration of clinical and theoretical issues.

The seminar program should go beyond the basic topics of psychoanalysis to include reference at least to certain aspects of other fields. In addition to sociology, anthropology, archeology, and literature, the developing knowledge of the neurophysiological and neurobiochemical basis of nervous-system functioning may ultimately be extremely relevant to psychoanalysis. Analysts must be aware of these areas to learn from them and possibly contribute to them.

We strive to encourage in our students the readiness to consider new ideas and to give up concepts shown to be replaceable by more suitable ones. The basic principles of psychoanalysis provide a frame of reference within which many changes of theory and practice have already occurred and will continue to occur. The ability to independently and critically evaluate these changes must be encouraged in the student. Such an ability does not arise out of the therapeutic success of the preparatory analysis alone; it is also integrated by the student out of the demonstrated attitudes prevalent among the institute faculty. By conveying a critical and scholarly attitude, we can effectively encourage the student to undertake appropriate research, an activity vital to the development of psychoanalysis as a scientific discipline.

Finally, as the commission so effectively emphasizes, there is a clear necessity for careful assessment at every level of progression from selection of applicants to review of faculty effectiveness. Meaningful evaluations of students' and teachers' performances are in themselves potentially educational rather than merely descriptive or administrative. There is still much progress to be made in developing a vocabulary of evaluation that is less subjectively impressionistic and more consensually accepted and objectively communicable.

SUMMARY OF CONFERENCE DISCUSSION

Over all, there was general agreement in all the discussion groups with the central positions and recommendations of the preparatory commission. The importance of close integration and continuing assessment of all three aspects of psychoanalytic education—the training analysis, academic curriculum, and supervised analysis—was strongly endorsed.

The discussion repeatedly addressed certain questions: How well are we now performing our educational tasks and achieving our educational goals? How much better could we function with increased systematic efforts of integration and assessment? What particular policies, methods, or new approaches might contribute to possible improvement in these areas?

The tripartite system itself was generally acknowledged as a logical and appropriate model for the education of psychoanalysts certified as competent to apply psychyoanalysis clinically, to do research in psychoanalysis, or to apply the theory and data of psychoanalysis to a related field of study. The tentative and provocative suggestion of the plenary discussant, that the personal analysis might be delayed, at least for certain students, until after their supervised work made their need for analysis more apparent, received no support in the discussion groups.

One participant suggested that the required personal analysis of the student be accepted by the institute if it were undertaken with any recognized psychoanalyst rather than only with an officially designated training analyst. The rationale behind this was that the complete separation of the personal therapeutic experience from the necessary educational assessments might clarify and strengthen the faculty obligation to evaluate a student's educational and professional development on the basis of actual academic and clinical performance. The preparatory commission had not specifically discussed the requirement that the personal analysis must be undertaken with a training analyst, and there were no other references to it during the course of the conference. Since the preparatory commission recommended the educational advantages to be gained by better integration rather than by greater separation of the personal analysis, its position presumably would be that the training analyst should be someone actively participating in and closely identified with the educational work and objectives of the institute, hence an appointed, experienced faculty member, rather than a member of the psychoanalytic community not so involved, however professionally competent he or she might be.

One of the discussion groups mentioned the need for a so-called quadripartite system, with research as the fourth component, to underline the objective of more systematic emphasis on the teaching of research methods and the encouragement of research interests and activities. It was clear from the nature of most comments, however, that research as a topic for instruction should be considered an integral part of the tripartite system rather than additional to it. The introduction of specific courses on research methodology was widely supported.

Teachers do not attend educational conferences primarily to express complete satisfaction with the status quo, and little if any time was spent in an effort to recite undeniable accomplishments or to balance for the record justifiable self-criticism with possibly well-deserved self-congratulation. Although it was agreed by all that there was room for improvement in every aspect of teaching and learning, very few with much experience in the institutes could agree that continued efforts at integration of the various educational components and proper assessment of teacher and student performance have been seriously neglected. Everyone, however, testified that, in one way or another, major educational problems have not yet been satisfactorily solved, even with an already large collective investment of time and attention.

The commission's recommendation for closer educational integration of the training analysis reopened the much discussed question of the confidentiality of that analysis, particularly as it pertains to whether the training analyst does or does not report an evaluation of analyzability or analytic progress of the student in analysis. The question remained unresolved. Those who were concerned about confidentiality felt that any transmitted assessment of the student's personal analytic experience endangered the therapeutic outcome, and they thought that proper educational assessments could and should be made entirely independently by teachers and supervisors. Those who sought greater integration of the student's personal analysis stressed the reality of the professional objective and the educational setting for the training analysis, no matter how separate it might be made to seem by nonreporting, and they saw great promise for more meaningful assessment of the student if the training analyst's evaluation could be added to that of other teachers. There was general appreciation for the difficulty of defining an appropriate communication from the training analyst, which would respect confidentiality and also contribute usefully to faculty decisions.

A number of discussants referred to the commission's discussion of the training analysis as an educational as well as personal therapeutic experience. There was considerable disagreement with the possible implication that the training analyst should explicitly teach analysis to the student-patient. Apparently the correct interpretation of the commission's statements was that by intention and in fact the training analysis was an educational experience in a general sense, rather than in the specific sense that the training analyst functioned in an instructional mode. Notwithstanding the ambiguous traditional term "didactic analysis," the predominant view is that the training analyst should analyze, not teach analysis.

Regarding supervision, the discussion groups agreed that our teaching and evaluation methods could be improved with systematic attention to the problems involved. The responsibility of the supervising analyst to assist the student's integration of the clinical experience with theoretical concepts was recognized and affirmed. However, the suggestion that the supervisor might go beyond indicating a problem area to the student, and actively and explicitly "analyze" the personal source of a student's problem, was rejected. Most discussants continued to support the view that training analysts should analyze but not teach analysis, while supervising analysts should supervise and teach analysis but not attempt to analyze their student's difficulties. Of course, it was generally understood that there was a difficult to define but valuable spectrum of supervisory techniques in between merely indicating a problem area and actively "analyzing" it. Supervisory tact was considered an essential component of supervisory skill. As in the discussion of reporting by training analysts, many references were made to the problem of developing an effective form and language for the supervisor's reports that would be helpful to student progression and graduation evaluations.

The section on the academic curriculum was the least discussed of the tripartite system report, perhaps because the objectives of the curriculum, as outlined by the commission, were so thoroughly accepted in principle and, according to many discussants, in widespread practice. Similarly, the poor pedagogical practices that were warned against seemed so obviously defective and inappropriate, as to make further disavowal or discussion unnecessary.

Consistent with the commission's insistent emphasis on careful individual evaluation was its repeated recommendation against a "lock-step" progression in the academic curriculum; the discussion groups uniformly endorsed these educational principles and recommended their implementation.

Child Analysis

Calvin F. Settlage, M.D., Chairman
Selma Kramer, M.D., Recorder
Herman S. Belmont, M.D.
Virginia Lawson Clower, M.D.
Robert N. Emde, M.D.
Phyllis Greenacre, M.D.
Marjorie Harley, Ph.D.
J. Cotter Hirschberg, M.D.
Marianne Kris, M.D.
Margaret S. Mahler, M.D.
Irwin M. Marcus, M.D.
Humberto Nagera, M.D.
Gerald B. Olch, M.D.
Fred P. Robbins, M.D.
Morton Shane, M.D.
M. Jeanne Spurlock, M.D.
Samuel Weiss, M.D.

Child Analysis

ORIGINAL CHARGE

To what extent should child and adult training be integrated with each other? Should psychoanalytic education move toward a core curriculum as a basis for a track system with specialization in either child, adolescent, or adult analysis? How can the psychoanalytic institute contribute to the dissemination of knowledge about family, child rearing, child development, and the psychogenesis of psychopathology in differing cultures and subcultures? Does psychoanalysis have a responsibility to participate in the education of teachers, mental health workers, and child-care personnel? How can the psychoanalytic understanding of child development and behavior best be shared and taught in undergraduate and postgraduate education in social work, psychology, medicine, and psychiatry?

PREPARATORY COMMISSION REPORT

As we undertook our task, we found ourselves engaged as much in a review and assessment of the field of psychoanalysis as a whole as of child and adolescent analysis alone. What emerged from our deliberations was an awareness that psychoanalysis has reached a degree of maturity that not only permits but calls for a shift of emphasis within our conceptual framework. The psychoanalytic treatment of the neuroses continues to be of central importance, but it is not adequate as an exclusive frame of reference for understanding and evaluating advances in theory and analytic method. The thesis and theme of this report is that the developmental orientation and approach provides a broader frame of reference, one wherein the psychoanalytic theory and treatment of neuroses occupies a position of prominence in an expanding spectrum of theories of psychopathology and treatment modalities.

HISTORICAL PERSPECTIVE

Support for our position comes first of all from a review of the evolution of the science of psychoanalysis, which indicates that the need for a broadened frame of reference evolved from the theoretical and technical advances associated with two trends: direct observational studies of psychological development in the first years of life, and the widening scope of psychoanalysis as a clinical-theoretical instrument for understanding and treating the more severe forms of psychopathology.

From the time of its inception by Freud, psychoanalysis as a method of treatment has been firmly linked to psychoanalysis as a psychological theory of human development. Freud's epoch-making formulation of the Oedipus complex and the psychosexual stages of development provided the precedent, now a paradigm, for understanding normal development as an essential basis for understanding pathological deviations and their resolution in treatment. The concepts of traumatic experience and psychogenesis in relation to the formation of psychopathology, and of transference and reconstruction of childhood in order to realize therapeutic objectives, make it obligatory that every psychoanalytic clinician be an expert in development.

Initially, insight into psychological development was gained from reconstruction of the individual past on the basis of data from the psychoanalytic situation with adult patients. Following Freud's case studies of Dora (1905a) and Little Hans (1909), developmental understanding began to be derived as well by reconstruction from the data of the analytic situation with adolescents and children. In his indirectly-gained observations of Little Hans, as well as from his own informal first-hand observations of children growing up around him, Freud forecast direct observational studies of children. As psychoanalysis evolved into a general psychology of human development and behavior, psychoanalysts sought understanding of both normal and pathological development from planned observational studies of children in interaction with their parents and environments. Still more recently, psychoanalysts have begun to study and integrate developmental data and concepts derived from nonanalytic work.

Advances in developmental theory, and particularly their implications for psychoanalytic treatment, have been the focus of considerable controversy in which child analysts were caught up from the very beginning as they adapted psychoanalytic technique to the child's level of development while retaining the basic concepts, principles, and goals of the analytic method. Often they were in the position of trying to persuade their colleagues trained only in adult analysis that child analysis, while modified in technique from adult analysis, is also psychoanalysis. In addition, child analysts, although by no means only child analysts, have been participants in the controversy because of their special interest in development and their commitment to studying its earliest manifestations. In recent years, the emergence of new formulations from observational studies of development during the first three years of life has stimulated much discussion on the significance of preverbal and preoedipal development for psychoanalytic treatment. Most child analysts quickly realized that the new observations should be brought to bear on our understanding of later development and the psychogenesis of all varieties of pathologic formations, as well as on formulations of prevention and treatment methods.

Freud derived the basic theoretical and therapeutic concepts of psychoanalysis from clinical observation of neurotic patients. The theory conceived of psychological forces in conflict. If such conflicts became too intense and overwhelming the consequences were psychopathological. In the therapeutic attempt to solve these conflicts the objective was to bring them to conscious awareness and resolve them by a working-through process. Classical analysis focused exclusively on the transference neurosis and its resolution and was applied to the treatment of psychoneuroses.

Psychoanalysts then began to address themselves to more severe pathology and it became apparent that, in contrast to the neuroses, areas of symptom formation might lie outside the area of conflict and be related to developmental deficits and deviations, including impaired development of self, object relations, and ego functions. In these patients, the transference neurosis often develops incompletely and sometimes only after a prolonged treatment. Therapeutic endeavors are directed at facilitating the further development of distorted or only partially developed object relations.

In light of increasing attention to the developmental aspects of severe pathology, the psychoneuroses were reconsidered, and their therapeutic analytic resolution was recognized as involving more than the transference neurosis. It was recognized that the achievement of certain ego functions and object relations must have proceeded sufficiently to make a therapeutic alliance possible, which in turn enhances the evolution of a transference neurosis. The analytic process promotes that further development resulting from the resolution of the transference neurosis.

From work with patients suffering from severe psychopathology, we can distinguish theoretical and technical issues pertaining to those clinical conditions resulting from structural conflicts and those resulting from structural malformation. Work with both adult and child patients demonstrates that arrest in the process of self-object differentiation can impede the formation of the typical oedipal transferences, and can also result in transferences of the preoedipal dyadic relationship. Therapeutic work with such transferences is designed not only to resolve structural conflicts, but also to facilitate resumption of developmental processes impaired by innate or experiential factors during the preverbal and preoedipal periods.

Insights provided by the study of developmental processes within the framework of psychoanalytic theory are germane to the understanding and treatment of all forms of developmental deviation and pathogenesis in every stage of the life cycle. The commission therefore wishes to underscore the central importance of developmental concepts for psychoanalytic psychology, treatment, education, and research.

The Developmental Orientation and Approach

Freud's (1905b) first psychoanalytic developmental outline, that of the psychosexual phases of development, extended through adolescence. In later elaborations of ego psychology, psychoanalytic developmental theory was carried into adulthood. Erikson's (1959) postulation of adult stages in the evolving ego identity stressed the continuing, reciprocal relation between the individual and the surrounding culture. As psychoanalysis moves toward delineating a general psychology of human behavior, analysts are interested in studying in greater detail the developmental phases of the entire life cycle. Viewed in the context of the individual life cycle, psychological change or development can be understood as stemming from three interrelated tendencies: the tendency toward neurotic repetition; the tendency toward recapitulation of earlier developmental issues in later stages of development; and the progressive tendency of normal developmental forces.

Neurotic repetition is a nuclear psychoanalytic concept. The unresolved repressed conflicts of childhood tend to surface repeatedly, evoked by situations and relationships that stimulate the wishes for gratification and the fears of painful frustration. It is, of course, this tendency that psychoanalytic treatment utilizes to effect beneficial psychological change in the carefully defined and controlled circumstances of the psychoanalytic situation. The possibility of therapeutic change, of relief of arrested development, may be seen in the fact that issues of earlier development, including neurotic issues, are recapitulated in the different context of each of the later phases in the life cycle. The decreasing dependence on the parents during adolescence is accompanied by a reworking of the psychic structures of ego, superego, and ego ideal. Similarly, the renewed confrontation with one's own childhood conflicts on becoming a parent or grandparent may, with more mature ego resources and perspective, allow for further resolution of those conflicts.

The concept of normative recapitulation of the opportunity to re-experience and further resolve a normal developmental issue is well illustrated by Mahler's (1968, 1972a) separation-individuation theory. This new psychoanalytic developmental theory complements the theory of the psychosexual phases and focuses on the development of the capacity for object relations and adaptation, arising from progressive ego development and self-object differentiation. The separation-individuation process takes place most crucially during the first three years of life. However, the central issues of actual, threatened, complete, or partial loss of the love object and the correlated internalization—what Freud characterized as the residue of abandoned object cathexes—are confronted again in each of the later developmental phases throughout the entire life cycle, including its terminal phase of death.

The progressive thrust of developmental forces has been well demonstrated by both developmental research and clinical experience. Biologically determined processes of differentiation and integration go on whether or not psychic development is adequate. The direction of psychological development is toward higher levels of organization and qualitative changes resulting from reorganizations such as the transformations of puberty. Child and adult development differ in certain respects. Early development proceeds much faster than later development, when basic structures and functions have already been established and there is less plasticity. Particularly during early childhood, the parents function as temporary auxiliary ego and superego for the child, optimally relinquishing these functions as the child's own capacities emerge and develop.

In both children and adults, normal development is characterized not only by progression but by temporary regression in the face of phase-specific developmental conflicts. It is essential to our understanding of normal development and functioning and to our treatment of patients that we appreciate the interplay of developmental and psychopathologic processes. It is also important to be mindful of the essential continuity of human psychic development, despite the quality of discontinuity that may be associated with transformations to higher levels of organization and function.

The implications of the developmental orientation for clinical work stem from the view of individual human development as a continuous and lifelong process. Mental illness is thus conceptualized as a disturbance that not only impairs current functioning of the individual but impedes further development of still-evolving psychic structures and functions. Defining mental illness within the broader context of the ongoing developmental process emphasizes treatment as a process enabling psychological development to proceed.

The nature of developmental continuity is conveyed in Anna Freud's (1954) formulation. She observed that, with the step from intrauterine to extrauterine life, need satisfaction becomes incomplete; there is never as much as the infant demands, and it never arrives quite as quickly as expected. Wish fulfillment is delayed and pleasure is rationed and curtailed. These disappointments and frustrations make an indelible impression on the infant's unformed mind and become imbedded in the ego structure. Later on, it is the task of the ego to react in a similarly restricting, delaying, rationing function toward the strivings of the id. These are probably the first beginnings of what will later develop into the reality principle. The implication of this view is that even the earliest experiences, occurring in the preverbal period and before the advent of conscious memory, enter into the determination of psychic structure and function. We must thus attempt to discern just how such experiences or their derivatives are represented in the analytic situation and material. While it is true that such early experiences cannot gain direct representation and expression in psychic function, and that the events and activities of later developmental stages tend to conceal earlier events; nevertheless, better understanding of early development increases the possibility of identifying derivatives of early psychogenetic factors. The assumption that what emerges in the psychoanalytic situation is what is important for reconstruction and interpretation has as its counterpart the assumption that we possess sufficient knowledge of development to recognize that which emerges. That the psychoanalytic method for the treatment of neurotic patients is at present limited in its ability to systematically address preverbal problems should not deter the effort to understand them and the attempt to develop appropriate psychoanalytic techniques for coping with them.

Within the realm of psychopathology, the newer theoretical formulations of earliest development hold the further promise of greater precision in our psychoanalytic nosology of psychopathologic conditions. We can now begin to correlate the timing and consequences of traumatic deprivational and stage-arresting experiences with the recently delineated phases and subphases of infantile development.

PSYCHOANALYTIC EDUCATION

Psychoanalytic education should be seen as a part of the analytic student's continuing personal development. Such a view may facilitate understanding of the interplay of the many factors, both within and surrounding the formal training experience, that influence student development.

The teaching of psychoanalysis changes, with an understandable conservative lag, as new knowledge leads to modifications in psychoanalytic theory and practice. The initial emphasis was on drive representation, the dynamic unconscious, preconscious thought, and the topographic model of the mind. Later, there was an additional emphasis on structural theory and ego psychology. With the accumulation of clinical analytic experience with children and greater knowledge of early biological and psychological development gained from direct observation of normal and pathological growth, the area of developmental processes has been particularly highlighted in the expansion of psychoanalytic theory and its clinical application.

It is apparent that psychoanalytic education already recognizes the new developmental insights; the institutes' standard courses on development now include the new developmental data and concepts. Training standards have been revised to endorse elective clinical work in child analysis in basic analytic education. Currently, developmental concepts are being integrated into the fabric of basic theoretical and clinical courses, demonstrating clearly the value of continuing re-evaluation of our approaches to teaching and to curriculum planning.

The historical approach to teaching psychoanalytic theory, psychotherapy, and technique serves an important purpose in teaching the evolution of psychoanalysis. We propose that human development as a lifelong process provides a better frame of reference for the organization and the teaching of our subject. For example, data from research in biology, physiology, and psychology can be included in discussions of drive and ego development. Direct observations of normal human beings in all stages of the life cycle, of children with illness or handicaps that influence maturation and development, and of mother-infant interactions are an appropriate part of the study of theories of ego and object relations. Psychopathology should be taught in terms of vicissitudes of development rather than in terms of outmoded psychiatric diagnostic nomenclature.

The developmental approach to teaching psychopathology begins with the integration of all observational, reconstructive, and theoretical knowledge about normal development, the organismic and environmental requirements, and the interplay of the innate and the experiential as they shape personality. The basic concepts regarding libido, aggression, object relations, structure, conscious-preconscious-unconscious, psychodynamics, adaptation, and defense formation can be reviewed from the standpoint of developmental emergence. Against the background of psychosexual progression and the separation-individuation process, the concept of psychic trauma and defense formation can be introduced to explain the origin and onset of pathological formations.

The elements of psychopathology can be discussed under two major headings: those impairing formation of structure and those disturbing function. Broadly speaking, these categories of psychopathology are seen as resulting from developmental failure occurring before and traumatic influence occurring after the attainment of object constancy. The concept of psychogenesis can then be addressed more pointedly, by taking up such subjects as the impact of trauma and deprivation in relation to their occurrence in the developmental progression, structure formation, phase-specific vulnerability, conflict, repression, symptom formation, etc. Specific generic forms of psychopathology such as psychoses, atypical ego development, borderline states, narcissistic disorders, character disorders, neuroses, situational reactions, and transient developmental disorders can then be discussed in relation to the degree of development of structure and object relations and the relative attainment of object constancy. Finally, the varieties of clinical syndromes within each of the generic psychopathologies can be studied.

A new dimension is now added to our teaching of analyzability. With the focus on the capacity for therapeutic alliance and ability to participate in the psychoanalytic process, each developmental line may be assessed as being either completed, somewhat less than completed, or clearly not completed. This is well illustrated by the adaptation of the analytic method for child analysis.

The very young child in the preoedipal phase has what might be termed a pre-analytic potential, development being incomplete in all lines. There is only a limited capacity for verbal expression, an imperfect attainment of object constancy, a limited degree of reality testing, and a phase dominance that, although age appropriate, is nevertheless easily vulnerable to regression in both drive and ego functioning. Other developmental achievements optimally necessary for analysis are not attained until the oedipal and latency phases: the establishment of a cohesive self-image, the triadic relationship, the capacity for signal anxiety, more adequate reality testing, relative autonomy of the superego, and the capacity to recognize and tolerate depressive states. These are, of course, not permanent attainments even in older children or adults. Even when there is no pull from pathological fixations, each subsequent phase of development puts previous developmental achievements to the test. For example, a traumatic latency may disrupt a developing superego autonomy, a stormy adolescence may lead to a loss of a previously established cohesive sense of self or of the capacity for drive regression without the involvement of ego and superego regression. The same may be said for the effects of extraordinary stresses in parenthood, middle age, or old age. Consequently, analyzability must be continuously reassessed as current and phase-specific developmental conflicts strain existing structures. What must also be assessed, at all ages, is the extent to which these underdeveloped capacities or temporary regressions from an attained phase dominance can be supplemented or aided to develop within the analytic situation. In the experience of child analysts, an initial supplementation of the child's capacities by the analyst, or analyst and parent, may lead to their being developed sufficiently for the goals and purposes of analysis.

We believe that the described concepts and viewpoint warrant the formulation of an explicitly developmental curriculum. The original conceptualization of such a model curriculum was by Lustman (1967), who noted that development is not disease-oriented but process-oriented. He felt that the teaching of pathology should serve the purpose of highlighting underlying formative processes, that the technique of analysis and observation could be introduced in relation to normal and pathological developmental processes, and that research and treatment could thus be integrated more closely, as they were in Freud's mind.

In a developmental curriculum the core courses would attempt to delineate individual differences in terms of age or developmental stage while conveying the continuities and commonalities in those stages, thus providing the basis for an appropriately flexible, discriminating, and valid application of the psychoanalytic method. Defining a core curriculum should make it evident that the growth of understanding and skills for a career emphasis on work with any given age group—children, adolescents, or adults—is built upon a basic understanding of psychoanalysis as it pertains to all age groups. It is also clear that professional qualification rests heavily on the clinical teaching in the case conferences, the continuous case seminars, and the supervised analysis.

The proposed curriculum (set forth below) illustrates the use of a developmental approach for courses throughout the curriculum. The unifying emphasis is on formative processes throughout the lifespan, encompassing what is now known about the significant factors that make for healthy or pathological development in individuals of every age. The aim is to integrate developmental concepts and basic metapsychological concepts not only in courses, but in supervised clinical work. The fundamental aspects of psychoanalytic education covered in the core curriculum are pertinent for both adult and child analysis.

There is, of course, the possibility of many variations in the design of the curriculum and individual courses, their timing and sequence, and the relation of coursework to other aspects of training. The structure of any program will inevitably depend upon the institute's teaching resources and its administrative and educational arrangements for conducting training analyses, clinical supervision, and coursework. The purpose of the presented outline of courses is to convey what is regarded as basic. The indications regarding content and teaching time are necessary to this purpose, but should not be understood as rigid specifications.

A Developmental Core Curriculum

This core curriculum is designed to be taught over a period of four years. The academic year is considered to be 32 weeks long and divided into two semesters. Although we acknowledge that certain courses may best be taught weekly and others on alternate weeks, each course is presented as being taught twice a month in alternation with another course. A semester-long course will thus consist of eight two-hour sessions (sixteen hours), and a year-long course of sixteen two-hour sessions (32 hours). Courses listed under the same Roman numeral in successive years reflect implementation of the spiral progression in learning.

As the basic curriculum incorporates concepts of human development in every phase, it provides the fundamental preparation necessary for both adult and child analysis. Students in child analysis, however, will take additional courses in aspects of theory and technique of the analysis of children and adolescents.

The student starting coursework in this curriculum is one who, by whatever process the institute uses, has been approved to be in classes. This student should be well established in personal analysis so that the inevitable transference responses to the instructors are, so far as possible, minimized.

FIRST YEAR (192 HOURS)

I. Theory

Basic Concepts (two semesters): Presentation of the basis for contemporary psychoanalytic theory. Beginning with Freud's early views on infantile sexuality, phases of instinctual development, the topographic model of the mind, and defense, the course continues with development, revisions in metapsychology, early concepts of narcissism, aggression, psychic energy, sadism, masochism, anxiety, and conflict, and concludes with early structural theory.

Readings in Theory (two semesters): Readings selected for the purpose of complementing the course on basic concepts. Ideally, the same instructor, or closely collaborating instructors, will teach both the basic concepts course and the correlated readings.

Introduction to Theory of Dreams (one semester): Study of Freud's *The Interpretation of Dreams* (1900), with emphasis on Chapter Seven.

II. Human Development (two semesters)

In the first year, this course covers development from the neonatal phase through the latency phase. Discussions of theory and literature are correlated with direct observation of newborn infants, older infants, toddlers, nursery school children, and early elementary school-age children. The value of direct observation in understanding human growth and development is incontestable.

Over the first and second years of the curriculum, this course spans the entire life cycle. It conveys an understanding not only of the details of psychic development but also of the nature of developmental processes. In order to highlight the interplay between biophysiological and psychological development, the course includes pertinent information about physical growth and development and the anatomical and physiologic changes occuring in the successive stages.

III. Psychopathology

Freud's Case Histories (one semester): Study of the five case histories, with the aim of correlating clinical material with Freud's early concepts of psychopathology.

Assessment of Analyzability (one semester): Study of criteria for analyzability of adults, children, and adolescents on the basis of assessment of the level of drive and ego development, including the capacity for object relations. Consideration should be given to having the students attend conferences in conjunction with the institute clinic, perhaps periodically throughout the span of training. In addition, an account of the assessment period should be given for each of the cases presented in the continuous case seminars. This course could be the basis for selection of the first supervised case, and might appropriately involve participation of the supervisor.

IV. Technique

Principles of the Psychoanalytic Method and Technique (one semester): Emphasis on the basic principles and the beginning of an analysis, with consideration of therapeutic alliance, development of the transference neurosis, clinical use of dreams, and the analyst's therapeutic attitudes and posture.

V. Clinical Case Conference [Adults, Adolescents, and Children) or Continuous Case Seminar (Adult) (two semesters)

Selection of a beginning case or cases emphasizing the opening phase of the analysis.

SECOND YEAR (192 HOURS)

The beginning of second-year coursework should, if possible, coincide with beginning the first supervised analytic case. In this curriculum the first case is an adult patient with a classical neurosis. While some institutes permit selected students to have a child as a first case, there is not enough experience with this approach to suggest it offers any advantage to the student in basic training. The advantage for the student in child-analytic training has been the opportunity to get started earlier in treating children, thus shortening the often prolonged training of the child analyst. With the model core curriculum, the child-analytic training requires no more than one extra year of required course work, and supervised work with children and adolescents can begin at the same time as the second adult case.

I. *Theory* (two semesters)

Study of structural theory in depth, including, whenever possible, correlations with recent contributions from experimental work in biology, psychology, and ethology, as well as appropriate reading.

II. *Human Development* (two semesters)

The second-year course covers development from adolescence through old age with continuing study of phase-specific developmental tasks, crises, conflicts, and the interaction of individual and environment.

III. *Psychopathology from the Developmental Viewpoint* (two semesters)

Presentation of basic concepts of psychopathology, embodying the approach outlined earlier in this report and thus focusing on development rather than nosology, emphasizing psychogenesis and psychodynamics and studying pathological formations as vicissitudes of development. Pertinent reading is included, and the concepts are illustrated by clinical material.

IV. Technique

Adult Analysis (one semester): Continuing from the first-year course on technique, this course focuses on the technique of adult analysis in the middle and later phases of the analysis.

Introduction to Child Analysis (one semester): Presentation of the distinctions and comparisons of analysis during different age periods and the principles of child analysis, including the following: a resume of the history of child analysis, emphasis on recent changes, the initial consultations with parents and child, assessment, preparation of child and parents for analysis, the role of the parents, the opening phase, adaptation of technique to different developmental levels, therapeutic alliance, transference, resistance, reconstruction, dreams, and termination. Reading is integrated with the course and includes important contemporary and early papers. Because of its overlap with the course on adult technique, this course should be taught by an experienced child analyst also experienced in the analysis of adults.

V. Continuous Case Seminar (Adult) (two semesters) and VI. Continuous Case Seminar (Child) (two semesters)

Ideally these seminars will be scheduled on alternate weeks throughout the year. If possible, in the child case seminar a prelatency-age child should be presented in alternation with a latency-age child. Similarly in the third-year adolescent case seminar, an early-phase adolescent would be alternated with a later-phase adolescent. Cases of both sexes would be represented in both seminars. The seminars should be viewed as vehicles for explorations beyond the material of the particular case under discussion.

THIRD YEAR (160 HOURS)

Those students who elect training in child analysis should by now be engaged in the supervised analysis of children and adolescents. For other students the supervised analysis of a child, although encouraged, is elective and its timing may vary.

I. Theory—Metapsychology (two semesters)

Review of earlier presented theoretical concepts in the light of the student's actual analytic work with patients and presentation of new concepts.

II. Psychopathology from the Nosologic Viewpoint (two semesters)

Presentation of psychopathology in the diagnostic terms of the classically described syndromes and also in the light of current knowledge. Discussion of neuroses, narcissistic disorders, borderline states, character disorders, psychosomatic illness, and psychoses in adults and children.

III. Technique

Adult Analysis (one semester): Discussion of technical issues in the use of dreams in adult analysis (including comparisons from the analysis of adolescents and children) and in the psychoanalytic treatment of patients in whom the developmental failure or deviation exists alongside neurotic psychopathology. Presentation of the rationale for variations in technical approach based on the patient's level of ego development.

Introduction to Adolescent Analysis (one semester): Presentation of the concepts of adolescent analysis, including: differing views on the analyzability of adolescents, the role of parents as contrasted with their role in child analysis, initial contact with the adolescent, analyzability and special problems of technique with the early and late adolescent, preparation for analysis, phase-specific areas of vulnerability and resistances in males and females, transference, criteria for termination, and technique of termination. Reading is integrated within the course. Ideally, this course should be taught by a child analyst also experienced in adult analysis.

IV. Continuous Case Seminar (Adult) (two semesters) and *V. Continuous Case Seminar (Adolescent)* (two semesters)

Ideally these seminars will be scheduled on alternate weeks throughout the year.

FOURTH YEAR (96 HOURS)

I. Technique

Advanced Technique—Clinical Case Conferences on Technique (one semester): Review and integration of the earlier technique courses in terms of both concepts and application. Clinical cases are used for comparison of adult, adolescent, and child cases with neurotic and other disorders.

II. *Continuous Case Seminar (Adult)* (two semesters) and III. *Continuous Case Seminar (either Child or Adolescent)* (two semesters)

Attendance at continuous case seminars is required until the student is approved for unsupervised work. The student in adult analysis attends the adult seminar, but may elect the child or adolescent seminar. The student in child analysis attends both the child and adolescent seminars.

IV. *Electives*

Electives vary from year to year and consist of courses or study groups offered on the basis of interest among faculty and students.

It is clearly the hope and expectation of the members of this commission that a developmental core curriculum will be evolved and refined, and that the shared ground of clinical understanding and technique between adult and child analysts will thereby be much enlarged. There will, of course, continue to be those who prefer to work primarily with children and those who prefer to work primarily with adults. For analysts in the first category, further training in the analysis of children and adolescents, beyond the core curriculum, will be required, as will further training in work with adults for those in the second category.

TRAINING IN CHILD AND ADOLESCENT ANALYSIS

Despite its difficult beginnings and the continuing shortage of child-analysis supervisors, child analysis in the United States has had a rapid and substantial development in recent years with regard to the number of training programs and child analysts. At present, most future child analysts are drawn from among trainees in child psychiatry. A smaller number are recruited from students in the adult curriculum who have been stimulated to undertake child-analytic training by a variety of factors. The usual adult-first, child-second training sequence in both psychoanalytic and psychiatric education tends to result in child analysts completing training some four or five years later than their colleagues in adult analysis; hence, the question of age at the time of admission to formal training deserves careful study. It includes the important questions of development, emotional maturity, and whether we can train significantly younger analysts whose quality, competence, and professional commitment compares favorably with that of today's graduates.

These considerations enter into planning for the future of child analysis. It is important that child analysts further extend their teaching activities into areas of learning where potential analysts will be exposed to psychoanalytic concepts at an early age. Indeed, all analysts should contribute as much as possible to such teaching—in adult and child psychiatric residency programs; in the pediatric, psychiatric, and child psychiatric curricula of medical schools; in universities; and even in college and high school programs.

The analyst of the future will continue to be a specialist in developmental theory, and because of the more direct access of child analysts to data from child-hood, they can and should play an important role in teaching and research on the interrelation between psychoanalytic treatment and developmental processes.

THE CHILD-ANALYSIS CURRICULUM

Observational Experience: In addition to the aims represented in the developmental core curriculum, the child-analysis student has the aim of learning the child's verbal and nonverbal language. This is best achieved by participation in nursery and elementary school activities. The experience should be discussed in a small group led by a child-analysis supervisor.

Further Considerations of the Principles of Child and Adolescent Analysis: In contrast to the case-oriented approach of the child continuous case seminar in the core curriculum, this course is topic-centered and considers principles of child and adolescent analysis pertaining to case selection, the beginning and the termination of analysis, differences in technique due to the age and developmental stage, and special problems in technique. Selected sequences of hours from cases in analysis are presented and related to theoretical problems and the pertinent literature.

Clinical Case Conferences (Children and Adolescents): This course allows the discussion of a wider variety of cases, reflecting different developmental stages, than is possible in the core continuous case seminars. Continuing this course until graduation permits review of the same cases at various stages of treatment.

Continuous Case Seminars in Child and Adolescent Analysis: The student in child and adolescent analysis will usually attend these seminars until graduation. Given implementation of a developmental core curriculum, there will probably be the need for a separate continuous case seminar for advanced child and adolescent students, to be taken in place of one of the core child continuous case seminars.

Child-Analysis Supervision

Requirements for starting adult or child cases vary considerably from institute to institute. Due to institute policies and other factors in the lives of the students, supervised work in child analysis usually begins relatively late in the educational process. This results in older students and later graduation from child programs as compared to adult programs. There is the further disadvantage that some students may complete their personal analysis before they even begin supervised work with children. Because of the possible specific impact of child-analytic work on the student, the supervisor may, in these instances, be more concerned than usual with the continuation of the therapeutic and developmental process set in motion in the student's analysis. Not unusually, there may be a revival in the student analyst of childhood conflicts with parents accompanied by an under- or overidentification with them, which may be reflected in the conduct of the child analysis. Certain typical residuals of childhood conflicts are encountered frequently in supervision of child-analysis students: the wish to rescue the child patient from the "bad" parent, hostility toward or the need to placate the child's parents, fear of possible aggression toward the child, discomfort with the child's aggressive behavior and with the empathic response it evokes. Finally, the face-to-face presence and the real demands of the child may diminish the maintenance of the usual optimal analytic distance. These difficulties must be worked out through the supervision, continuing self-analysis, and, if necessary, further personal analysis.

Child-analysis supervision should enhance the capacity to recognize and understand childhood events and dynamic factors that are studied only by way of reconstruction and the transference in adult patients. Child-analysis students observe the ongoing interaction between the developing child and the family, and come to know directly and appreciate the importance of specific familial and cultural influences on children. A sensitivity to these matters, facilitated in analyzing children, certainly enhances their use in analyzing adults. The child-analysis student also learns to employ the developmental approach to diagnose the child's level of ego development and to adapt psychoanalytic technique to the child's particular capacities and limitations: for example, the characteristic proclivity for action, a limited capacity for verbal free association, and a less complete or less intense transference neurosis. Such understanding also contributes to the treatment of adults with defective ego resources.

PSYCHOANALYTIC EDUCATION IN CHILD AND ADOLESCENT ANALYSIS: A HISTORICAL REVIEW AND SURVEY

THE VIEW IN 1960

In their survey of psychoanalytic education in the United States, Lewin and Ross (1960) reviewed the development of training in child analysis. American child analysis was directly stimulated by Anna Freud and her followers, especially Berta Bornstein, Dorothy Burlingham, Marianne Kris, Margaret Mahler, and Jenny Waelder-Hall. Lewin and Ross presented a somewhat pessimistic outlook on child-analytic training in this country. Child analysis did not appear to be moving toward fulfillment of the promise of its "golden age," that period in the early thirties culminating in the publication of Anna Freud's epic *The Ego and the Mechanisms of Defense* (1936) and the *Psychoanalytic Quarterly* special issue on child analysis (1935). Following that period, child analysts seemed to devote less and less time to child analysis and more and more time to work in child-guidance clinics and with social agencies, with the result that services for children improved greatly while programs for training in child analysis suffered.

Although courses in child analysis were being given as early as 1938 in New York, Boston, and Chicago, the first published minimal curriculum requirements of the Association made no mention of courses in child analysis. Probably the first official recognition of child analysis as an integral part of the curriculum was published by the Association in the 1950 *Bulletin of the American Psychoanalytic Association*. It cited the 1948 adoption of standards for the training of physicians in psychoanalysis (Kaufman, 1948) and included the following statement under the heading "Child Analysis":

> Designed to direct attention to therapeutic procedures with children, instruction is given on child analysis and therapeutic emergencies.
> The course is devoted to *The Neuroses of Children; The Instinctual Development of the Child; The Theory*

of Education; and to *The Indications and Criteria, Child Analysis and other Techniques of Psychiatric Treatment of Children. . . .*

Advanced lectures, clinical seminars and supervision are obligatory for those desiring to specialize in child analysis. The special requirements for specialization in this field are elective additions to the curriculum and correspond approximately to the type of instruction for therapeutic work with adults [pp. 4-5].

At the time these standards were adopted, only the Boston, Chicago, Philadelphia, and New York Institutes had established training programs in child analysis.

Lewin and Ross thought that a lack of definition of child analysis as a specialty was holding back the development of formal training, and suggested that there was indifference, possibly even opposition, to child-analysis programs on the part of the institutes. They noted that the field of child analysis seemed overshadowed by other psychotherapeutic approaches to children and by scientific investigation into general problems of child development. The goals of child-analysis training were unclear and there was even uncertainty about the long-range commitment to child analysis by child analysts themselves. There seemed to be a problem of scarcity of child patients and a serious question about how much child analysis was being done.

In 1960 Lewin and Ross presented certain questions as still needing to be answered: What is an ideal child-analysis curriculum? When should a student start child training? How much of the child curriculum should be open to the general student and how much should be required? Lewin and Ross concluded their chapter on child-analysis training by quoting Ives Hendrick (1958), who raised doubt that child analysis would survive as a subspecialty at all.

THE VIEW IN 1974

A more recent view of child-analysis training in the United States is given in the report of the work of the committees of the Board on Professional Standards (Panel, 1973). This report, which presents a summary of the work of the Committee on Child Analysis during the 25 years of its existence, provides an augmentation of the Lewin and Ross survey, as well as an interesting comparison. The work of the Committee on Child Analysis has included: the definition of child analysis and child-analytic technique; the setting and maintenance of standards for child-analysis training; the development of child-analysis training programs; and the contribution by child analysts and child-analytic research to psychoanalysis and psychoanalytic training.

The history of the committee can be divided into four periods. The first period, from about 1948 to 1951, was actually a period of "prehistory" for the committee as a committee of the Board on Professional Standards. The then Committee for the Psychoanalysis of Children and Adolescents was appointed by the President of the Association and functioned as one of its scientific committees. As its initial undertaking this committee formulated a consensus definition of the analytic treatment of a child, a definition that distinguished child analysis from psychoanalytically oriented child psychotherapy. Because it felt that the analyst's personal analysis followed by psychoanalytic work with adults was not adequate preparation for the analysis of children, the committee initiated discussion of the requirements for psychoanalytic work with children and forecast the establishment of specific training programs in child analysis. The first comprehensive plan for the training of child analysts was brought forth during this period.

During the second period, from about 1951 to 1957, a Subcommittee on Standards of Training in Child Analysis was appointed under the Board on Professional Standards. This committee formulated a tentative statement of minimal requirements for a training program in child analysis. In formulating this statement, the committee surveyed individual child analysts and studied the requirements of the four institutes with training programs in child analysis (Boston, Chicago, New York, and Philadelphia). The committee proposed to the Board that the training of all analysts should include both a course in child development and a clinical case seminar in child analysis. It also established that training in child analysis should be in addition to training in adult analysis. In December, 1954 the Board authorized the committee to develop procedures for accreditation of child-analysis training programs.

The third period, from 1957 to 1965, was governed by the recognition that the tentatively specified minimal requirements for a child-analysis training program were in actuality closer to ideal requirements. Because of the shortage of qualified child-analysis supervisors, insistence that an institute meet these requirements before initiating a program would have precluded or long-delayed the development of new child-analysis training programs. Accordingly, the committee recommended that while these requirements should be fulfilled in time, they would not have to be met prior to initial accreditation. It also recommended that the committee establish close liaison with the institutes for learning about and fostering the development of local child-analysis training programs. These recommendations were approved by the Board in May, 1958, and the annual meetings of the committee with institute representatives began at that time. In recognition of the committee's broadened responsibilities, in 1959 its name was changed to the Committee on Child Analysis.

The committee then served as a clearing house and forum at the national level for the discussion, evaluation, and dissemination of information regarding training in child analysis and the training and research activities of child analysts. At the same time, the committee, through its administrative functions, sought to ensure a high quality of training by working closely with the institutes.

By the beginning of the fourth period, from 1965 to the present, the number of training programs in child analysis had increased from the original four in 1952 to a total of fifteen, and there was a clear consensus regarding training standards, arrived at on the basis of a considerable body of knowledge and experience. The committee formulated proposals leading to the development and establishment of training programs in child analysis. After reviewing the earlier training requirements and practices, the committee drafted a revised statement of training standards in child analysis. This statement was submitted first to the institutes for their comment and criticism and then to the Board for its approval. It contained a section on "Enabling Procedures" that reflected the committee's experience with the development of new training programs. Although the number of child-analysis training programs had increased, the number of child analysts with the five years of postgraduate experience needed to qualify them for appointment as supervising child analysts was still small. Enabling provisions and procedures were thus necessary to permit the development of training programs in those institutes without programs, including the new institutes developed under the aegis of the Committee on New Training Facilities.

The proposed standards and enabling procedures were approved by the Board in December, 1966. By May, 1970, applications from all of the fifteen institutes with established training programs had been received and approved by the Board. The Board's 1954 declaration of intent to adopt standards for training and to accredit child-analysis training programs had thus been realized.

A comparison of early and current statistics provides one measure of the growth of child analysis in the United States. At the time of appointment of the original committee in 1948, there were no training programs in child analysis. By 1953 four institutes had programs; now (in 1974) there are sixteen approved training programs in child analysis. In addition, three institutes are in the process of developing training programs in consultation with the Committee on Child Analysis and its enabling subcommittees. Two other institutes have indicated their wish to develop child-analysis training programs as soon as their circumstances permit.

In regard to growth in the number of child analysts trained in institutes, the Lewin and Ross survey (1960) indicated that in 1958 there were 41 students enrolled in child-analysis training programs. The data submitted between 1969 and 1972 by the sixteen institutes with approved training programs show that, during this time, there were 170 students in training in child and adolescent analysis. In 1958, the child-analytic student body constituted five per cent of the total student body; today it is between fifteen and twenty per cent. In 1958 there were 31 supervisors in child analysis; today there are 79.

CONCLUSION

We want to stress the importance of a continuing review, assessment, and delineation of psychoanalysis as a science and as a therapeutic modality. It seems evident that the accelerating accumulation of data on the first years of life and the increasing number of child and adult patients with primary developmental deviations require the extension of our conceptual frame of reference to include more precisely the nature and interplay of developmental processes. We must attempt to integrate expanding knowledge of the preverbal stage into our analytic techniques and broaden our therapeutic aims to include patients whose pathology is essentially not secondary to neurotic conflict but rather the consequence of primary structural maldevelopment. While this is not meant to imply that all pathological formations are amenable to psychoanalytic treatment, it does suggest that we should attempt to broaden the valid criteria for analyzability and sharpen our diagnostic and prognostic skills. A revision of psychic structures and functions that involves more than the resolution of neurotic conflict is compatible with the concepts and principles of psychoanalysis or the analytic method. We also suggest that our analytic techniques may be adapted to preverbal reconstruction and work with the "basic transference" (Greenacre, 1971) and manifestations of primary structural deficiencies.

It is equally evident that, along with the need for broadening criteria for analyzability and increasing the repertoire of analytic techniques, there is need for continuing delineation of psychoanalysis lest the demarcation between it and other forms of psychotherapy become increasingly blurred. Such a delineation should rest on a fidelity to the basic concepts and principles of psychoanalysis as distinguished from the particular techniques devised to implement it therapeutically.

PLENARY DISCUSSION— EDWARD M. WEINSHEL, M.D.

The report of the Child Analysis Commission is, indeed, a comprehensive and far-ranging review of the field of psychoanalysis, and as such it deals with a variety of topics in a somewhat general fashion rather than focusing more intensively on the central issues. I believe the report would have been even more valuable if it had been more explicit about the nature both of the pathology that the group recommends psychoanalysis include within its scope and of those therapeutic approaches that can be predicated on the developmental orientation and approach. Also, it would have been most helpful if the commission had more sharply delineated which of its recommendations are already accepted psychoanalytic theory, practice, and training; which are new; and which of those are specifically derived from the developmental approach.

The most challenging recommendation is the statement: "psychoanalysis has reached a degree of maturity that not only permits but calls for a shift of emphasis within our overall conceptual framework.... The thesis and theme of this report is that the developmental orientation and approach provides [that] broader frame of reference." Insofar as the commission's initial assertion is not meant to imply that we now understand all we need to know about the neuroses, I do agree that our own scientific development requires another review of the relation of theory to therapeutic practice and further attempts to delineate the relation of the traditional "psychoneurotic model" of treatment to the treatment of other pathological formations.

It is important to differentiate between psychoanalysis as a theory and as a therapy. When we talk about psychoanalysis as a treatment, we are referring to the treatment of a psychoneurotic condition, utilizing the traditional model of psychoanalytic technique. It is by no means necessary to limit our conceptualization of psychoanalytic therapy to that kind of model and to those psychoneurotic conditions as long as we are clear about *what* we are treating and *how* we are using psychoanalysis in that treatment.

The traditional psychoanalytic model together with its specific techniques and procedures did not arise *de novo* in its present form. Freud experimented with a number of technical approaches and modifications that evolved into the therapeutic technique we utilize today. This evolution of technique was the result of specific theoretical formulations and, even more, of particular clinical observations. Freud's goal for psychoanalytic therapy was the uncovering of material repressed under resistance; and a therapeutic method was devised and employed to facilitate the recapturing of that repressed material.

I am not concerned here with whether the early cases Freud described were indeed "classical," as some writers have seriously questioned; instead I want to emphasize that he was attempting to understand and influence the result of certain conflicts, the repression of certain derivatives associated with those conflicts, and the return from repression in the form of certain symptomatic manifestations. The technique he developed was determined by his intent to understand and to retrace those processes leading to repression and the return of the repressed in these characteristic forms. This particular therapeutic experience produced cathectic and structural shifts, particularly in the ego. Freud (1937) wrote, "The business of analysis is to secure the best psychological conditions for the functions of the ego: with that it has discharged its task" (p. 250). At the same time, it was clear that for an individual to undergo this experience and to benefit from this treatment, a certain level of ego development was necessary.

I present this familiar material because I believe that a psychoanalytic therapy must involve more than a belief in psychoanalytic theory, and, as illustrated by the evolution of Freud's model, should reflect a rationale for the relation among pathology, theory, and technique. I therefore hope that any emerging models of a psychoanalytic theory for the treatment of pathology other than the neurotic will include the following:

1. A definable psychopathological constellation that derives from specific psychological conflicts, even if not altogether intrapsychic in origin, and that demonstrates a specific defensive configuration.

2. Some reasonably clear-cut therapeutic goals.

3. A therapeutic rationale and approach that indicate some consonance among the pathology, specific techniques utilized, and goals of treatment.

4. Evidence that what actually occurs in the treatment is consistent with the above.

I have not referred to the couch, free association, fixed frequency of sessions, types of interventions or activity that could be used, or the neutrality of the psychoanalyst. These familiar components of the psychoanalytic model for conducting an analysis involving primarily psychoneurotic structures may not be useful or relevant in the psychoanalytic treatment of other conditions, but their application or the utilization of other technical procedures should be based on a sound consideration of the factors mentioned above.

I believe that the traditional model of psychoanalytic therapy can be used for only a limited segment of possible psychological difficulties; furthermore, this model can be abused if applied to pathology for which it was not intended. I also believe that there is sufficient flexibility and comprehensiveness in our theory to enable us to devise therapeutic approaches to work with conditions other than adult neurotic pathology and where, therefore, the goal of treatment might well be other than the lifting of repression.

The most striking, best-known, and most carefully validated therapeutic innovation is that of child analysis. The question of whether child analysis should be considered a psychoanalytic therapy has been discussed, and certainly most of us now agree that child analysis is indeed a valid form of psychoanalytic therapy. I cannot, however, agree with those who insist that there is no difference between child and adult analysis, and that child analysis can be conducted in essentially the same manner as adult analysis. The technique of child analysis is appropriately based on an assessment of the child's psychosexual and ego development, the particular kinds of interruptions or distortions that occur in that development, the psychological resources of the child, and the reality situation in with the child lives. While the treatment of adults is based on similar assessments, the goals of treatment for the child are not and obviously cannot be exactly the same as those for the psychoneurotic adult. The therapeutic model for psychoanalytic work with children thus differs from that for adult psychoneurotics.

Constructing effective psychoanalytic models of therapy for adult non-psychoneurotic pathology may be considerably more difficult than doing so for child psychoneurotic pathology. One reason for this is that in the former group one often observes psychopathology, from several early levels of development, whose source and severity may be considerably clouded by the overlay and interaction with material from later stages of development. This can produce an exceedingly complex clinical picture in which it is difficult to delineate the specific foci to be dealt with in the therapy. On the other hand, the presence of the consequences of psychoneurotic conflict makes it possible to deal, at least in a limited way, with such patients using the traditional technical model. The work of Kohut and Kernberg provides examples of the serious attempts being made to establish theoretical, clinical, and therapeutic criteria for dealing with pathologies other than the neurotic, and such attempts are to be applauded and encouraged.

The developmental orientation and approach is the main theme of the commission's report. Although the commission's search for a broadened frame of reference and an extension of our therapeutic applications is praiseworthy, it is difficult to understand the emphatic statement that the developmental orientation and approach provides the basis for such broadening and extension, and the proposal that the developmental orientation and approach should be the central one for psychoanalysis seems questionable. The commission does explicitly disclaim an intention to downplay or discard other viewpoints; nevertheless, the tone of the presentation makes it clear that the developmental orientation and approach is not to be viewed as only one of a number of equally important points of view in psychoanalysis and psychoanalytic thinking. It is necessary to clarify the distinction being made between the traditional genetic point of view and the developmental point of view, especially because it has been some time since psychoanalysts considered development only in terms of childhood. There is no question that psychoanalysis has always been a developmental science and that the developmental orientation has always enjoyed a central position in its conceptualizations, but this position has been shared with the dynamic, the structural, the adaptive, and the economic points of view (despite the attacks leveled at the latter in recent years).

While there have been tremendous advances in the last decade in our understanding of human development, the understanding of psychoanalysis and its application affirms that the several points of view are really inseparable and must all be considered. One of the factors that has contributed most to both the elegance of psychoanalysis as a theory and the rigor it demands of its practitioners is the simultaneous application of all these perspectives to any particular psychological phenomenon. We have considerable historical evidence and experience that when there has been an inordinate emphasis on any one approach at the expense of the others, confusion and blurring of psychoanalytic theory and practice tends to occur.

The elevation of the developmental approach to a primary position in our thinking has its potential complications and does not necessarily provide us with better tools to cope with some of our tasks. There is, for example, the question of diagnosis and assessment, whether it be of patients or of applicants for psychoanalytic training. It is very doubtful that a still greater attention to developmental aspects will help clarify some uncertainties or facilitate decisions. It is true that what is known about a patient's development, the obstacles to an orderly development and the trauma that contributed to various developmental difficulties, has always been extremely important in understanding and assessing the patient; but it is not evident that such information is categorically more useful than a careful assessment of the patient's current capacities and liabilities. Early in the assessment process it is not too difficult to learn something about the major developmental events and to get a fairly good picture of what's currently going on in the patient; however, it is extremely difficult to get a precise and comprehensive picture of how the past has become the present. Often the links do not become available until after many months or years of treatment, and, if the original assessment has not been reasonably accurate and the patient is not actually amenable to classical analysis, that kind of data may never be obtained.

The commission would surely agree on the need for great care in differentiating what is known about a person on the basis of extra-analytic developmental observations from what is learned in the course of analysis; and just as there is the need for circumspection in using extra-analytic data in diagnosis and assessment, the same is even true in regard to reconstruction and interpretation. If the developmental approach is overstressed, it may lead to an excessive utilization of genetic interpretations, which may mesh with the intellectualizing and isolating resistances of the patient or even stimulate certain iatrogenic resistances of this nature. Also, in the utilization of developmental data from pregenital and particularly preverbal periods, what we consider reconstructions may, in effect, become constructions with a high suggestive potential. Finally, the genetic fallacy—here entitled the developmental fallacy—should be included among these caveats. This is the tendency to believe that if the analyst understands how a certain piece of pathology developed, then a comparable understanding can be conveyed to the patient, or that if the analyst understands something, it is therefore treatable by analytic means. This developmental fallacy warrants special attention with regard to very early material, particularly preverbal material.

I am in general agreement with most of the positions and recommendations that have been expressed in regard to psychoanalytic education; but again I question whether the central position of the developmental orientation and approach is necessary. Certainly, enthusiastic endorsement is in order for the recommendations to give

developmental material a prominent position in the institute curriculum; provide all students with some experience in working with children; increase emphasis on the
teaching and learning of basic principles of psychopathology rather than nosological categories; emphasize relatively fewer courses in the curriculum and a sequential organization, consistent with the "spiral" concept of
learning; make training analysis central in the training
experience and conduct it along the lines of the traditional model of psychoanalytic treatment; give all students
sufficient experience in working with that traditional
model; encourage and view re-analysis with a positive attitude; take cognizance of the fact that regressive tendencies do appear in students during the course of training;
and provide for the essential continuing assessment of our
work as psychoanalytic educators.

The proposed curriculum is a sound one. However, I
am sure that it is not intended as the only curriculum that
could be utilized, and each institute will necessarily
construct curricula not only on the basis of pedagogic
philosophy but also in terms of available teaching
resources. It is not clear why this curriculum is presented
as a primarily developmental one, or predicated on the
basis of the special developmental approach. Rather, it
seems to me, that it is an excellent curriculum that, at
least in general outline, has long been used in most of our
institutes.

The commission has not limited the concept of
development to infancy and childhood, and certain
apparent parallels are drawn between the child's
development and that of the student in training. It
would be unfortunate to overemphasize these similarities and translate them too literally into formula-

tions for establishing and conducting training programs. Analytic students are adults, and they should
be and want to be treated as adults. Institutes, of course,
should not set up artificial obstacles and frustrations for
students, nor treat every aspiration or complaint as symptomatic in nature. Nor should the institutes be converted
into therapeutic communities wherein libidinal or
narcissistic gratifications are self-consciously provided.
Our responsibility is to establish an average expectable
environment in which the student can obtain an optimal
personal analysis and a reasonably effective psychoanalytic education. Adapting to such an environment, as to
any reality, inevitably entails frustration, transient loss of
self-esteem, regressive tendencies, and individual vulner-
abilities. It would be remiss if overconcern for the latter
superseded dedication to the former. I believe that this
view is valid for all stages of the student's course in the
institute: for the selection procedures, personal analysis,
didactic seminars, clinical supervision, and graduation
requirements. The fact that some of the students we
select for psychoanalytic training eventually fail to meet
our rigorous but not unrealistic standards for graduation
and certification, and that we cannot be more accurate in
our predictions or more effective in our work, is one of
the painful realities with which we live and struggle.

RESPONSE TO THE DISCUSSANT BY
CALVIN F. SETTLAGE, M.D., CHAIRMAN
COMMISSION ON CHILD ANALYSIS

I wish to make clear that our emphasis on the
developmental orientation and approach does not
attempt to introduce a totally new concept; rather, it

proposes the use of an old concept in a new way. As our report affirmed, psychoanalysis has always been a developmental science. From the time of its inception, psychoanalysis as a method of treatment has been inextricably bound to a psychological theory of human development. In T. S. Kuhn's (1962) terms we are operating within the framework of normal science, attempting the further articulation and refinement of an existing theoretical paradigm rather than suggesting a new, revolutionary paradigm. Our view that development can provide a broadened frame of reference for understanding and evaluating advances in theory and particular adaptations of the analytic method certainly does not minimize or discard other viewpoints or relegate any basic psychoanalytic concepts to a subsidiary position. Indeed, we fully agree with the statement that the understanding and application of psychoanalysis demand the simultaneous consideration of all viewpoints.

At the heart of the issue is the question of the necessary distinctions between the genetic point of view and the developmental one. The terms "genetic" and "developmental" have indeed been used quite interchangeably in psychoanalytic thinking and writing. This is so despite the fact that from the beginning they have had implied differences in meaning.

In his 1913 paper, "The Claims of Psycho-Analysis to Scientific Interest," Freud chose a separate heading, "The Interest of Psycho-Analysis from a Developmental Point of View," to indicate that psychoanalysis was from the very first directed toward tracing developmental processes as well as the genesis of neurotic symptoms. In speaking of developmental rather than genetic processes, Freud was, I believe, drawing a distinction between the retrospective, reconstructive view of developmental processes, the genetic point of view, and the view of on-going and evolving developmental processes — the developmental point of view.

Hartmann and Kris (1945) noted that the emergence of psychoanalytic ego psychology required distinctions that seemed irrelevant when Freud first formulated his genetic propositions. They were, of course, referring to the maturation and development of ego structure and functions outside the sphere of conflict. They also introduced the concept that conflict was inherent in normal as well as pathological development, and suggested that cultural influences come to bear on these nonpathogenic maturational conflicts in the shaping of human personality. These formulations made it apparent that much of what takes place in normal development may not be accessible to genetic reconstruction in the psychoanalytic situation. Although it contributes importantly to our understanding of normal development, the primary contribution of the genetic approach is to our understanding of pathogenesis.

Hartmann (1950), referred to the necessity for greater refinement in the use of early developmental data as indicators of actual or potential conflict and pathology, and pointed out that they are not the same. He indicated that the concept of developmental phases is indispensable for genetic research. He further noted that the analytic method had the limitation of not providing information on the undifferentiated phase or preverbal stage, and called for building the psychoanalytic theory of early developmental stages on the basis of data derived from both reconstruction and direct observation. Drawing the distinction in still another way, Hartmann

and Kris (1945) stated that however rich the data sup-
plied by the psychoanalytic interview, the thus-derived
view of the child's development is on the whole not sufficient to allow for the full and detailed formulation of
genetic propositions. Their thinking takes on increased
importance as the widening scope of psychoanalysis
includes concern with psychopathology stemming from
the preoedipal phases of development and requires
conceptual distinctions that did not seem particularly relevant before.

Whereas the genetic point of view is on the same
level of abstraction as the dynamic, structural, and other
metapsychological concepts, the developmental orientation and approach is, as the commission defines it, at a
lower level of abstraction, closer to clinical and direct
observational data. By way of illustration, Anna Freud's
(1963, 1965) concept of developmental lines is at this
lower level of abstraction. It would be incorrect to suppose that the commission places the developmental orientation and approach in an elevated primary position and
the other approaches and points of view in subordinate
positions. Rather, it provides a conceptual framework
that studies the individual in the light of all the basic
concepts and viewpoints, while emphasizing the longitudinal continuum of development. The genetic point of
view enabled psychoanalysis to bring the study of personality development within the scope of developmental psychology; however, it alone cannot unravel all the
complexities of the developmental processes.

I shall now respond to some of Dr. Weinshel's more
specific comments. He suggests criteria to be met by
emerging models of psychoanalytic therapy for the
treatment of non-neurotic pathology, and proposes that

any such model should include a clearly circumscribed psychopathological constellation derived from relatively specific psychological conflicts. I believe it is inconsistent to use the long-standing definition of neurotic psychopathology, namely structural conflict, to define essentially non-neurotic psychopathology. Similarly, when it is suggested that the traditional psychoneurotic model of therapy is misused or abused when applied to pathology for which it was not intended, one can only agree that the model should not be used where it does not apply. The call for the delineation of clearly circumscribed psychopathological constellations must be tempered by the frequent observation, in the same patient, of psychopathology derived from several levels of development. It is this very circumstance of mixed psychopathologies that prompted the commission to advocate the special value of the developmental orientation and approach.

The question thus raised is whether it is more useful to conceptualize in terms of a series of discretely different psychopathologies and of equally different models for their treatment, or in terms of one basic psychoanalytic model, which can be adapted technically in accordance with the nature of the psychopathology and the patient's capacities. I agree that there are differences between adult and child analysis, but I disagree with the view that child analysis requires or constitutes a different model from the traditional adult model. Child analysis treats psychoneurotic structural conflict, and it employs the same concepts and principles and has the same fundamental goals as adult analysis, namely the lifting of repression and the effecting of favorable psychological structural change. It also has the same theory of technique, differing only in the specific technical adaptations made in accommodation to the child's level of development. These techniques are not parameters employed in deviation from the analytic method or model, but variations and adaptations required to adhere to it.

The commission did not address in detail the question of the specific technical use of developmental knowledge in the analytic situation. Had we done so, we would not have proposed the techniques Dr. Weinshel thought might result from the developmental approach — namely, the frequent use of extra-analytic observations, excessive use of genetic interpretations, use of developmental data from pregenital and preverbal periods in the formulation of suggestive recommendations, or the notion that an analyst's hypothetical understanding can or should be conveyed to the patient simply because the analyst is capable of constructing it. Our thoughts in this regard are contained in the view that the greater the precision and extent of our understanding of early development, the greater the possibility of our more fully discovering the representation of early psychogenetic factors in the psychoanalytic material. I believe that Hartmann (1950) had that in mind when he suggested that direct observational studies of early development would lead to a growing awareness of the sign or signal function that behavioral details may have for the observer in the psychoanalytic situation.

Our recommendation that we take cognizance, through a developmental orientation, of different modes and rates of progression and avoid uniform progression in training does not mean that our institutes should be converted into therapeutic communities, or that students should not be treated as adults but provided with artificial sources of libidinal and narcissistic gratifications. On the contrary, the suggestion concerns the need for continuing attention to individual differences in our students as adults in the adult developmental phases of the life cycle.

Understanding why the commission regards the proposed curriculum as an example of a developmental core curriculum, predicated on a developmental orientation and approach, requires an understanding of the presented concepts. As was stated, a developmental core curriculum is not simply an aggregation of traditionally offered courses and seminars in psychoanalytic education. The particular sequence of courses is planned to convey a continuing and expanding understanding of human development and its relevance to psychoanalytic theory and practice, and the developmental approach is utilized in the teaching of the curriculum with the aim of providing a similar understanding within all topic areas.

SUMMARY OF CONFERENCE DISCUSSION

The several group discussions of this commission's report were almost exclusively concerned with evaluating the significance of the commission's designation and strong recommendation of a so-called developmental approach and orientation. The dominant response within the several discussion groups was an enthusiastic appreciation of the commission's effort to organize and underline the importance of accumulating data on early human development and maldevelopment. All such knowledge, whether from an observational or clinical therapeutic setting, was naturally viewed as most welcome having great value for increasing fundamental understanding of both psychology and psychopathology.

However, certain questions and reservations about the commission's presentation did arise. One objection was to the postulation that the new data required a new approach, neglecting the fact that psychoanalysis has always been a developmental psychology and has always stressed the relation between normal and abnormal development. It was therefore suggested that the designation of a special developmental orientation and approach was superfluous and potentially confusing conceptually. Another objection expressed in one form or another by several discussants, was that the commission seemed to claim too much immediate practical usefulness for the new developmental data. As indicated, everyone agreed to the obvious potential value of the new information in this area, but it was felt that much further thought and work remained to be done in the clarification of concepts and the translation into valid therapeutic, educational, and prophylactic methods to warrant the commission's rather encompassing claims and conclusions. It is clear, then, that although there was an eagerness to assimilate and utilize the contributions of developmental observation and research, there was some reluctance to accept the commission's narrow definition of the so-called traditional psychoanalytic approach, which seemed to justify the addition of a new developmental approach.

A spectrum of opinion was expressed regarding the importance of child-analytic clinical experience for all students of analysis, whatever their future specialization. Some discussants seriously questioned its necessity for those students who did not intend to analyze children after graduation; however, most others felt that direct clinical experience with children could not fail to be broadening for future analysts of adults, just as it is generally held that analytic work with adults is important for future child analysts. The discussion indicated an awareness that much further carefully reasoned rather than impressionistic consideration of the topic is essential.

There was certainly no objection to the recommendations that clinical and theoretical seminars on the analytic treatment of children and systematic child observation experience should be integrated into the general curriculum for all students.

Two aspects of the report received very little attention in any of the discussion groups: the developmental core curriculum and the specific application of developmental understanding to the education and evaluation of the analytic student. As to the curriculum, the general opinion seemed to be that the proposed curriculum and its philosophy were not radically dissimilar from that already in use in most institutes. Whatever the shortcomings in actual practice because of insufficient personnel or time, the objective has always been an educationally effective and well-integrated presentation of psychoanalytic knowledge. With regard to the analytic student, it was apparently thought by many that the commission's recommendations offered little that was specifically useful beyond what has long been accepted as sound educational practice.

The commission earned high praise in each discussion group for their attempt to describe the many implications of their proposed point of view in almost every aspect of psychoanalysis and psychoanalytic education. It was remarked that in doing so they risked spreading the argument too thin; nevertheless, the very active debate stimulated by the report was proof of its great value to the conference.

Psychoanalytic Research

Morton F. Reiser, M.D., Chairman
Peter H. Knapp, M.D., Recorder
Samuel Abrams, M.D.
Elwyn James Anthony, M.D.
Jacob A. Arlow, M.D.
Charles Fisher, M.D.
Mrs. Selma Fraiberg
Merton M. Gill, M.D.
Leo Goldberger, Ph.D.
Mardi J. Horowitz, M.D.
Mark Kanzer, M.D.
I. Charles Kaufman, M.D.
Lester Luborsky, Ph.D.
Peter B. Neubauer, M.D.
George H. Pollock, M.D.
Lewis L. Robbins, M.D.
Alfred H. Stanton, M.D.

Psychoanalytic Research

ORIGINAL CHARGE

What are the obstacles in the way of stimulating a more vigorous research involvement within analysis, about analysis, and in psychoanalytically sophisticated approaches in related behavioral sciences? What is the best mixture of prior backgrounds, experiences, and commitments in the student body? How can the research perspective best be integrated into the training of all analytic students? What is the proper place of scientific research training in relation to individual progression in regular training? What and how much should be taught of "soft" and "hard" research ideologies and technologies?

PREPARATORY COMMISSION REPORT

This report concerns psychoanalysis and research more than psychoanalytic research, which might denote some unique enterprise. Psychoanalysis is a professional discipline with many aspects, social-organizational as well as scientific. Research, as scholarly investigation, is also multi-faceted. In general, we will direct our attention to all research that is relevant to psychoanalytic practice, theory, or education.

The purpose of research is to gather evidence under conditions of maximum feasible specification of the conditions of observation and data collection, to make inferences according to communicable rules, and to draw theoretical conclusions that enlarge the existing understanding of the world as well as our capacity for further productive inquiry. Variations of research overlap in subtle ways. A distinction between experimental and naturalistic investigation is useful but not absolute. It is incorrect to see experimental methods as constituting the essence, or even the ideal goal, of research since they may not be applicable in many areas, including much of the research germane to psychoanalysis. Psychoanalytic investigation may span a wide range of questions, from systematic examination of psychoanalytic process and outcome to studies whose main focus lies beyond the confines of psychoanalysis but which are informed in some way by the theories of the psychoanalytically sophisticated investigator.

Actually, certain recognizable categories have emerged, so that a rough classification of studies can be offered, while still allowing for considerable overlap:

1. Studies of psychoanalysis itself (largely naturalistic)

a. Studies of the processes involved in psychoanalysis

b. Studies of the outcome of psychoanalytic treatment

2. Applications of psychoanalysis (both naturalistic and experimental)

a. Use of the psychoanalytic method, as in some psychosomatic studies and investigations into special states, e.g., delinquency and psychosis

b. Use of psychoanalytic theory as a broad explanatory frame of reference, as in child development research, some psychosomatic and many social-historical investigations

3. Studies (largely experimental) testing specific propositions derived from psychoanalytic theory, as in investigations of cognitive controls and studies of dreaming, suggestion, memory, etc.

Our report does not aim to review comprehensively what is now a substantial body of publications. Several surveys (Luborsky and Spence, 1971; R. Jones, 1970; Kohut, 1970) summarize specific studies in these areas of inquiry. Instead, we will address the following general questions: Does psychoanalysis face problems in developing and maintaining scientific productivity? If so, do those problems call for changes within the profession? A preliminary answer to these questions was provided recently by an ad hoc committee on scientific activities of the Association (Kohut, 1970). This body concluded that all was not well in the scientific life of psychoanalysis. A suggested remedy, already acted upon, was the establishment of a standing committee concerned with scientific activities in the Association.

The present commission discerned three separate but related problems, and accordingly divided itself into three subcommittees: (1) the state of research into psychoanalysis; (2) the interface between psychoanalysis and other branches of science; (3) the scientific ambience within psychoanalytic institutes. In each area we endeavored to survey past accomplishments and current problems and to make recommendations for the future.

RESEARCH INTO PSYCHOANALYSIS

Throughout the history of psychoanalysis attempts have been made to assess its therapeutic impact on outcome as evidenced by earlier surveys (Hendrick, 1958) and more recently by an attempt of the Association to conduct its own large-scale investigation of the question (Hamburg et al., 1967). Several groups have contributed to this complex issue (Kernberg et al., 1972; H. Klein, 1960; Wallerstein, 1968; Weber et al., 1967), and in several institutes further studies are currently in progress (Greenspan and Cullander, 1973). However, in an over-all sense, the effort, time, and funds devoted to such investigations have been relatively limited and the yield insufficient. Clearly, there is still an imperative need for research in this crucial area.

Difficulties are, in part, substantive and methodological: lack of generally acceptable criteria for illness and health; problems in assessment of change; clinical-ethical considerations—namely, that in order to elicit the requisite information it may to some extent be necessary to reopen processes already brought to some resolution, whether entirely successful or not, in psychoanalysis (Pfeffer, 1959). These methodological obstacles, though real, are by no means insurmountable, as evidenced by the laborious but definitive advance in the related general field of psychotherapy research. Our conclusion is that a second group of obstacles, social-organizational in nature, have prevented more psychoanalysts from undertaking the arduous process of systematic self-scrutiny. To do so requires some detachment from the clinical task, readiness to examine it both critically and sensitively, familiarity with techniques of scaling and measurement of subtle variables, and ability to utilize appropriate statistical measures. The task calls for a multidisciplinary approach, which is always complex and which frequently carries with it attendant organizational difficulties.

We recommend that all levels of psychoanalysis, national and local, strongly support further serious and informed efforts to assess psychoanalytic results. Some commission members pointed out that such efforts were congruent with trends in the national medical scene toward peer review and self-evaluation. Although skepticism prompted the question whether those procedures alone could accomplish the necessary scientific task, it should be emphasized that attempts at self-appraisal are now becoming mandatory in serious professional groups. Our national organization must take the initiative in stimulating and supporting these endeavors, and assume responsibility for ensuring that the work is as competent and as relevant as available methods permit.

There has been a considerable effort to study the processes involved in psychoanalytic treatment. A large part of the literature has been devoted to elaborating the psychoanalytic process. As a result, there has been a steady growth of knowledge about the psychoanalytic situation: transference, resistance, interpretation, and the symbolic modes of expression and concealment. However, inquiry has not been sufficiently systematic or reproducible, or carried out in ways allowing satisfactory scientific comparison between competing views. Conclusions often seem to stem from assertion more than from evidence and reasonable inference; they thus frequently fail to persuade other psychoanalytic scholars, much less those from different disciplines.

The most important gains in information about the psychoanalytic situation have been made by the treating analyst who contemplates and reviews his or her own clinical observations. Involved in the production of data, the analyst selects from them, although often in ways that are not made explicit. Some questions may be susceptible only to this research method, and some analysts are particularly gifted in doing it; certainly, the commission agrees with the many who believe that this mode is a most important one for continued efforts in the future.

However, in addition to the traditional clinical mode of investigation, other research avenues should be pursued. Efforts are now being made to elaborate new approaches, located somewhere between the existing methods of so-called hard science and purely descriptive efforts adapted to the unique requirements of psychoanalysis itself. These new approaches involve various ways of observing the analytic situation by analytically informed observers who are not themselves directly involved in the treatment. Review and utilization of data is made possible by the retention of information through notation, recording, or some form of third-party observation. Electronically recorded data may be used to great advantage (Bergman, 1966), although evidence has also been offered for the advantages of notes (Dewald, 1972) or quasi-supervisory reports, the technique of consensual analysis (Windholz, 1972). Investigators have focused on clinical samples selected systematically according to the various contexts they represent (Knapp et al., 1970; Luborsky, 1967); they have also sought ways to examine the structure of the psychoanalytic interchange using clinical research approaches (Gill, 1972) and computer methods (Dahl, 1972; Spence, 1970).

Some argue that such recording, retention, and review of data may modify the situation so that it is no longer psychoanalytic. Proponents of the newer methods reply that significant distortion of the psychoanalytic process can be avoided through careful attention to and working through the implications of the research methods for transference and resistance. Still others maintain that even were the resultant situation found to be somewhat altered, important research could still be done, in that the process would still be enough like the original to serve as a useful and relevant model while retaining a primarily therapeutic emphasis. The most important point is that by examining the raw data of psychoanalysis — and in our opinion only by this route — an observer can see and study patterns and phenomena virtually impossible to note by the analyst directly involved in the therapeutic endeavor. Unless such independent observation plays a role in our research approach, further investigation of the psychoanalytic process will be severely limited. Psychotherapy research was greatly assisted by introduction of tape recording more than twenty years ago. We should allow no less a methodological advance for our own form of therapy, since every effort must be made to deal with the problems of recording and studying primary psychoanalytic data.

The intentions to provide optimum treatment and to obtain reliable data for the development of valid theory may coexist but require consideration of ethical issues and the need for safeguards. The psychoanalytic situation is unlike any other in the degree of privacy required and the nature of the information revealed. If the usual situation must be altered in some regard for scientific purposes, the patient must and can have safeguards. This is also true for the analyst, whose work may be adversely affected by the experience of being observed, to the detriment of the patient.

Most important, we must enlist individuals who have both the necessary skills for conducting psychoanalytic treatment and the temperament to commit themselves to scientific study of it; the joint exercise of these functions may be enhanced by training. This training must include painstaking analysis, not only of the impact of research upon transference, but also of the countertransference effects. Work with a group of colleagues can be most helpful in this respect. Further, if a broad pool of data can be collected the task of preserving anonymity of both patient and analyst becomes simplified. Finally, we suggest that the practice of accumulating data and postponing its use for research until after the treatment has been completed — as recommended by Freud himself — is a further aid, particularly if it is combined with assurance to the patient of his or her ultimate control over use of the material.

Informed consent is, of course, necessary, even though such consent, given at the start of the analysis, may be based on only fragmentary knowledge on the part of the patient. Nevertheless, it is ethically mandatory that a person consent to participating in a research project whenever some experimental procedure is anticipated as part of treatment. We should note that although third-party observations are not a usual aspect of research, electronic recording has become more frequent. The major objection to it comes from the analyst more often than the patient. Informed-consent procedures may be facilitated and, in fact, made more relevant, if they center not on the fact of recording, but on the safeguards over access to and use of the recorded data. Psychoanalysis itself, being a psychologically determined effort, may inevitably be affected by the act of consent itself—or by the act of not giving consent, if that eventuates. The dilemma will not disappear and should not be avoided, but it may be minimized by freedom from conflict on the psychoanalyst's part and by implicit and explicit reassurances to the patient. Its effects can then be described and rational choices made.

The sheer volume of data obtained in an analysis creates a problem. With electronic recording, storage needs are great and retrieval systems imperative. Editing to preserve anonymity poses further problems. Undoubtedly, much of what is stored will not be used. A projection of the anticipated needs of investigators committed to study of psychoanalytic material is thus necessary in order to provide incentive and rationale for data-collection efforts.

Perhaps the most important difficulty facing psychoanalytic investigators is the complexity of psychoanalytic material—the lack of accepted ways of reducing data and making inferences from them. More basic research is needed in this area, including: (1) studies and descriptions of the phenomenology of conscious and unconscious mental life and of our ways of deriving the meanings of behaviors, thoughts, and emotions in both patient and analyst; (2) development of methods for segmenting information into meaningful units as well as correlating these with each other or independent variables, taking as a point of departure the efforts at content analysis already available; (3) examination of the processes of inference, especially those by which analysts go from manifest material to conclusions about unconscious processes, making an effort to stay close to clinical rather than metapsychological theory; (4) studies of emotion and the subtleties of its communication; (5) examination of characteristics in the therapist, such as empathy, sensitivity, and incisiveness; (6) investigation as to how these elements interact with the development of insight and personal growth in the psychoanalytic experience. The list could be greatly expanded and it is clear that the processes of psychoanalysis present a host of researchable problems.

RECOMMENDATIONS

1. Efforts should be made to retain the data from analyses. Toward this end every training institute should maintain files on supervised cases. A general file, preferably national in scope, should be maintained of recorded analyses. These files should, given appropriate safeguards, be available to qualified researchers. Conceivably they could be coded into particular diagnostic, operational, theoretical, and therapeutic categories (Schwartz and Rouse, 1961), though in view of the diverse use to which they might be put, such codings would at best be of limited and preliminary value.

2. Safeguards should be developed for protecting confidentiality, including anonymity of both patient and therapist. Measures must be developed for securing informed consent of patients and insuring some degree of patient control over the use of the data on a continuing basis.

3. Careful planning for research into the processes of psychoanalysis is necessary and should include: plans for sampling the large volume of raw data; specification of research goals, so that there is a fit between time available, topics selected, and technology used; a sequential approach to large goals.

4. An awareness of multiple possible paradigms for study of the psychoanalytic situation is needed. It may well be that to capture certain crucial aspects of the psychoanalytic encounter we must develop uniquely appropriate methods, capable of better exploiting the rich data. Such methods could ultimately prove to be less like those of the natural sciences and more like approaches used in the social, political, and historical sciences, or in linguistics, literature, and art. For this reason psychoanalysis must recruit into its research ranks scholars from a wide variety of fields and continue to examine the interface between itself and other behavioral sciences.

The Interface between Psychoanalysis and Other Sciences

Empirical studies of child development have modified our views of the first years of life; the formation of libidinal ties; specific characteristics of libidinal, cognitive, and ego development; and the timetable for unfolding developmental events. Comparative psychology and animal ethology have both been informed by and enlarged the scope of psychoanalytic thought. The field of psychosomatic medicine received its initial impetus from psychoanalytic observations and hypotheses. Using psychoanalytic methods to a limited extent and psychoanalytic theory both in clinical and animal experiments, the field has expanded widely and in many areas has maintained fruitful interaction between psychoanalytic concepts and a variety of experimental approaches. Psychoanalysis has applied itself to studying other clinical states such as delinquency, the addictions, and the psychoses. Research into dreams and dreaming, which received great impetus from the discovery of the electrophysiological concomitants of dream activity and the various stages of sleep, has also developed an extensive body of knowledge that has both modified psychoanalytic theory and been enriched by it (R. Jones, 1970). Contributions of psychoanalytic investigators have been prominent though far from exclusive in this investigative arena (Fisher, 1965). Study of perceptual psychology and of cognitive controls has grown into a body of experimental work, to which psychoanalytically trained investigators and psychoanalytic hypotheses have added extensively (G. Klein, 1954; Schwartz and Rouse, 1961). Psychoanalytic principles have also been widely applied in literary, historical, and social inquiry.

This area is by no means free of problems. The majority of practicing psychoanalysts, although well equipped by virtue of clinical skills and knowledge, remains apart from participation in these interface activities. To clarify the relation of psychoanalysis to other disciplines, it may help to indicate several relevant factors:

1. Psychoanalysis from its inception has had to struggle against criticism, often hostile and irrational, from other fields. It has consequently tended to remain somewhat isolated and outside of organized academic investigation.

2. Its clinical theory is closely tied to its unique observations, so that colleagues from other fields never

before exposed to psychoanalytic data, trained primarily in laboratory methods, or committed to therapeutic approaches stemming from other theories, find it uncongenial. Furthermore, psychoanalytic language and terminology, based on the interlocking between theory and clinical findings, has inevitably become so specialized that clear communication with other disciplines is often difficult for both participants in the dialogue.

3. An inexperienced psychoanalyst interested in obtaining data from other disciplines might naïvely assume that the appropriate interpretation of these data can only be derived from the psychoanalytic point of view. He would thus convey to his colleagues in other fields a sense of superiority or defensiveness, further increasing difficulties in joint work.

4. In an attempt to overcome some of these problems, psychoanalytic institutes have developed programs for training colleagues from other professions. However, these programs have occasionally resulted in further difficulties. Most nonmedical graduates have continued to apply their psychoanalytic training in the area of original interest; a few, however, have changed their orientation, and partially or totally moved away from their primary field to become analytic practitioners. Such outcomes have caused concern in both psychoanalytic and academic circles, although the gradual shift from early absorption in research to other pursuits, whether clinical or administrative, is a fact of life in the careers of many scientists.

These factors have led some psychoanalysts to take the position that an interchange with other disciplines may still be premature, probably unrewarding scientifically, and might only dilute the core of psychoanalytic thought. Others, including this commission's members, hold that the intellectually wide interests of psychoanalysis demand constant interchange of data for the continual development of psychoanalytic theory and practice. Surely one of our ultimate goals is to formulate a general theory of human psychology compatible with expanding biological and sociological knowledge.

More specifically, psychoanalysis is interested in how complex behaviors originate both phylogenetically and ontogenetically. To discover general developmental principles, it is necessary to consider all the factors involved, to relate the innate to the experiential, to describe and account for the maturational timetable, and to account for exceptional instances and discontinuities in development. All this requires familiarity with the accumulating knowledge from many related fields, including animal behavior, behavioral genetics, and the neurosciences.

We are reaching for an integrated theory of psychology. Such an interdisciplinary ideal, we firmly believe, will not lead to the reduction or even subordination of psychoanalytic knowledge to physiologic or mechanistic views, but rather will greatly enrich and stengthen psychoanalysis.

RECOMMENDATIONS

1. We must develop interface structures, that is, organizational forms of sustained interaction between psychoanalysts and other behavioral scientists. We do not mean occasional symposia or workshops but groups devoted to serious interdisciplinary and collaborative investigation.

2. Scientific rigor needs to be a part of training. The tradition of a scientific paper or case report as a requirement for graduation is praiseworthy, but these exercises need more exacting standards of evidence and inference.

3. Although the psychoanalytic institute's task is not to provide basic instruction in behavioral sciences, it should foster a broad outlook and respect for the contributions of other disciplines. To that end, the curriculum should include exposure to interdisciplinary knowledge along with psychoanalytic theory and practical instruction. In the case of institutes lacking requisite faculty, we suggest the use of visiting lecturers, supported as far as possible by the Association. It is equally important for the student body to be interdisciplinary in order to amplify the impact and widen the range of course instruction.

4. Publication policies promoting interdisciplinary review and expanding the exchange between psychoanalysis and other sciences should be encouraged. This trend is already manifest in several annuals and could be extended in other psychoanalytic journals.

Institute Ambience and Administrative-Organizational Factors

Certain institutes have made deliberate efforts to maintain a research ambience, often centered around talented research leaders. There have been various patterns, such as a research committee, informal research groups within a psychoanalytic society, or a separate research institute. In some instances contributions from these groups have been notable, as in the case of those analysts, most of them nonphysicians, who gathered first at

Topeka and later at Stockbridge, under the aegis of the late David Rapaport, who exemplified the force of a single gifted research leader. However, generally institutes themselves have not been systematically active in stimulating or sustaining research interests; it has been suggested that the atmosphere of institutes may even evoke an inhibitory effect (Engel, 1968).

Our impression, based on recent surveys, is that many institutes do not offer students much research stimulation. Curriculum plans rarely provide for research courses, nor do they reflect sufficient use of instructors with recognized research expertise. Teacher-models are almost entirely clinically oriented. Research committees exist without much activity, influence, or funding. Postgraduate seminars or training programs do not usually grant empirical research a high priority. Naturally such an atmosphere has a discouraging effect on the research interest and productivity of students and graduates. However, a report by recent graduates of an institute that prides itself on its research orientation suggests that in spite of attempts to generate an appropriate atmosphere, little research-directedness was actually created. Recent graduates frequently could not recall or identify the research courses in the program, and their postgraduate activities did not reflect a particularly enhanced research productivity.

Psychoanalytic research has existed in an atmosphere of financial deprivation. Today, with the suspension of much federal and other funding, the pursuit of research interests, always a potential hardship, has become extremely difficult. This is true for the regular medical analytic students and presents even more pressing problems for research analytic students who rarely have the equivalent opportunity to personally subsidize research interests through private clinical work.

The following are suggestions to help institutes create a more stimulating research atmosphere along the lines already begun by some. After all, it should justly be noted that some graduates do turn to research and some research analytic students have had an increased productivity following their training.

1. *Further study.* We suggest the study of four particular situations: (a) the institute that describes itself as research-oriented; (b) the regular student who goes on to an active research career; (c) the special student whose research pursuits are enhanced; and (d) the outstanding leader who develops and influences a large number of research workers. Such a study may find that a research-oriented institute fails in its clinical teaching, succeeds to an unusual degree, or requires certain special circumstances or a special source of applicants and faculty for success. Study of the regular student who overcomes the usual research disinterest may point to the influence of the training analyst, some of the supervisors, certain special circumstances outside or on the periphery of the institute, or only an individual personality tendency to overcome adverse circumstances. Interviews with those research graduates who have indeed enriched their own field or ours may also yield special data to aid future planning. Study of the charismatic leader may teach us how better to support such figures and how to utilize them more fully. Information accumulated in this way may help to clarify whether the institutes themselves or some special bodies apart from them should be the media of research stimulation.

2. *Organizational structure.* The development of special research divisions within institutes or parallel to them should be considered. Such divisions would be staffed separately and have different educational methods and objectives. The commission feels that this additional structure should not represent an exclusive direction of development, and should in no way diminish the responsibility of institutes as a whole to create a research ambience. In fact, a major responsibility of such a research division would be to stimulate research within the institute as a whole.

3. *Status of research members.* The commission feels that the present system of dealing with research students deters full scientific maturation. Research students should be admitted to training on the basis of talent and potential productivity. They should receive full training on the basis of continued scientific promise, coupled with clinical aptitude. Once graduated, they should be allowed to pursue their careers in whatever combination of formal scientific endeavor and further psychoanalytic clinical experience best suits their individual needs. We recommend emphatically that the Association work toward the goal of abolishing the distinction between the medically trained and nonmedically trained research analytic students.[1] This recommendation is not a sweeping endorsement of lay analysis, though some commission members were sympathetic to that notion, too. It refers to a special group of scientists, screened at three levels: at acceptance on the basis of their scientific promise; at advancement to supervised work on the basis of clinical

[1] *Editor's note:* A Bylaw Amendment, passed May, 1974, created a new membership category: Lecture Member (Research).

talent; at graduation on the basis of general productivity and maturation. Such individuals merit full certification.

4. *Foundation.* The commission recommends the establishment of a National Psychoanalytic Research Foundation whose primary responsibilities would include stimulating research interests, offering scholarships, funding projects, and (probably chiefly) raising money to support all these activities. The existence of such a foundation would be an explicit affirmation of the Association's genuine interest in research, and its activities could be the instrument of that interest.

CONCLUSION

The commission concludes that all is not as well as it might be with the scientific life within the Association. A flow of fresh data and new and solidly based additions to theory, particularly clinical theory, are needed; and these must come from an organized research effort. The commission feels that there is a dampening of research interest within the psychoanalytic profession at two levels. It occurs at the level of scholarly inquiry, where research is often inappropriately equated with restrictive experimental and laboratory models, rather than broadly defined and adapted to the particular discipline of psychoanalysis. It is also manifest at the socio-organizational level, where the major emphasis has been upon those training activities which are the source of important career rewards. As a result there are too few personal incentives or organizational structures to reinforce research activity.

The commission makes the following summary recommendations:

1. Psychoanalysis must make systematic efforts to study the outcome of psychoanalytic treatment. Such efforts might occur in conjunction with peer review and with efforts at systematic evaluation of the quality of service provided by member psychoanalysts, but they must utilize independent, objective, and scientifically tested methods of assessment.

2. Psychoanalysis must continue to study the processes involved in the psychoanalytic situation and develop methods suited to that special task. Such methods should add more systematic data collection and evaluation to the present form of clinical study. These systematic methods may differ from those found in the natural sciences and be more like objective approaches in the humanities and social sciences, but this does not mean exemption from the canons of research. The nature of psychoanalysis demands that special attention be paid to the ethics of the collection and utilization of data.

3. Psychoanalysis must develop a sustained exchange with other scientific disciplines, providing for interdisciplinary discourse and collaborative investigation.

4. Psychoanalytic institutes should introduce research into their curricula and insure that qualified faculty members are available to provide research knowledge, as well as a student body recruited in part because of research interest and demonstrated research talent.

5. Psychoanalytic institutes should, under guidance of the Association, move toward development of methods to encourage and train research-minded psychoanalysts; in particular, it should allow full equality in all respects to nonmedical research psychoanalysts after acceptance and graduation from training.

6. The Association should develop a National Re-

search Foundation, which would give symbolic and material support to group research projects or individual research workers.

PLENARY DISCUSSION —
PHILIP S. HOLZMAN, Ph.D.

I have prepared two discussions of the commission's report that directly contradict each other. My purpose is to underscore the dialectic confronting us in contemporary psychoanalytic training, which has not been made sufficiently explicit, thus delaying resolution and synthesis. I believe that any response to the commission's report must reflect a basic conception of where American psychoanalysis should be going and, therefore, what the institutes should be doing.

To simplify the argument, let us say that there are two models for the psychoanalytic institute. The first holds that the function of the institute is to train practitioners through the teaching of psychoanalytic treatment. The second holds that psychoanalytic treatment is merely one aspect of applied psychoanalysis and that the institute should be a center for scholarly activities in psychoanalysis, including research, disputation, and interdisciplinary exchanges as well as training for clinical psychoanalysis. I will present both discussions in the hope that they will catalyze argument rather than foreclose discussion prematurely.

First, I will take the point of view that the task of the psychoanalytic institute is to train people to acquire professional skills. Since the institute's function is to train analysts, can one expect institutes to do an equally effective job in training researchers, scholars, or those who apply psychoanalysis to other fields? One might argue that these tasks are secondary, if not irrelevant, and we should not criticize the psychoanalytic institute for failing in these functions. Since therapy can be taught effectively only by those who regularly practice it, it is reasonable that the faculty should be composed mostly of practitioners. Like practitioners in other fields, the psychoanalyst need not be a researcher at all. The physician, for example, does not need to be a physiologist, anatomist, or cytologist, although it helps clinical practice to know the relevant results of research conducted by such scientists, and the field may lose nothing if the practicing physician does not engage in basic research. Some physicians, of course, may be researchers as well as practitioners, but their research activities are generally separate from their clinical practices. At this time, psychoanalytic treatment cannot be taught in any other academy of learning than an institute. To bring it into another setting, such as the university, would subject it to a leveling process in which its uniqueness would be gradually eroded as it became assimilated with other therapeutic techniques. It would probably die of its own success, as departments of psychiatry appropriated the training functions for themselves.

We should therefore not lament that institutes train too few researchers, since that is not their province. Rather, we should concentrate on correcting deficiencies in technique, establishing models of effective technique, and planning studies of outcome. These studies could be done in collaboration with those who know how to evaluate outcome. Certainly, we could continue to train some students who intend to do part-time practice but whose major interests are either in teaching, research, or administration. The more such persons we train, the more effectively will psychoanalytic ideas be represented in other academies where the scholarly integration of psychoanalytic ideas with other currents in social thought can take place. Thus, the various nonclinical applications of psychoanalysis should be left to others. These others may actually be practitioners of psychoanalysis who are also working in other contexts and not only in the psychoanalytic institute. The evaluation of the success of psychoanalysis could then be gauged by the visibility of its ideas in the intellectual forum, just as, for example, one evaluates the success of Darwinian ideas or Newtonian ideas.

Our concern, then, is to provide the most effective training for treatment and to provide a center for the continual improvement of our treatment. But the teaching of research methods and the training of researchers is not our province. If our task is the training of practitioners, then we can be reasonably satisfied with our educational structure.

However, if our task is more than the teaching of a therapy, if we maintain that psychoanalysis is a part of behavioral science, then we are deficient. The following remarks stem from the second premise—that psychoanalysis is a scientific paradigm and that research and other scholarly enterprises belong in the psychoanalytic institute's training curriculum.

Our presence here signifies our general concern and some dissatisfaction with psychoanalytic research and education, and I think we are secure enough to ask the probing questions about what is wrong. This meeting is no place for a modern Dr. Pangloss, that absurdly comic creation of Voltaire, who went to his own execution convinced that this is the best of all possible worlds. All of the commission reports reject the Panglossian view that all is right with psychoanalytic education and research or that criticism should be ignored since it is only motivated by hostility toward psychoanalysis.

As far as the Research Commission's report is concerned, the nature of the trouble may be summed up as follows: psychoanalytic institutes are failing to stimulate or sponsor sufficient psychoanalytic research or a significant number of capable psychoanalytic researchers. Clearly, the issues the commission sets forth are all important matters for discussion. We do need to know more about the psychoanalytic process, the nature of outcome, the methods by which psychoanalysis can be investigated, and the difficulties in the path of such investigations. Not the least of these difficulties is the resistance of analysts themselves to submitting their own work to more detailed research scrutiny than is possible in the usual clinical case reports. It is of course crucial to preserve the confidentiality of the analytic relationship, yet analysts discuss their cases with colleagues, supervisors, and in case conferences, where control over dissemination of information is not as careful as it would be in a research context. It is necessary to prevent the contamination of the psychoanalytic situation, and Gill's (1972) studies suggest that it is indeed possible for a recorded analysis to meet the criteria of a psychoanalysis. But the analyst's pride and self-esteem are often wounded when his work is critically scrutinized, and it is true that collectively we have not learned well enough how to be critical without being condemnatory, or how to be criticized without feeling condemned.

I agree with the commission that it would be advantageous to have more attention paid to problems of data storage and utilization; to this end, files of supervised cases and of recorded analyses might be helpful. I am very uncomfortable, however, about setting such organizational priorities for ourselves. All of us know research seldom proceeds by fiat, and that its most productive outcome emerges from the inner motivations of individual investigators working in a setting that nurtures the work, unhindered by dogma or burdensome administrative responsibilities. Research is not a some-time job; it demands full-time preoccupation, and this is the crux of the difficulty. For us to call for research to be done, to point to areas of research that need work, to conclude that we need to know how psychoanalysis works and how to apply psychoanalytic principles to other areas, are signs of the difficulty we are experiencing. Essentially, the call is for research; a scientific discipline should not need to be reminded of that obligation.

I believe that the commission's recommendations go only part way toward remedying the basic problem in psychoanalytic research diagnosed by the commission — that the institute structure has not adequately fulfilled its scientific obligation. There are striking similarities between this diagnosis and that reached by almost every other commission: a dissatisfaction with the institute ambience, and a need for modification of the educational structure for psychoanalytic training and research.

Historically, the psychoanalytic institute emerged in response to a social, intellectual, and scientific constellation generally hostile to Freud's discoveries. Most scientific revolutions emerge from within the academic structure, and all scientific revolutions disturb the older members of the community. Darwin, for example, wrote to Joseph Hooker in 1860, "Nearly all men past a moderate age, either in actual years or in mind are, I am fully convinced, incapable of looking at facts under a new point of view" (p. 243). According to Feuer (1963), new views, and especially revolutionary ones, are experienced as generational insurgence, provoking opposition. Yet this opposition is not without its benefits, for it tests the strength, flexibility, and durability of the theory or hypothesis. And if the evidence for the theory finally becomes overwhelming and convincing, the theory then assumes its place in the established order. Mendeleev's formulation of the periodic table of elements ultimately won acceptance because its predictions were accurate. The empty boxes in the periodic table were filled in by hitherto unknown elements with properties almost exactly like those Mendeleev predicted, elements that were discovered independently by others. We do not hear of a Mendeleev institute, or an institute for training in Darwinian evolution, or a theory of relativity training center. The findings and the paradigm are part of the scientific enterprise.

But the psychoanalytic revolution was different from any of these. New journals, new societies, and new academies or institutes arose in response to the official ostracism of psychoanalysis by the medical academies and universities of the day, after the first Breuer and Freud publication in 1893. Several new psychoanalytic journals appeared: in 1910 *Zentralblatt* was established, *Imago* appeared in 1912, *Internationale Zeitschrift* in 1913, and there were occasional issues of *Jahrbuch für psychoanalytische* and *psychopathologische Forschungen*. Although these new publications opened up opportunities for dissemination of new psychoanalytic discoveries to psychoanalysts, they effectively closed the forum to others. It is well known that Freud was suspicious of the brickbats from official science—the doctrine that regards itself as the protector of social and scientific stability, and which, in the pursuit of its function of preserving established social institutions, makes use of arbitrary, nonscientific, repressive measures. The opposition of official science was not, however, unique to psychoanalysis. In all science what is new establishes itself only with difficulty and against much resistance. Freud believed that the attitude of official science reflected not only the natural resistances to new views, but a defense against the anxiety aroused by the specific content of psychoanalytic discoveries: the threat to narcissism and the unsettling of sexual repression.

While the new training institutes and publications bolstered the new psychoanalytic endeavors, they had certain negative consequences as well. First, they increased the isolation of the psychoanalytic paradigm from the intellectual mainstream, a separation that was increased by the inevitable development of a vocabulary that became ever more specialized, particularly in the language of metapsychology. Such a development has occurred in other sciences, and although it is accompanied by some narrowing of vision and scope, it may nevertheless result in deeper probing into the specific field, provided new investigators can be recruited and properly equipped to continue the quest. Second, the measures taken for the protection and preservation of psychoanalysis tended to displace the goals of developing and testing the theory.

Today the academic establishment is not monolithic. The nature of the university's response to psychoanalytic ideas is somewhat different from what it was 50 to 70 years ago. Indeed, psychoanalytic ideas are today taught not only in departments of psychiatry in medical schools, but also in many other university departments. They are taught in departments of psychology, sociology, anthropology, English literature, in law schools, and schools of business. They may be taught badly, and often without crediting the source, but nevertheless, they are being taught. The hostility with which psychoanalytic ideas have been met within the university is not altogether different, as mentioned before, from the rough reception accorded most theoretical positions, be they behaviorism in psychology or Keynesian theory in economics. Such challenges for survival in the marketplace of ideas are appropriate and valuable and not merely to be decried as attempts to suppress. The issues are clarified and the new contribution potentially strengthened in such cross-fire.

Can psychoanalytic institutes be modified into full-time academies, with a cross-disciplinary faculty, with adequate funding for research activities, and with an atmosphere that encourages challenge, doubt, and disputation? Can institutes respond by opening themselves to members of other disciplines? What kind of institutional arrangements can be provided in order to make this possible? Many, including the Research Commision, see great difficulty in attracting nonpsychiatrist scholars into psychoanalysis. Not the least of these difficulties is the financial burden of the training. It now costs some $35,000 to train a psychoanalyst, and this is an unrecoverable sum for those who will not practice clinical psychoanalysis privately. Scholarships, fellowships, and grants do not seem to be the answer, for too few can receive this magnitude of financial support to make a significant impact. Moreover, insofar as the rationale of this solution is to import scholars into psychoanalysis and then expect them to do the research for the rest of us, it will not work.

The ambience of institutes would need to be that in which a psychoanalyst is a member of a community in which there is the guaranteed financial support for those who wish to pursue that activity. A move into universities is an obvious suggestion. The nature of such a move, the quality of the universities into which such moves would be made, the status of clinical training, the various models for the relationship, all call for vigorous debate and judicious experimentation. For, apart from the overwhelming job of creating a full-time faculty, the financial support of research in institutes seems an insurmountable problem. No scientific discipline can support research by contributions from practitioners. Although there are large corporations that sponsor specifically targeted research, society has taken upon itself the support of most research, and it is done principally through the university.

But there are grave problems with such a solution. How can the practice of psychoanalysis be taught in a university? What about the selection of students, the opportunity for supervised analysis, the student's personal analysis, relations with the Association, and a host of other problems? I do not see the move to the university as the complete answer. I do believe, however, that the institutes as now organized and functioning are relatively unsatisfactory for supporting research and other scholarly activities in analysis. We thus need to debate what the psychoanalytic institute should be: an academy to train effective practitioners of psychoanalysis, an academy to train scholars, or an academy that could achieve both objectives. Can 'psychoanalysis continue to carry out its

functions by itself? Must it move toward the more traditional institutions? How can this be done without sacri-
ficing that which is unique in our field?

SUMMARY OF CONFERENCE DISCUSSION

A summary of the group discussions on this topic can be
relatively brief since there was virtual unanimity in
support of the views and proposals of the commission. In
every discussion group there was a rather similar candid
and searching exploration of the socio-economics of
psychoanalysis significantly influencing commitment to
individual or institutional research activities. The
complex relation between institute selection policies and
individual self-selection for psychoanalytic careers, as
well as the effects of institute encouragement, individual
teacher example, and student talent for reserach, were
reviewed in an attempt to formulate more successful
approaches to the problem.

As in the discussion of other topics, several participants pointedly balanced the description of the present
situation by suggesting that in their view the state of
affairs in psychoanalytic research was not necessarily as
critical as the dominant tone of the discussion and the
commission's report might indicate. While supporting all
reasonable efforts to fund and encourage more research
in psychoanalysis, they wanted to acknowledge the
important past and present work of a great many individual psychoanalytic clinician-researchers for its affir-
mative testimony to the success of psychoanalytic education and the vitality of psychoanalytic research. It was
strongly urged by many that this unity of clinician and researcher should be maintained and fostered in the future,

that such psychoanalysts held the greatest promise for psychoanalysis, whereas too much subspecialization during and after training into exclusively clinical or exclusively research groups would weaken rather than strengthen psychoanalysis.

The Ideal Institute

Stanley Goodman, M.D., Chairman
Herbert J. Schlesinger, Ph.D., Recorder
Norman B. Atkins, M.D.
Frances J. Bonner, M.D.
Homer C. Curtis, M.D.
Bernard D. Fine, M.D.
Heinz Kohut, M.D.
Maimon Leavitt, M.D.
Joseph M. Natterson, M.D.
Haskell F. Norman, M.D.
William R. O'Brien, M.D.
Ishak Ramzy, Ph.D.
Miss Helen Ross
Louis Shapiro, M.D.
Malvina Stock, M.D.
John J. Weber, M.D.

The Ideal Institute

ORIGINAL CHARGE

The ideal institute — is it just a utopia, or a possibility for some analysts and students? How could psychoanalytic training be structured differently in such a setting? How might it be supported? What would be the advantages and the disadvantages? Would there be a full-time faculty? What should be their optimal relation to clinical practice? Would the ideal institute train for the same careers as the present-day institute or for a different range of careers?

PREPARATORY COMMISSION REPORT

The commission responded to the task implied by its title by disclaiming any interest in defining perfection or designing utopia, and indicated sober awareness that human affairs were not easily susceptible to perfect arrangements in any sphere, including psychoanalytic education. Ideal was then redefined to mean the best possible arrangements, in the actual circumstances at a particular time, to encourage movement toward a desired goal, even if that goal was not immediately or even ever completely achievable. The self-specified charge was to consider the important implications and consequences of the structure of psychoanalytic education. Obviously, the assumptions, both explicit and implicit, of any system's organizers will strongly determine its form and function. We are familiar with those assumptions, not only because of direct testimony from early organizers of psychoanalytic education, but also because later generations of analytic educators have inherited and endorsed them.

The commission soon realized that its deliberations would necessarily overlap those of other preparatory commissions; however, it was concluded that such jurisdictional considerations were quite secondary to the need for full consideration and discussion of all relevant aspects of the subject. Indeed, it was thought there might be added value to the conference in the observation of significant convergences and divergences in the commission statements. It seems we all have been concerned with, talking about, and self-consciously or otherwise trying to move toward, without certainty of arriving at, the ideal institute.

We usually refer to psychoanalysis in three senses: as a body of knowledge, as a method of investigation and research, and as a method of treatment. In all its discussions, the commission was mindful of this triple meaning. The primary goal of the psychoanalytic institute is to structure its teaching methods and content to assist its students most effectively toward a sound understanding of psychoanalytic theory, competence in applying psychoanalytic technique in treatment, motivation to develop psychoanalytic knowledge through research, and motivation for continuing development as an analyst.

The institute structure over the past several decades has served moderately well in the education of competent professional psychoanalysts, although there is some dissatisfaction with the frequently lower level of commitment to research in contrast to clinical practice. The institute has been less effective in offering relevant systematic teaching to allied mental health professionals: psychiatrists who do not intend to become psychoanalysts, physicians, social workers, teachers, and psychologists. Despite the often well-taught and well-received courses and symposia for these groups offered through the extension division of many institutes, this activity is conceived as definitely peripheral to the central task. Finally, the institute structure has apparently been least effective as a means of achieving a continuing dialogue and mutually influential exchange with the wider world of science and scholarship housed in a quite different structure, the university. This is not to deny the profound cultural impact of psychoanalytic ideas, as well as their specific though often disavowed, influence on the behavioral sciences and professions.

A number of questions may be raised: Is the usual structure of the institute, designed as a professional school for the education of psychoanalysts, the most advantageous one for accomplishing even its declared primary goal? Is the further development of psychoanalysis as a science best served by the present institute organization? How does the institute structure, as such, affect the relation of psychoanalysis to other sciences, professions, and the academic world? As psychoanalysts we have several collective goals, not only to educate more professionals, but also to develop our science and to share our ideas with others. As the commission discussion continued, and particularly as some dissatisfaction was expressed with the relative degree of attainment of each of these goals, the essential concept of an institute was itself called into question.

Various negative connotations that have been attached to the idea and to certain realities of the institute were reviewed. The attitudes and policies associated with the term "training" are important in this regard. The parochial structure, functioning in partial isolation, without easy access to and by other disciplines, has tended to cast psychoanalysis, in its educational, professional and scientific activities, into the appearance of a guild, seeming to avoid open discourse to protect a fragile doctrine, which it also seeks to propagate.

The commission affirmed that a school for the development of professional clinical psychoanalysts was certainly one of the most important concerns of psychoanalytic educators, and that whatever else might enhance the future contributions of psychoanalysis, clinical practice, clinical competence, and clinical data would continue to be most essential. The questions remain, however, whether the presently constituted institutes provide the best possible setting for the development of the professional, and whether the present institute structure sufficiently favors the broader scientific and educational goals of psychoanalysis. It would appear that psychoanalysis either needs to develop new educational agencies, in addition to its professional schools, to accomplish its several declared aims, or it must evolve a single educational agency capable of encompassing all its aims more effectively.

Even though a perfectionistic quest for the ideal institute was abandoned, it was evident that the traditional concept of an institute may contribute to certain current dissatisfactions with psychoanalytic education. In this sense, even the ideal institute wouldn't be ideal as long as it remained an institute. The following remarks suggest some possible evolutionary trends in psychoanalytic education. Who might be taught by whom, in what kind of school, in which setting, to do what in psychoanalysis or in related fields of knowledge and practice?

WHO WILL BE TAUGHT?

The commission discussed at length the idea that a significant gradual reconstitution of the institutes would probably follow from a single specific change in their admission policies. If applicants were evaluated with primary concern for their personal and intellectual qualifications and motivation, without an overriding regard for their possession of a medical degree, far-reaching and probably beneficial consequences for psychoanalysis might ensue. The altered mixture of students, while still including a majority with medical background, would then include a significant number from the behavioral sciences and the humanities, with a sufficiently different background to suggest fresh questions and answers, and to stimulate further developments in teaching, practice, research, and application. While most commission members reacted favorably to this suggestion, a minority held that there was little actual evidence available to support the positive expectations expressed.

The medical domination of psychoanalysis, at least within the American Psychoanalytic Association, has been much discussed through the years. The time has come to discuss it once again in the light of our continuing attention to psychoanalytic education and its inevitable effect on the development of psychoanalytic science and the psychoanalytic profession. Such a discussion is urgently needed to clarify the underlying sources and assumptions of a variety of attitudes on this subject. Has our traditional attitude, viewing psychoanalysis almost exclusively as a medical specialty, been based entirely on a concern for the development of psychoanalysis? Have we not also been influenced by a wish to maintain a formal identification as medical doctors for reasons of social prestige and economic advantage? Do we still, or did we ever, have sufficient reason to believe that a complete medical school curriculum and degree is so important for the development of a psychoanalyst that it should continue as an absolute prerequisite for regular admission to the psychoanalytic professional school? There is now an increasing conviction that the present policy may have unnecessarily restricted the choice of suitable applicants, and may have excluded many who would have been admitted if the primary consideration had been psychoanalytic aptitude, judged by the applicant's personal qualities, intellectual capacity, and motivation. Those who recommend the modification of admission policy, while generally accepting the importance of certain attitudes and experiences usually afforded by a medical education, have suggested the practical possibility that specifically designed programs, both clinical and preclinical, might prepare otherwise qualified nonmedical applicants at least as effectively as those with the medical degree.

The implied widened responsibility of the psychoanalytic school should be considered. The psychoanalytic school need not wait for the usual channels of the educational system, primarily the medical schools and psychiatric residencies, to produce applicants who are assumed to only require a personal analysis, advanced psychoanalytic seminars, and supervision in their clinical psychoanalytic work to complete their formal psychoanalytic education. The psychoanalytic school could conceivably take responsibility, or at least participate, at an earlier stage in the development of analytic students. This proposal is relevant whether the students intend to become professional clinical psychoanalysts, wish to use psychoanalytic knowledge in another discipline or profession, or are interested in psychoanalysis for general cultural purposes.

It is necessary to avoid idealization of the academic and depreciation of the medical doctor. Nonmedical academics are equally susceptible to the attractions of increased income and prestige. We would not expect to be ennobled somehow by closer association with nonmedical colleagues; however, as students and as teachers, it seems probable that we would be influenced in many ways. Conversely, the medical psychoanalytic teachers and students would have an important influence on the nonmedical students, particularly in the areas of clinical experience, the appropriate role of therapeutic intention, and professional responsibility to the analysand. Incidentally, the commission was reminded that certain attitudes often brought from a medical background require significant modification for the optimal functioning of a psychoanalyst (e.g., the general use of suggestion and persuasion, active management focused on the disease rather than the person, etc.). Some measure of heterogeneity of background would thus have a salutary effect on both the medical and nonmedical psychoanalytic students and on their eventual contributions to psychoanalysis and other fields of knowledge.

The advisability of attracting younger applicants for psychoanalytic professional education, and the many problems connected with this potential group of students, has been mentioned repeatedly in recent years. This question is obviously closely related to that of the non-medical psychoanalytic student. A significantly younger applicant in medical training might not have begun a psychiatric residency or possibly even an internship, and a younger nonmedical applicant would almost certainly not have achieved the Ph.D.

The major apparent problems in this area are:

1. *Selection*. At a much earlier stage of academic or professional education there would certainly be less of the data usually available for evaluation. Actual research activity or clinical experience might be minimal or even entirely absent; thus, an estimate of potential creative and therapeutic talent would be even less certain than at present. In addition, the capacity for coping with certain critical developmental and maturational problems is particularly difficult to measure and predict in this age group.

2. *Time*. The limited time available for psychoanalytic education away from the simultaneous full-time pursuit of medical or academic curricula would be an even more difficult problem for this group than for our present students, who have to arrange time away from psychiatric residencies or private clinical practice. This factor would of course be minimized if the institute were not physically and, more particularly, organizationally isolated from the university and medical school.

3. *Immobilization*. There may be a special, difficult-to-calculate handicap for younger students in the premature geographic immobilization necessitated by

psychoanalytic studies. Transferring from one psychoanalytic teaching center to another during the personal
analysis or during supervised analytic work has very serious educational disadvantages, not altogether removable
administratively. It may be that this younger age group's
need for mobility to pursue personal goals or for the
optimal development of ongoing academic or medical
studies may override the assumed desirability of earlier
involvement in psychoanalytic professional education.

4. *Economics*. Finance is a problematic consideration affecting all aspects of psychoanalytic education,
but it has a particular importance for the younger student, whether medical or nonmedical. It is at this point
that many are tempted to yearn for utopian solutions.
Training subsidies, foundation grants, health insurance,
and individual private donations are all extremely
unlikely sources of adequate, dependable, long-term
support for the psychoanalytic student or school. This
problem might become much more manageable if the
psychoanalytic professional school or department functioned within the university. A short-term proposal is that
psychoanalysts themselves should subsidize psychoanalytic education even more than they so liberally do at
present, optimally in some shared equitable manner,
with direct financial contributions to the institutes and
markedly reduced fees, when necessary, for the personal
analysis and supervision of their students.

The commission members expressed little confidence that many younger applicants would be well prepared for all the demands of the psychoanalytic professional school (in contrast to graduate and undergraduate
nonprofessional studies in psychoanalysis). Most discussants agreed that the central considerations in evaluation
of an individual applicant of any age should be his or her

personal maturation, motivation, general educational background, and capacity for the demands of a psychoanalytic career.

Who Should Teach?

The ideal institute would be engaged in a continuing effort to recruit, develop, and encourage excellent teachers. Such teachers would certainly possess a variety of teaching styles and present competent, creative approaches to psychoanalysis, thereby also conveying the sense of fulfillment and gratification in a life of psychoanalytic study, practice, and teaching.

On this question as well, it seemed probable that if in the near future our eligible applicants and actual students came from a somewhat different mixture of educational backgrounds and professional experience, our faculties would also gradually be transformed and manifest an increased diversity. Obviously, it would be useless to exhort our present faculties to teach research or encourage creativity if they didn't already do so, and there is no reason to believe that institute teachers have been discouraged or prevented from doing this, insofar as they have been capable of it. However, teachers can only teach what they know, what they do, and who they are. It is true, of course, that good students of good teachers often develop independently and function differently from their teachers, not just in spite of them but because of them.

This speculation suggests that a gradual change in psychoanalytic teaching would occur with the development of future teachers who, in addition to those entering psychoanalysis from the world of medicine and psychiatry, came from and retained their association with other fields. Our intention is certainly not to minimize or abolish medical influence in psychoanalysis. Nor do we deny the great value the medical model has had in the development of American psychoanalysis and psychoanalysts. However, there is a growing consensus that the almost exclusive domination of psychoanalysis by the medical and psychiatric points of view may have, to some extent, slowed progress in psychoanalysis and limited the perspective of psychoanalysts.

The commission warns the conference not to view such possible eventual changes in the faculty and student population as a panacea for psychoanalytic educational problems. Many nonmedical psychoanalytic students, particularly at first, when almost all their teachers are engaged primarily in the private practice of psychoanalysis, will be strongly attracted to similar careers. The demands and gratifications of clinical practice would encroach, just as they have for so many medical psychoanalysts, on time and energy that might be available for scholarship and research. Nevertheless, not all of them will be so influenced, if a gradual diversification of career models and goals occurs, and as even the organizational setting of psychoanalytic education may be modified. It is not possible to transform psychoanalytic education instantly, nor would most of us wish to bring that about, but there is at least the opportunity to facilitate its development in certain desired directions.

What Kind of School?

The commission's early attempts to describe the ideal institute resulted in a picture bearing a striking resemblance to most present institutes in essential structure and function, only better. Subsidies or endowments would allow for a full-time director and several paid full- or part-time faculty positions. Stipends or scholarships would be available for the anticipated younger students in need of financial aid. Educational policy would be flexible, carefully considered, and frequently reviewed. Optimal educational standards would be rigorously maintained. Many elective study possibilities would be offered and the school would be open to desirable change. There would be much more systematic encouragement of research. An active low-fee psychoanalytic clinic program would provide an ample number of suitable patients for students' supervised work, and it would simultaneously offer a valuable service to the public at large as well as to various community agencies.

The commission reviewed the anticipated advantages and disadvantages of the so-called full-time institute. The supporting argument pointed out the acknowledged value of full-time serious study in any area of knowledge or practice. Medical schools and specialty residencies have not considered part-time training practical, desirable, or even tolerable; serious academic careers have rarely been pursued on less than full-time commitment. There is no reason to believe that psychoanalysis is a unique subject that may be adequately mastered while making lighter demands on its students' time and energy. The principal objections, on the other hand, were that full-time psychoanalytic teachers might have insufficient opportunity for maintaining and developing their own clinical experience and skills, thus reducing their value as teachers, and that full-time

students often would be in difficult economic circumstances. It was also thought that a full-time arrangement
might tend to increase the infantilization of students and,
particularly in the younger group, might seriously interfere with the pursuit and completion of their medical and
academic studies elsewhere.

In listing desirable features of the ideal institute, the
wish was frequently repeated that it should become more
like our *ideal* image of a univeristy graduate school, and
less like our *harshest* image of a craft-training school. At
first, it seemed that the atmosphere rather than the
actuality of the graduate school was being sought. Only
as we continued to survey possible means of achieving our
broad scientific, educational, and professional objectives
did it become apparent that, in addition to the university
atmosphere, we might be seeking and needing the university itself.

What Is the Best Setting?

At the present time psychoanalytic education within the
Association is carried on by accredited institutes in various localities. These institutes are essentially professional
schools, designed specifically to provide post-medical-
school, post-psychiatric-residency, subspecialty training
of psychiatrists who wish to become psychoanalysts and
enter the clinical practice of psychoanalysis. This is not to
disregard the current existence and acknowledged importance of extension programs and special research-
candidate programs; however, even the titles of these
activities reveal their peripheral or at least secondary
position in the institute. A number of psychoanalysts have
considered the possibility that this single educational

focus and organizationally isolated setting of the institute may have played some difficult-to-measure role in limiting the development of psychoanalysis and its continuing contribution to human knowledge.

There is need to clarify further in what setting psychoanalytic teachers would be most effective in contributing to general education, sharing knowledge with scholars in diverse fields of inquiry, or offering their knowledge and making themselves accessible on many levels to students, graduate or undergraduate, who may have a wide variety of personal, educational, and professional goals. Certainly, we will continue to be interested in the best possible setting for the education of the professional psychoanalyst.

The suggestion that emerges from our consideration of the optimal setting for psychoanalytic education is that psychoanalysis might begin to think about the possibility of moving, at whatever cautious and practical pace, toward increased participation in the mainstream of general and professional education—the university. The policy decisions regarding our institutional evolution require thoughtful review and assessment of our resources and objectives, such as is now being attempted at this conference. Certain short-range actions might then be initiated, such as admitting to our present educational facilities qualified students with a variety of career goals related to psychoanalysis, without overriding regard for the prerequisite medical degree. A long-range program might be developed for the eventual establishment within the university structure of a department of psychoanalysis, composed of a professional school as well as undergraduate and graduate divisions. Such a university department would not only recruit, possibly at an earlier age or in greater numbers, suitable students for professional specialization, but would be available and accessible to the nonmedical as well as medical student, and would attempt to contribute systematically to medical education in the medical school and to the later specialization of medical doctors. Its main responsibility, however, would be to the students of the related but independent profession of psychoanalysis. A psychoanalytic professional school could assume an active, early, and primary role in helping its students become professional psychoanalysts rather than rely on medical schools and psychiatric residencies to supply it with ready-made students presumably already prepared for professional responsibilities. The important implication here is that the psychoanalytic professional school should develop psychoanalytic residencies for its students, both medical and nonmedical, as distinct from psychoanalytically oriented psychiatric residencies.

Further observations of present relations between psychoanalysis and the university support the above recommendations. Even those institutes now attached to departments of psychiatry in medical schools tend to lead a shadow existence, share a chronic concern for their autonomy, function completely separately in the specific professional psychoanalytic education of their own students, and tend not to participate *as an institute* in an organized, systematic relationship with the medical student and resident. While individual teachers who are psychoanalysts may have considerable influence, that seems quite unrelated to the presence or absence of the institute, as such, within the department of psychiatry. The experience of the several institutes attached to medical schools has not clearly demonstrated an

advantage for psychoanalytic education and psychoanalysis, as distinguished from a certain convenience for
the department of psychiatry, psychiatric education, and
individual faculty members. Perhaps we should not be
too impatient or overly critical of this model, since it does
represent at least some significant move toward the more
public institutions of education. It may be valued as a
transitional stage, however, rather than as a sufficient
end in itself.

Individual psychoanalysts have long participated,
sometimes quite actively, within the university in various
departments. Such affiliation could become more frequent in the future, particularly if nonmedical psychoanalytic graduates continued their work in their original
fields of interest rather than devoted themselves exclusively to private clinical practice. Such increased
individual participation in the unviersity would almost
certainly precede organizational participation. As psychoanalytic teachers and scholars become more visible,
the value of developing an academic department prepared to offer regular instruction at undergraduate and
graduate levels might become more attractive to the university itself.

Some of the problems reflected in our collective hesi-
tation, as well as in our eagerness, for fruitful association
with the university, may be related to the often opposed
idealizations of academia and medicine. Medical psychoanalysts have experienced chronic difficulty in their
attempts to determine an appropriate professional niche
in society. This is obviously demonstrated in certain
organizational ambiguities, and often in the suggested
solutions to these ambiguities. The several idealized
self-images of medical doctor, practitioner, therapist, re-

searcher, psychologist, professor, philosopher have, to say
the least, not yet been comfortably reconciled. Of course,
just as there may well be more than one kind of ideal
institute, there certainly may be more than one kind of
ideal psychoanalyst. Among the difficulties for an individual may be the temptation to realize all these idealizations within one mere mortal—hence, the often well-
rationalized but not well-managed tension between
the medical doctor and the nonmedical scientist, and between the private practitioner's office and the university
campus.

What Kinds of Competence Should Students Acquire?

The institute has long required an extended learning
experience, including a personal analysis, a several-year
curriculum of theoretical and clinical seminars, and
sufficient supervision in conducting clinical psycho-
analyses to assure satisfactory clinical competence. The
official ideal has always been that graduates of such an
educational program would be able and motivated to
apply and advance psychoanalytic knowledge through
clinical practice and research. The commission members
differed to some extent in their views of the relative
importance of the personal analysis, seminar program,
and supervised analytic work as well as of each area of
expected competence. These matters have been under
almost constant study and re-evaluation by the institutes,
so it was to be expected that in our discussion the personal
analysis, the seminar program, and the supervised analytic work were each thought perhaps insufficiently emphasized by some discussants and possibly overempha-

sized or prolonged by others. However, there was a high degree of consensus that, whatever the professional purpose of a psychoanalytic education, whether clinical practice, research in or on psychoanalysis, serious application of psychoanalytic knowledge to research in other fields, or the appropriate application of knowledge from other fields to psychoanalytic practice and theory, it was not possible to specify any aspect of the usual tripartite sequence as entirely dispensable or even significantly modifiable in any precise way for particular career activities. Although everyone was aware of the hope that specifically designed curricula would be possible in the future; nevertheless, there was very little certainty that at present psychoanalytic educators know how to specify the appropriately different training for analysts with different special interests. The commission therefore wished to affirm strongly the importance of clinical competence and the need for continued clinical experience whatever the intended psychoanalytic specialization.

In further consideration of the so-called multiple educational tracks, designed to take students toward different professional goals within psychoanalysis and allied fields, it should be noted that currently many institutes do, in a sense, have two tracks of professional study. The second track is represented in the special additional programs taken by those students wishing to qualify as child analysts. Students in the so-called regular program have not been thought to need any clinical experience with children, and only in some institutes have they been encouraged to participate in a continuous case seminar on a child patient or to analyze a child patient as an elective. There should be much further discussion about whether this particular tracking represents an educational refinement or handicap for our regular students. It could be argued that every student, whatever his or her primary psychoanalytic interest, should have at least some clinical psychoanalytic experience with a child, some opportunity for systematic observation of infants and small children, and a clinical conference on a child analytic patient. Perhaps, in the ideal institute a waiver would be required if a particular student is not expected to acquire significant clinical experience with children before graduation as a competent psychoanalyst. It is hoped that future planning for possible specific tracks in psychoanalytic schools will proceed with greater sophistication than has been demonstrated in our established approach to the different training for those who do and those who don't intend to specialize in child analysis.

Those who seek out psychoanalytic schools with an interest in studying psychoanalytic ideas do so for a variety of serious purposes. This group includes undergraduates, graduates in various university departments, psychologists, social workers, physicians, and lawyers. Some might benefit greatly from a systematic curriculum of psychoanalytic instruction—even though they do not wish to be professionally trained, they do wish to achieve a deeper understanding of psychoanalytic ideas. The commission members generally favored an increased effort by the psychoanalytic establishment to offer its knowledge broadly, and not only for specific professional purposes. Perhaps, if the traditional perspective were modified, such phrases as full training, partial training, and extension programs would become obsolete. The institutes might begin their own eventual transformation by reconstituting themselves as university-like structures, including both a professional and nonprofessional school.

Obviously new organizational labels will have little consequence unless they actually reflect changed conceptions and objectives. The nonprofessional school could be made more easily accessible to serious students, and could offer a high standard of systematic instruction rather than episodic programs. Of course, psychoanalytic teachers could be more easily and effectively available, particularly to the curious nonprofessional undergraduate and graduate student, if they actually functioned within the university itself.

CONCLUSION

The ideal psychoanalytic school lies beyond the ideal institute; it may evolve through the gradual transformation of the earlier, historically determined institute form. The transformation would occur as the institute moved away from its functional isolation and parochial organization, which have tended to encourage an apprenticeship attitude in its students and subsequent guild-protective concerns in many of its graduates. The design of the psychoanalytic school and the distribution of effort by its teachers should more adequately reflect all of the objectives of psychoanalysis in order to achieve any one of them more successfully.

The commission has attempted to articulate and consider a number of observations, speculations, and recommendations offered by many psychoanalytic educators in recent years. It is hoped that some approximate balance has been maintained between short-range recommendations, longer-range evolutionary perspectives, and more lofty, possibly utopian, fantasies.

PLENARY DISCUSSION—ALAN. J. EISNITZ, M.D.

This commission has been successful in its aim of stimulating thought in its area of inquiry and has made some very interesting proposals. It agrees with the usual definition of the goals of psychoanalytic education, and offers the opinion that "whatever else might enhance the contributions of psychoanalysis in the future, clinical practice, competence, and data would continue to be most essential." It is gratifying to see the special emphasis placed upon clinical work. The single criterion most widely employed for graduation from our institutes is the demonstration of clinical competence. Similarly, Association membership, the only form of national professional certification available at this time, relies most heavily on the requirement to demonstrate clinical competence in psychoanalytic treatment. Clinical psychoanalytic work provides us with the basic foundation of our psychoanalytic data and the opportunity to test hypotheses, including those derived from other sources.

Another important conclusion inferred from this report is approval of the present tripartite system of psychoanalytic education. The importance of the personal analysis is not questioned, the need for an organized curriculum is accepted, and there is no suggestion for any modification of the system of supervision.

The recommendation of movement toward a structural relationship with the university presents many exciting prospects and challenges. It would bring us into contact with a much younger group of students, there would be an opportunity for greater interchange between psychoanalysis and other fields with which we usually do not have contact, and students who might otherwise know little about psychoanalysis would learn something about its contributions. Some of these students might choose to study psychoanalysis further, and many would at least have the opportunity to gain a less distorted view of psychoanalysis than is currently offered at many universities.

However, there are major problems in developing university departments of psychoanalysis. The universities and the existing departments may not want departments of psychoanalysis. Tremendous energy and time will be needed to manage these programs; this may lead to a new model, the academic psychoanalyst, who would begin to replace the clinician. What effect would this ultimately have on psychoanalysis? Individual psychoanalysts who now teach in universities have an independence that a department, subject to a variety of pressures, might not find as easy to maintain. How would a psychoanalytic department respond when required to compete against rivals whose appeal may be more consistent with cultural and other influences accepted by the adolescent and immediate postadolescent population? Psychoanalysis must be careful not to aim for too broad a base of acceptance. Does the commission suggest, despite their emphasis on clinical practice, that we shift our major orientation away from clinical work so that more psychoanalysts would be available for university teaching? My own preference is for some university psychoanalytic departments coexisting with psychoanalytic institutes as we now know them. I see no advantage or necessity for abandoning the present institute structure. The institutes must be retained if we wish to maintain our roots in clinical psychoanalysis and to avoid having all psychoanalysis become applied psychoanalysis. Another major problem is that the greater the shift toward universities, the less might be the influence of the Association in establishing and maintaining training standards.

Medical school institutes do represent a step away from isolation but are not considered in the report as an ultimate model. According to the commission, these institutes offer advantages mainly for psychiatric education and for some faculty members, but the advantage for psychoanalytic education is questioned. While psychiatric education has benefited greatly from the participation of a psychoanalytic institute, I do not see this as a disadvantage, and there have been direct benefits to psychoanalysis in terms of increased respect and interest. Medical school institutes are among the finest and most creative; our concept of what is the ideal should encompass them.

In considering this commission's recommendations, one can reasonably ask whether there could be a single ideal type of institute. A university-based department of psychoanalysis is a most attractive concept and I hope it will be tried. However, it does not represent the only ideal; local needs and resources would dictate what the local ideal institute would be. In some places this might be a university institute, in other places, a medical school institute, in still others, an institute as we know it now, or a separate school or division in a group of health-science schools, an institute sponsored by a hospital, foundation, or clinic. In each case the overriding concern should be for the training program that best promotes psychoanalysis and could best prosper in the particular environment. Even now, institutes vary greatly in their characteristics. This heterogeneity has a value that should be retained as part of our ideals.

The question of the relation of psychoanalysis to medicine is a most important one. It underlies the question of nonmedical psychoanalytic students and the idea of an independent profession. Psychoanalysis is, in my view, essentially one of the healing arts, and thus should always be closely connected with medicine. At the present time of contemplated changes in health-care systems it seems almost a matter of survival as a profession to retain our medical orientation. The commission bases its recommendation for modifying the current medical perspective in psychoanalysis upon little demonstrable evidence. Certainly, the commission is not proposing that a change in the mixture of students would cure all existent weaknesses in training programs. In fact, many more analysts have come to medicine and to psychoanalysis from the behavioral sciences and humanities than is generally recognized. Medical school requirements are presently being broadened so that others from those backgrounds can more easily enter the programs. Experimental track systems are being devised so that medical students can follow a more rational path to their ultimate goals in medicine. Such programs are also being considered for specialization in psychiatry. In some medical schools, it is now possible for psychoanalysts to make contributions to teaching even during the early phases of medical training. Experience in clinical medicine has a genuine and not-to-be-depreciated value for future psychoanalysts.

If psychoanalytic students do not have a firm foundation of psychiatric knowledge, it will have to be provided for them. No patient should undergo psychoanalysis without a careful evaluation from the psychiatric point of view. The psychoanalyst must be able to perform this evaluation and to rely confidently on his or her own psychiatric judgment repeatedly during the psychoanalytic treatment of patients. The commission's recommendations would impose the obligation to provide a *psychoanalytic* residency, which, for obvious reasons, would have to include a considerable amount of psychiatry. However, we already know that psychoanalysts can make useful contributions to residency programs and to the design of these programs; I consider this alternative a far more economic approach to the goal. The task of providing an entirely new psychoanalytic residency with sufficient facilities for psychoanalytic and psychiatric patients is a vast time- and energy-consuming undertaking. It becomes almost overwhelming when considered in conjunction with the recommendation that we might also assume responsibility for the preclinical training of students.

The commission report suggests that the institute structure maintains isolation from other branches of the scientific and academic community. However, we must consider that we psychoanalysts are, after all, the most specialized and best trained mental health scientists. Would it not seem at least as gross an isolation if we were to move ourselves even farther away from psychiatry and the problems of serious mental illness?

SUMMARY OF CONFERENCE DISCUSSION

The several discussion groups responded in much the same manner as the preparatory commission responded to its charge. After the initial unavoidable exchanges about the relative value of an idealistic or realistic viewpoint, the discussions moved to the familiar inventory of problems possibly inherent in the objectives, methods, and organizational setting of most psychoanalytic institutes.

There was a rather positive response to the recommendation for considering the possible advantage of increased educational or professional heterogeneity of psychoanalytic students and teachers. The stimulating effect of such a change on the educational, scientific, and professional aspects of psychoanalysis was stressed. It was repeatedly noted that if the institutes were freed from the restriction of selecting psychoanalytic students primarily from psychiatric applicants, they would then be able to concentrate exclusively on selection of students with regard only for the personal and educational qualifications deemed essential for psychoanalytic training. Discussants were mindful of the long history of the issue of nonmedical psychoanalysts within the Association. Judging from the several position papers, the comments of most of the plenary-session discussants, and the range of opinions expressed in the discussion groups, there has been a significant shift away from the traditional categorical opposition to the training of nonmedical analysts. But practical concerns and cautions were also expressed in every discussion. Some speakers were uncertain about the development of a sense of therapeutic responsibility in persons without a medical background; others pointed to the possibly negative consequences of losing a close identification and relationship with medicine if the profession became more heterogeneous in composition. This aspect of the discussion included references to economic considerations, problems of health insurance coverage for psychoanalysis, and the possible diminution of a vitally important commitment to clinical psychoanalysis in the more active pursuit of scholarship and the increased interest in nonmedical fields of applied psychoanalysis.

With regard to some form of relationship with the university, there was a cautious readiness to consider the possible implications. The very great difficulties, even hazards, as well as the conceivable benefits of moving closer to society's acknowledged primary center for intellectual exchange, scientific research, and professional training — the university — were generally well recognized. Some comments reflected the view that psychoanalysis, even now, might require the protection of a completely separate and totally autonomous institutional form. The opposing view suggested that analysis was sufficiently robust to defend itself and might even be strengthened more in exchanges with challenging academics in the university than by overprotective support.

The discussions revealed an awareness that any of the possible evolutionary changes in the institutes depended on local factors such as the institute's teaching resources and interests or the currently prevailing attitudes in the local university or medical school. It was clear that most conference participants were open to change compatible with the maintenance of our professional and scientific standards. Further, it seemed acceptable, even desirable, that the ideal institute might exist in several forms: (1) an independent institute in its present form, only improved in function; (2) an independent psychoanalytic university with the resources to support preclinical, clinical, and research activities, and including programs for training professional psychoanalysts, courses for undergraduates and graduate academics, courses on the application of psychoanalysis to allied disciplines, and courses for the interested general public; (3) an institute somewhat modified from its present form, so as to support a full psychoanalytic residency for its medical and nonmedical students; (4) a psychoanalytic institute within a medical school department of psychiatry—several examples of this model have existed for some time, and it has been proven viable with proper safeguards; (5) an independent department of psychoanalysis within the university with undergraduate and graduate divisions and professional training programs; (6) a cross-disciplinary institute within the universities.

The question of adequate financial support was realistically confronted in the discussion of the ideal institute, and it was quite clear that there are no easily available solutions. Everyone was painfully aware that this problem was crucial for most of the plans to improve and expand psychoanalytic education. Even a moderate expansion of low-fee clinics would require more support than the already very considerable amount contributed by psychoanalysts and psychoanalytic students themselves, and the training of nonmedical students would require additional funds for trainee stipends as well as support, even at greatly reduced fee, of the personal analysis.

Only a few of the institutes have been able successfully to raise funds privately to support a variety of programs. It seemed doubtful to most conference participants that sufficient money would be available, even with very large contributions of both time and money by psychoanalysts themselves, for the plans envisioned by several of the reports. It was suggested that one very practical consequence of a relationship with the university, experienced by the medical-school-related institutes, would be some measure of dependable funding for the educational and scientific work that is so essential.

Age and the Psychoanalytic Career

Samuel Ritvo, M.D., Chairman
Marshall Edelson, M.D., Recorder
Martin A. Berezin, M.D.
Daryl E. DeBell, M.D.
Ruth S. Eissler, M.D.
Frances Gitelson, M.D.
Janice Norton Kaufman, M.D.
Leo S. Loomie, M.D.
I. Floyd Mallott, M.D.
John B. McDevitt, M.D.
Arthur J. Ourieff, M.D.
M. Barrie Richmond, M.D.
Marshall D. Schechter, M.D.
Clarence G. Schulz, M.D.
Gertrude R. Ticho, M.D.

Age and the Psychoanalytic Career

ORIGINAL CHARGE

What are the consequences for psychoanalysis, for analytic training, and for the lives of psychoanalysts that training characteristically takes place in the fourth decade of life? What information do we have both from other disciplines and our own experience on norms of peak scientific creativity and what are the implications of these data? What about the necessary maturity, the life experience that Anna Freud has called "human authority" in the training of analysts? What would be the consequences for psychoanalysis if training were to start ten years earlier, at age 21? What would be the problems raised — psychological, psychosocial, practical?

PREPARATORY COMMISSION REPORT

Psychoanalytic training starts later and lasts longer than any other scientific or professional endeavor, and this has an extensive impact on psychoanalysis as a career. The commission approached these issues under three main headings: (1) factors delaying the beginning of psychoanalytic training or resulting in its not being undertaken altogether; (2) factors unduly prolonging training; (3) problems of the aging analyst.

CURRENT AND FUTURE ISSUES IN PSYCHOANALYSIS AS A CAREER

After psychoanalysis was introduced into this country in the early 1900's by psychiatrists it had a slow but steady growth until the end of World War II. After the war there was a rapid increase in the number of individuals seeking psychoanalytic training because of the demonstrated effectiveness of psychoanalysts as teachers and psychotherapists in the military service. Starting in the mid-sixties there was some decline in the popularity of psychoanalysis as a therapy and as a career choice for psychiatrists. The reasons most commonly cited for this are: (1) disillusion with the inability of psychoanalysis to fulfill the exaggerated expectations of persons unfamiliar with the difficulties and limitations of psychoanalysis as a treatment for a broad spectrum of mental ills; (2) the enthusiasm of the psychiatric profession for newer therapies; (3) new careers in community and social psychiatry; (4) the reluctance to undertake long and expensive institute training and possible further prolongation of training stemming from interruption for military service; (5) the improved educational programs of psychiatric residencies, with extensive participation of psychoanalysts since World War II, which satisfied a need for knowledge about psychoanalysis that earlier could be obtained only in the institutes.

All these factors have somewhat lessened the attractiveness of psychoanalysis as a career. Of course, there is no way of knowing whether the people attracted to other careers are a great loss to psychoanalysis. It is conceivable that we are now getting applicants and students who have a stronger interest in psychoanalysis.

In its deliberations and recommendations the commission kept in mind the different career lines of psychoanalysts and how these are affected by socio-economic conditions, differing social and professional images and conceptions of the psychoanalyst, differences in atmosphere from institute to institute, and differences in the developmental phases of a psychoanalytic career. Although questionnaire studies done by the Association have shown that very few analysts devote their time exclusively to treatment by psychoanalysis, the most common model is still the analyst as primarily clinician and practitioner. Many analysts combine analytic practice with medical school and psychiatric teaching and administration. However, rarely, if at all, can a psychoanalyst find support for a career of psychoanalytic scholarship and research. Certainly, this is not an established model in psychoanalytic institutes. The training programs of the institutes and the training standards of the Association are aimed primarily at the psychoanalyst as clinical practitioner.

In order to counter the influence of the economic factors that restrict and even coerce career choices and range of professional activity, we will need to consider subsidization of analytic students in two main categories: young psychiatrists who are not yet able to support their own training from private practice or salaried positions in psychiatry and individuals from other fields in research training who have no way to support training from their own earnings. The burden for such subsidies fall mainly on the training analysts unless additional support could be obtained from psychoanalysis as a whole and the public. Enlisting such support would probably be easier if there were existing career lines other than the analyst as private practitioner.

The fact that most analytic students in training expect to achieve an economic status comparable to colleagues in psychiatry or other branches of medicine affects many aspects of analytic training. For some, it is a deciding factor in not electing such training with its financial strains and inevitable sacrifices over at least a several-year period. For others, it prolongs the training because the student's financial situation becomes a factor in whether additional supervised patients are undertaken, particularly clinic or low-fee patients.

The professional and social setting of analytic training is, therefore, an important determinant of the individual psychoanalyst's career. The elements to be considered in this regard are:

1. The function and the image of the psychoanalytic institute and psychoanalysts in contributing to community mental health services.

2. The role of psychoanalysts in informing the community about psychoanalysis, especially in reaching high school and college students. Several commission members stressed the importance of psychoanalysts teaching in undergraduate psychology courses where those nonpsychoanalysts who do teach about psychoanalysis are often inadequately prepared to do so competently.

3. A favorable climate for psychoanalysis is more likely to exist if the senior analysts in the institute ac-

quaint themselves with the talents and aspirations of younger colleagues and make efforts to provide opportunities for their career development. An active and stimulating scientific forum, study groups, opportunities for teaching, and clinical conferences are developmentally necessary forms of participation for all colleagues and students in the institute.

Factors Leading to Unnecessary Delay in Starting or to Deciding Against Psychoanalytic Training

Considerations Regarding Early Training

The question of the age at which a student begins psychoanalytic training has come to the fore recently because of the shortened period of medical training in some schools and the elimination of the internship. The earliest age at which one can begin psychoanalytic training now is determined by the time it takes to complete medical school; in the accelerated program, the age might be lowered by a couple of years, but with our present requirements of complete medical training there are not many eligible applicants below age 25 or 26. However, even at 26, these possible applicants would be about five years younger than the most recent average applicant age.

Five years of added lifetime productivity is an important consideration; even more important is creativity. Creativity in some fields of endeavor reaches a peak in late adolescence and early adulthood. Although this has not been documented for psychoanalysis, it is worth considering.

Despite the apparent advantages of starting training at a young age in Europe in the 1920's and 1930's, we do not currently have empirical evidence for a minimal (or optimal) developmental age for starting analytic training in this country. Utilizing developmental considerations and the usual selection criteria, however, it appears that the minimum age for starting training is somewhere in the twenties. These considerations suggest that not until the postadolescent stage can a meaningful assessment be made of the capacity to analyze and to be analyzed; and that not until that stage does there exist the capacity to form the kind of therapeutic alliance and transference neurosis necessary for successful training analysis. It should be pointed out that assessment of analyzability and assessment of potential for a psychoanalytic career are not identical. Our present ability to assess the analyzability of younger people is better than is our ability to predict their future capabilities as analysts. Assessment for acceptance for analytic training will thus be more difficult with younger applicants who are still relatively immature and almost certainly clinically inexperienced.

Developmental studies and informal conversations lead to the following generalizations in which chronological age is used as a rough approximation for developmental age. Some analysts believe that analytic training, or at least the beginning training analysis, should take place in the early twenties. They suggest that there may be advantages for further maturation in conjunction with personal analysis and beginning psychoanalytic work—the earlier the analysis, the greater the flexibility in the student, both with respect to personality development and in terms of choice of life situations, such as career line. Earlier analysis might also prevent adverse choices or commitments, such as the choice of an unsuitable marital partner. Others believe that the mid-twenties are the preferable time for training, that only then has intrapsychic development progressed sufficiently for the student to make the fullest use of the personal analysis and the training. This is partly due to having reached the time of life when major commitments to life tasks and roles have already been made and more energy for psychoanalysis is available. Thus, there are apparently contradictory considerations: there are advantages to having a personal analysis prior to major life commitments; on the other hand, the analytic work necessary for analysis and training may not progress as satisfactorily until these commitments have been made. Still others think that as a general rule the late twenties are preferable; only then can one be reasonably sure of adequate maturity, sound commitment, and conscious motivation that is reasonably related to the realistic features of the psychoanalytic career. Although these assessments are made primarily from the point of view of intrapsychic development, they also take into account the phase-specific psychological requirements that stem from consideration of productivity, creativity, research, and scientific achievement and specialization.

CATEGORIES OF TRAINING

Two groups of trainees need consideration with regard to age: those desiring full training and those for whom partial training is indicated. Future practicing analysts, including those who will utilize the psychoanalytic situation as a research method, will require full training. Partial training may be suitable for those who want to learn about psychoanalysis as a body of knowledge. The latter include graduate students, medical students, and professors in fields such as law, anthropology, and literature.

Let us consider some of the misgivings about early training. We are not advocating that all trainees should begin earlier or that there are inevitable and obvious benefits to starting earlier for all trainees. Rather, we are looking at those factors that contribute to unnecessary delays in starting or avoidance of training, while recognizing that many trainees should start later. We are concerned that undue emphasis on early training may eliminate those potentially good trainees who come to it later. Indeed, some might possibly make a premature decision concerning analysis as a career. We want to avoid a discussion that focuses entirely on chronological age and overlooks the fact that potential trainees have varied levels of experience prior to a particular age. If we are uncertain whether an early training might prolong late adolescence, we should observe some current attempts at early training and await the outcome of these experiments. On the other hand, we do have available experiences of some of the European-trained analysts who had their training in their early twenties.

FACTORS SPECIFIC TO THE YOUNG APPLICANT

1. *Family*. Responsibilities for care of young children lead some potential applicants to delay training. The spouse often resents the time consumed by the additional burden of the training program.

2. *Economics*. Medical students, residents in psychiatry, and graduate students are not in a position to take on the financial load required by psychoanalytic training.

This is especially true if they have already gone into debt for some of their education. Postponement is often decided upon until they are well established in practice, at which time some of the same factors may still lead to a decision against analytic training.

3. *Mobility*. Indecision about where one will want to practice after residency or where one will take one's residency following medical school leads to postponement of analytic training until these matters are settled. The possibility or fact of military service has also delayed the decision regarding where and when to begin institute training.

Recommendations. As psychoanalytic training is presently organized there are no recommendations that would ease or remove psychoanalytic training as an additional time burden on family life. The problem is that whenever it is undertaken it is added to either another concurrent full-time commitment, e.g., a psychiatric residency, professional career in private practice, or academic appointment. Basic changes to integrate psychoanalytic training with the psychiatric residency or establish a psychoanalytic residency seem a remote possibility at present, with governmental and public support of all training programs diminishing rather than increasing.

Subsidization of the training analysis is an obvious recommendation but there are complex and difficult problems connected with any plans for this. Who would bear the cost? The most frequent suggestions heard are: (1) each training analyst having one student at a low fee; (2) all training analysts in an institute sharing their training-analysis fees under equitable procedure that would not interfere with the analysis; (3) more loan funds for those students able and willing to assume debt; (4) scholarship support from a national fund to which all analysts would be asked to contribute — one possibility being to earmark a portion of the annual membership dues for this purpose: (5) scholarships for the subsidization of a certain number of promising young people in analysis regardless of whether they are or intend to become analytic students.

The problems connected with such recommendations are numerous. If the subsidy is provided by the training analysts, it may be too large a burden on a group of analysts who individually are already contributing a great many hours to the institutes' educational and administrative work. There are likely to be special difficulties for the analysis of the transference if the analysis is a large gift from an individual training analyst or even a small group of training analysts. The subsidization of professional training directly by the established group in the profession, particularly where the main and practically sole career line is private practice would be unique among professions and difficult to rationalize socially and economically. Nor, is it certain that subsidization of this type would have an entirely desirable impact on the self-selection for psychoanalytic training.

Loans to students also present problems. Those who need assistance frequently prefer to wait until they can support the training analysis from their psychiatric practice or academic positions, although the latter is usually more difficult. Students in training are understandably reluctant to go into debt, especially as many of them have already accumulated debts during their medical education. The soundest approach to the problem might be a national scholarship and loan fund administered by a representative board, which would make loans and scholarships available on favorable terms.

Special planning is needed for students in research training who are unable to support their training from private practice. A national loan and scholarship fund could serve this group as well. A national fund has the advantage over local funds in that it can draw on wider support for contributions and the aid given on a collective basis would have a smaller impact on the personal analysis.

INSTITUTE FACTORS

1. The psychoanalytic institute often appears remote to the potential applicant in contrast to the individual analyst who has functioned as a teacher or psychotherapy supervisor.

2. Institutes may be reluctant to consider younger applicants because of difficulties in assessing the younger applicant, who may be less stable, less reliable, less certainly motivated, and less consolidated as an individual.

Recommendations: The institutes, especially admissions committees, should review their procedures to see if they are too demanding in their requirements for clinical experience, maturity, or life experience, and in what way this policy may be contributing to delays in application or acceptance. A greater receptivity on the part of institutes would necessarily need to be combined with procedures facilitating easy withdrawal. Institutes would need to evaluate carefully the progress of younger students and review policies that tend to keep marginal students in the system. The fact that a student does not complete analytic training should be viewed in terms of what he has gained from his training, however incomplete it may be.

Studies could be made of institutes using a relatively easy-in/easy-out policy. It would be particularly interesting to study the consequences of such a policy. Studies could be made of important motivating factors for application or nonapplication as they are affected by the potential applicants' perception of the institute. The effect of the composition of the admissions committee on the selection of younger applicants also invites study.

PROFESSIONAL CAREER FACTORS

1. The practice of analysis seems to some potential applicants narrow and even incompatible with other psychiatric career choices. Popular activist attitudes run counter to the psychoanalytic approach.

2. There are more opportunities for rapid professional advancement in careers other than psychoanalytic psychiatry.

Recommendations. Analysts should remain actively involved in most areas of psychiatry. They should demonstrate the usefulness of a psychoanalytic background in other areas, particularly child psychiatry, child development, research, academic psychiatry, treatment of psychotics, group process, and community psychiatry. The analyst who is teaching in any of the applied psychoanalytic fields should be competent in that area as well as the area of special expertise — treatment by psychoanalysis.

ACADEMIC FACTORS

1. The interest of college students in psychoanalysis is often discouraged and may be turned into antagonism when psychoanalysis is poorly presented by analysts or misrepresented by nonanalysts.

2. Competing theories, such as behavior modification, frequently are more attractive to the uncritical person because of a certain simplicity of explanation and seemingly greater practicality and more rapid effectiveness.

3. The anti-analytic attitude of some medical school departments of psychiatry has a negative effect on the attitude of residents to psychoanalysis and psychoanalytic training.

Recommendations. Analysts should be encouraged to participate in college teaching and to develop effective methods of presenting psychoanalysis to college students and faculty. Analysts should not shun active teaching roles in departments of psychiatry, even when the leadership of the department may not be fully sympathetic to analysis.

THE OLDER TRAINEE

Adherence to a rigid upper age limit for applicants would exclude some with particular talents, abilities, interests, and potentiality for contributions to psychoanalysis.

Recommendations. If any institutes have a fixed upper age limit for applicants it should be reconsidered, especially for those scholars and teachers who will not be entering the practice of psychoanalysis. A flexible upper age limit is consistent with the principle that consideration of applicants should be on an individual basis. During and after World War II a number of older applicants were accepted for training; it might be useful to review this experience.

THE PROBLEM OF PROLONGED TRAINING

All institutes should regularly re-examine their progression and graduation policies to determine the extent to which these policies place an undue economic burden on students or delay their educational and professional progress. The Association should take notice of the difficulties in analytic training experienced by those with academic careers and promote nationwide institute policies that would recognize the often necessary mobility of such students and facilitate transfer of training from one institute to another.

THE OLDER ANALYST

In 1961 the Association advised the adoption of the following guidelines for retirement of training analysts:

1. No training analyst who has reached age 68 should start a training analysis.

2. Training and teaching analysts who have reached age 72 should usually be relieved of administrative, supervisory, and educational responsibilities.

3. Participation in educational and administrative activities after 72 may continue by mutual agreement but without vote.

These guidelines have been essentially adopted by almost all institutes with provisions permitting continuation of work beyond retirement age if the training analyst is in good physical and mental health. There are quite a few analysts at the age of 70 and older who are in good health, do not experience more than the usual effects of aging, and do creditable work. The age-appropriate fatigability and forgetfulness are compensated for by the valuable experience the older analyst has accumulated.

RECOMMENDATIONS

1. The retirement guidelines of the Association should be adopted by all institutes with no provision for exceptions. Most commission members felt exceptions only make management of the problem more difficult.

2. The Association should make provisions for local institutes to seek and receive help in difficult situations concerning retirement. This help could be provided either by an ad hoc committee or by members of the Ethics Committee. If possible, one member of such a consulting body should be a training analyst who has retired successfully.

3. There are many activities of the Association in which retired training analysts could participate, such as the above-mentioned Ethics Committee, professional and educational surveys, and other organizational functions. The Association should seek out and enlist the energy of such colleagues.

4. The several functions of the training analyst should be considered separately in relation to retirement.

5. Institutes should not permit situations in which a training analyst derives a large part of his income from training analysis or supervision. In anticipation of retiring from that function the training analyst should have developed other sources of practice or other professional

activities, both for personal satisfaction and economic security.

6. Analysts contemplating retirement should be encouraged in autobiographical writings, and efforts should be made to find funds to support them in this activity. Such records could provide valuable insights about who analysts are and why they choose a lifetime profession of listening to other people and attempting to understand their mental activity and behavior.

A rigorous application of retirement guidelines may seem unduly arbitrary to some but the commission sees an advantage in that training analysts will be stimulated to prepare themselves earlier, psychologically as well as financially, for retirement. Although such a policy may deprive institutes of training analysts who are still in full command of their faculties at retirement age, these analysts may continue to serve in several much needed roles, as indicated above.

The recommendations primarily concern training analysts and the commission is well aware that the problem of aging and retirement for psychoanalysts who are not training analysts is even more difficult, particularly since they are more isolated from their colleagues and the consequences of their disabilities may not come as directly to the attention of the society or institute. In this regard further studies and consideration are certainly desirable.

PLENARY DISCUSSION—
HENRIETTE R. KLEIN, M.D.

The commission essentially concerned itself with factors delaying the beginning of psychoanalytic training, or resulting in its not being undertaken altogether; factors unduly prolonging training; and problems of the aging analyst.

Regarding the late age at which psychoanalytic training usually begins, the report considered the consequences for psychoanalysis, psychoanalytic training, and the lives of psychoanalysts, and implied that if analysis is to flourish it must make itself available to a younger and wider range of students, especially since our teaching interests are not, or should not be, only in training of clinicians. The commission thus recommends, and I agree, that for some students psychoanalytic training should begin earlier, concurrent and if possible integrated with other aspects of their education, rather than be postponed until after the Ph.D. or an M.D. has been achieved. In the emphasis on earlier integration in career development it was kept in mind that this might induce premature career choice (Coker, 1960). However, other studies show that career-related choices are, in fact, usually made early in life. Of a group who were queried when they entered medical school, 50 per cent of those who said they were going into psychiatry did so (Bloom, 1973). The population is there to be tapped if desired, and if training is not artificially delayed.

Although I believe strongly that the analytic institutes should accept qualified nonmedical students, I shall confine my remarks to those analytic students who will be drawn from the medical profession. In a study (Becker et al., 1961) of 1,500 interviews with medical students, psychiatry and surgery were the two specialties named originally by the entering student, and retained as the actual career choice. All studies tend to show early selection of psychiatry and psychoanalysis where it becomes the final choice. In a study at Downstate Medical College (Bloom, 1973) where the students were asked to rate the specialties, psychiatry was the only specialty that did not shift its rating in the four years. Further studies of specialty choice based on psychoanalytic studies of students would be most useful.

Whatever the constructive changes brought about in the analytic institutes to interest younger students and those who intend to pursue academic analytic careers or research, these factors are negligible compared to what can be done through the crucial area of medical college admissions. Decisions by medical college admissions committees affect the future population of psychiatrists and psychoanalysts to some degree. If medical colleges accept more students with high verbal skills, strongly humanistic interests, and multiple cultural involvements, the percentage of those who go into psychiatry and psychoanalysis will similarly increase. Psychoanalysts should be more appropriately represented in the administrative processes of the medical college, including the admissions committee, rather than only engaged in postgraduate teaching.

The commission did not consider another change, not unrelated to age—the increased admissions of women to medical schools. In the past four years, at three medical colleges, Harvard, Cornell, and Columbia, women constitute over 30 per cent of admissions. The current most-favored specialty among women is no longer pediatrics and medicine, but psychiatry. Many residencies are now arranged with extension of training time to permit pregnancy and early child care; therefore, women's admission age for psychoanalytic training, and certainly their graduation age, will be raised. This is a crucial factor, especially since some believe that in the years ahead, admissions of women to medical college will increase to 50 per cent. If the largest percentage of the group continues to show a preference for psychiatry, women may eventually predominate in psychoanalytic training.

I urge institutes to continue re-evaluation of their policies along the lines of the commission's recommendations regarding the undue prolongation of training. For example, further follow-up studies should be made of the occasional practice of recommending to marginal students a second training analysis in the often vain hope that more analysis will help, or the tendency to refer such students to one supervisor after another on the chance that some kind of learning transfusion will be educationally catalytic. These actions may explain at least some of the lengthy training experiences.

I do not agree with the suggestion that it might be possible to bypass the current policy that a completed case should be experienced by every student before graduation. Whether one calls a case completed or interrupted, every analyst, sooner rather than later, must become familiar with and competent, preferably while still in supervision, to deal with separation, loss, fear of dying, and residuals of transference and countertransference feelings, as evoked in the termination process of an analysis.

The geographic immobility of psychoanalysis is intimately related to the age factor. By the time the average student has entered or completed psychiatry residency, started private practice, and enrolled in an institute, he or she is often geographically fixed (Potter et al., 1957). Studies from all institutes confirm that our profession has the lowest degree of mobility. In addition, the analyst stays close to his or her own institute for multiple emotional reasons.

And now to the last of the problems of the consequences of age, the aging analyst. The report indicates that psychoanalysts tend to continue to work as long as their capacities permit. I would say, rather, that in most instances they continue as long as their environment permits. The analyst's reluctance to retire is, of course, based on many factors, economic considerations being only one (Coker, 1960). Among the factors determining our organizational attitudes regarding the aging analyst is our greater or lesser personal identification with the aging, including our own fears of separation, helplessness, anonymity, and dying. In a sense, we might be somewhat less uneasy about an aging analyst analyzing a student than about his or her analyzing a private patient. An institute is able to exercise some influence on the training analysis in a variety of ways, but a private patient has little protection. The emotional life of the analyst who must forsake the practice of analyzing patients may be a precarious one. The separation from patients, the subsequent partial separation from colleagues, the feeling of not being needed and no longer appreciated, are universal problems that each of us will confront and must eventually attempt to solve for ourselves.

SUMMARY OF CONFERENCE DISCUSSION

All of the discussion groups responded favorably to the commission's presentation. There was a general recognition of the probable value of an early entrance into training, but there was equal awareness of the importance of adequate personal maturity in the analytic student, which makes careful individual evaluation a necessity. The problems attendant on both early and late entrance were reviewed in some detail, and the consensus was that although selection evaluation, preclinical preparation, and financial support would present great difficulties, the possible yield in flexibility, creativity, and diversity of career development of younger students and graduates should stimulate the effort to overcome the obstacles.

The discussion groups certainly agreed with the commission that the idea of younger students and younger graduates should not become an end in itself, overriding all other relevant considerations, but rather that careful attention should be paid to every factor that might unnecessarily delay or discourage application for training or prolong the training. The complexity of the issue was indicated by the suggestion that, quite aside from the question of personal maturity, a very early involvement in psychoanalytic training, before relative completion of either medical or nonmedical graduate preparation, might limit rather than enlarge what the younger student could contribute to or obtain from analysis.

The economic considerations involved in the training of younger analytic students, medical or nonmedical, were discussed at great length. It will be noticed that the topic of economics came up in the context of almost every conference presentation; perhaps there should have been a separate preparatory commission on the economics of psychoanalysis, psychoanalytic education and research. Difficult to state with any precision, at least it may be indicated that there were generous measures of both pessimism and optimism regarding possible financial support for the several programmatic recommendations of the conference. Most conferees agreed that individual psychoanalysts and organized psychoanalysis must make an even greater direct contribution in time and money than they do at present. This conclusion in itself generated a certain despair because of the wide recognition that the profession is already extremely generous in support of psychoanalytic education and may not be able to increase that support to the extent envisioned. It was clear that even if psychoanalysis were able to raise a sufficient fund from within its ranks to support younger students that very effort would further increase the necessity for psychoanalysts to devote their time almost exclusively to private clinical practice; thus, the model of the psychoanalyst as clinician would be still further emphasized to the very students being encouraged to exercise more varied career choices.

The considerations of individual maturation and development as well as economics were pertinent to the issue of the aging training analyst and the question of retirement from teaching and the responsibility for training analyses. As always in the discussion of topics involving an evaluation procedure or a personnel problem, there was the frequently expressed wish for flexibility and careful individual evaluation as opposed to rigid categorical decisions. There was also the realistic recognition of the almost impossible practical and personal difficulties that ensue from too much emphasis on individualization and too little attention to a sometimes unkind but at least impartially applied policy and procedure.

The discussion groups seemed to agree that equitable retirement policies for training analysts are appropriate, and that their systematic application by the institutes would effectively encourage training analysts to prepare economically and emotionally for retirement. Efforts to utilize the valuable experience and insights of retired senior analysts were universally recommended. It was recognized that the institutes as such had no direct responsibility or authority in regard to the retirement of nontraining analysts, but concern was expressed that the nontraining clinical practice of analysis has, so far at least, been less accessible than desirable to adequate peer review. Discussants felt that this matter was an appropriate concern of the psychoanalytic professional societies.

Relationship of Psychoanalysis to Current Changes in Medical and Psychiatric Education

Paul G. Myerson, M.D., Chairman
William W. Meissner, M.D., Recorder
Jose Barchilon, M.D.
O. Eugene Baum, M.D.
Samuel L. Feder, M.D.
Paul Jay Fink, M.D.
Theodore J. Jacobs, M.D.
Robert A. Nemiroff, M.D.
William S. Robbins, M.D.
Melvin Sabshin, M.D.
Joseph Sandler, M.D.
Elvin V. Semrad, M.D.
Roy M. Whitman, M.D.
Lyman C. Wynne, M.D.

Relationship of Psychoanalysis to Current Changes in Medical and Psychiatric Education

ORIGINAL CHARGE

Long-established medical educational practices are now being challenged and altered. The uniform student progression and the skilled craft orientation are being de-emphasized in favor of diversified curriculum models and core programs with greater range of electives; multiple-track systems with earlier specialization are becoming more frequent. Many medical schools and residencies are making serious efforts to transform the traditional passive learning methods into ones that aim for achievement of mastery through an active and more self-initiated process. How many of these alterations in principles and practice are applicable within the psychoanalytic training setting? How can preparation for psychoanalysis be connected with these evolving and altered medical and psychiatric educational structures? How much coordination or separation should there be in the medical-psychiatric-psychoanalytic sequence?

PREPARATORY COMMISSION REPORT

The formation of a commission to study the relation of psychoanalysis to changes in medical education and psychiatric training programs also serves as a response to the changes taking place in medical and psychiatric practice. The present report is based on a survey of past and present psychoanalytic involvement in medical and psychiatric education; on the results of three separate questionnaire surveys focusing on medical education, residency training programs, and the impact of changes in the policy and programs of psychoanalytic institutes on medical and psychiatric training programs; and finally on a survey of new approaches to the integration of psychiatric and psychoanalytic training.

Considerations

PRESSURES TO CHANGE

Current forces of social and economic change are having far-reaching effects on the organization of medical and psychiatric practice, and their corresponding training programs. These changes are related to two important developments. First, there is an increased emphasis on the distribution of adequate health care to all segments of the population, a most worthwhile policy which, however, should be accompanied by a continuing emphasis upon the quality of care and dedication to maintaining excellence of professional training, specialization, and research. Second, the rapidly growing cost of health care has necessitated greater reliance on third-party payment programs, both private and public. Already on the horizon is a national health insurance program and the federal supervision of the organization and operation of all health-care systems. There is also a trend toward organizing health care and training around regional academic medical centers, which may assume primary institutional responsibility. It appears likely that the future of self-sufficient training centers separate from university medical centers is limited.

The challenge to psychoanalysis is clear. The psychoanalytic emphasis on individual treatment extended over a long period of time and the relative unavailability of that treatment to many for economic reasons present many problems in relation to current and impending socio-economic changes. There is a danger that psychoanalysis may become isolated and move into an ever smaller role as a treatment modality as well as in medical and psychiatric training. Current versions of national health insurance programs offer little provision for either long-term intensive psychotherapy or psychoanalysis.

A number of factors may tend to reduce the capacity of psychiatric departments in medical schools and psychiatric residency programs to continue to fulfill their usual objectives, particularly in regard to adequate training in psychotherapy. First, cutbacks of funding at all levels will reduce the number of psychiatric residents and the time available for teaching both in medical schools and residency programs. Economic considerations will direct the training of residents toward those areas currently being given greater support, e.g., community psychiatry. Second, there now seems to be a trend for medical schools and residency training programs to appoint chairmen and directors who are at best neutral to psychoanalysis and psychoanalytically influenced psychodynamic psychiatry, e.g., biochemists. Third, the use of third-party payments with peer-review systems will probably emphasize short-term crisis-intervention approaches rather than long-term psychotherapy.

TRENDS IN MEDICAL SCHOOL EDUCATION

Along with these changes, the expansion of knowledge in the health sciences has created further demands for change in existing medical school curricula. The importance of the newly emerging sciences and fields of study has opened a wider variety of medical careers to new graduates. New trends include the abandonment of strict departmentalization, an emphasis on learning rather than teaching, greater flexibility in determining various paths to the M.D. degree, multiple-track undergraduate curricula, and more individualized postgraduate education in which greater individual choice is offered to the student in working out specialized fields of study.

Almost all applicants for psychoanalytic training now come from psychiatry, and it must be noted that psychiatry is currently beset by a severe shortage of qualified applicants and graduate specialists. Within psychiatry, psychoanalysis must compete with the many fields of study and professional involvement promoted by social demand and government support, and by medical schools and psychiatric departments dependent on government support. This situation is unlikely to change in the immediate future.

Where psychoanalysts are associated with a department of psychiatry, they have exerted varying degrees of influence upon the curriculum. This influence seems rather unrelated to any formal connection between a psychoanalytic institute and the department of psychiatry. Even where there is no institute in the same city as the medical school, local analysts have sometimes played an important part in the teaching. The inclusion of behavioral science as one seventh of Part I of the National Boards has exercised a considerable influence on the curricula of many medical schools in the United States. The basic science of psychiatry is presented in behavioral-science courses in the first year of medical school; whether concepts of psychoanalytic psychology should be and are being adequately presented in such courses is an important issue.

In medical schools where analysts have an influence, medical students do learn psychiatry and behavioral science with a psychoanalytic orientation. A survey of medical school departments of psychiatry generally favorable to psychoanalysis lends considerable support to the view that valuable contributions are made by individual psychoanalysts to these teaching programs, and there is general agreement that psychoanalysts have a unique contribution to make to the teaching of clinical understanding. However, there is a need for a nationwide survey and study of medical school departments of psychiatry in which psychoanalytic influence has been altogether lacking or insignificant.

TRENDS IN PSYCHIATRY RESIDENCY TRAINING

It seems clear that most residency programs are attempting to provide a broad spectrum of training in modern psychiatry. A decade ago, many programs made training in individual psychoanalytic psychotherapy the core of their residency experience. The trend today is to decrease that emphasis; nevertheless, the increase in experience and teaching of community psychiatry, family therapy, behavior modification, and group psychotherapy has not totally eliminated the psychoanalytic material.

In general, the interest of psychiatric residents in psychoanalytic training has remained rather stable — the application rate to psychoanalytic institutes averaging between ten and 30 per cent of the resident group in the institutions surveyed. The active participation in the residency teaching programs of enthusiastic and respected analysts is an important factor in generating interest in psychoanalytic training. In a number of programs many residents begin a personal analysis or individual psychotherapy during their psychiatric training. There have been some problems resulting from the initiation of psychoanalytic training during the course of the residency, particularly as the resident's personal analysis takes time from the working schedule. However, this difficulty has usually been surmountable and does not appear to be a crucial factor in determining whether a resident will apply for psychoanalytic training.

Opinions of the residency training directors have been divided about the elimination of the internship. Some educators feel that the elimination has created problems of professional insecurity and immaturity, such that those residents without an internship experience have had greater difficulty than their colleagues in developing a professional identity. Others, however, feel that these differences have been of consequence only early in the resident's training, and that by the second and third year the differences between the internship and noninternship groups have been insignificant. In general, the change in the internship requirement seems to have created no discernible effect on the interest of residents in psychoanalytic training.[1]

Surveys generally indicate that despite the changes in residency training during the past decade, psychoanalysis continues to be a major influence in modern American psychiatric education. The influence and the role that it plays can be attributed almost exclusively to the efforts of individual analysts and their active participation in all phases of the residency training program.

THE PLACE OF PSYCHOANALYSIS IN TEACHING AND TRAINING PROGRAMS

The participation of individual analysts in teaching and training programs has had several consequences: it has helped increase the awareness of medical students and physicians of psychological influences upon the course of both physical and mental illness, the effects of illness upon the whole person, and the influence of transference and countertransference phenomena on the patient-physician relationship; it has helped psychiatrists, psychologists, and other mental health professionals who do not obtain full psychoanalytic training to develop and improve their skills as psychodynamically oriented psychotherapists; and it has helped interest medical students and psychiatric residents in psychoanalytic careers.

Although on the individual level many psychoanalysts have played a significant role in the evolution of psychiatric training, organized psychoanalysis, as re-

[1] *Editor's note:* Internship requirement is to be fully re-established by 1977.

presented by the Association and its affiliate societies and approved institutes, has so far participated to only a minor extent. The committee concludes that the Association must take an organizational responsibility for maintaining the significant activity and contributions of psychoanalysis to the teaching of medical students and psychiatric residents.

THE ROLE OF PSYCHOANALYSIS

Psychoanalysts are being stimulated to explore innovative approaches to the integration of psychoanalytic and psychiatric teaching. The committee feels that it might be possible for particularly gifted and mature medical and psychiatric students to begin a modified program of psychoanalytic education at an earlier than usual point in their training. The feasibility of developing a combined psychiatric and psychoanalytic residency leading toward psychoanalytic as well as psychiatric certification should be actively explored by local institutes and directors of residency training programs. It would also be desirable for the institutes and societies to investigate the possibility of their membership making low-cost analyses available for medical students and psychiatric residents.

The committee recognizes the potential difficulties and complexities in working out arrangements for a joint program that would be acceptable to both the psychoanalytic institutes and the psychiatric departments or residency programs. Some analysts have expressed concern that the core of psychoanalytic training would be diluted if the institutes were to collaborate in this manner with medical school departments of psychiatry and with psychiatric residency training programs. The committee believes that these difficulties could be surmounted and that the feared dilution could be avoided if both institutions were sufficiently motivated for an earnest cooperative effort.

We are not suggesting that institutes should assume responsibility for the training of psychiatric residents, rather they should make their organizational resources available for the teaching of psychoanalysis to the extent appropriate in the over-all plan of the residency. Each institute will certainly contribute to the communication of psychoanalytic knowledge in its own way. Some may want to work through their existing extension school programs in offering courses to medical students, social workers, and psychologists; others may develop a group of psychoanalytic teachers willing to travel to understaffed residency programs; and still others may find that their most effective contribution is to offer low-fee personal analyses through treatment centers. Obviously, there are a diversity of possibilities for each institute according to the local situation.

RECOMMENDATIONS

In view of all these current social, economic, and professional changes and the resultant challenging difficulties as well as opportunities for psychoanalysis, the committee strongly recommends to the local societies and institutes that in each area committees be established for the following purposes:

1. To survey the current situation related to the psychiatric teaching and training programs in their area.
2. To mobilize teachers within the institute who

would be capable of more effective participation in those teaching and training programs.

3. To arrange for possible participation in teaching and training programs that may even be outside of the institute's immediate geographic area.

4. To develop an appropriate organizational structure to offer low-fee psychoanalysis to students in local medical schools and psychiatric programs.

5. To review the success of methods for developing such programs and the relative effectiveness of programs that have been developed.

We also strongly recommend that a joint committee of the Board in Professional Standards and the Executive Council be established to review and encourage such programs on the national level.

PLENARY DISCUSSION — ELIZABETH B. DAVIS, M.D.

This commission used questionnaire surveys to obtain data on several aspects of psychoanalytic involvement in medical and psychiatric education: in medical schools; residency training programs; and psychoanalytic institutes themselves, in particular how changes in their policies and programs have affected medical and psychiatric training programs. Two additional reviews were made: one, of the history of psychoanalytic involvement in medical and psychiatric education, and the other, of progressive approaches to the integration of psychiatric and psychoanalytic training.

The commission expresses appropriate and valid concern about the possible downgrading of emphasis on quality of care, specialization, research, and excellence of training that might be associated with a suddenly widened demand for health care supported by national health insurance programs. The commission predicts that health care and training will increasingly be organized around regional academic medical centers. This developing situation is seen as a challenge, if not a threat, to psychoanalysis.

Characterization of these developments as threatening requires further consideration. The view is advanced that, because of the expense and the limited availability of psychoanalytic treatment to the community-at-large, psychoanalysis will become increasingly marginal in medical and psychiatric training. In order to support this view, we must determine in what ways national health insurance and better distribution of health care will change the psychoanalytic practice situation. Currently, persons primarily dependent on third-party payments for psychiatric care are, with few exceptions, unable to obtain psychoanalysis privately. Long-term intensive psychotherapy is frequently available under prepayment plans, but only a small fraction is provided by psychoanalysts. It is my impression that psychoanalysis has been and probably will continue to be a mode of treatment restricted to the relatively affluent who do not now and will not in the future rely entirely on national health insurance or third-party payments for access to medical care, and to those who need psychoanalysis for training and research purposes. Long-term intensive psychotherapy will remain available to those willing and able to pay for it beyond reimbursement limits, out of personal resources, often at the cost of real sacrifice. If its cost-effectiveness could be documented, psychoanalysis might also become reimbursible as an alternative mode of care.

Will the wider availability of acute psychiatric care reduce the need and desire of people for therapy requiring greater investment of time and money? I think not, and, furthermore, I believe that access to acute care earlier in the course of psychiatric illness will probably increase the demand for long-term intensive treatment since early diagnosis would allow for more options in treatment modality and setting. Will it reduce personnel available to supply intensive psychotherapy if demanded? It certainly could if training for psychiatry is decreased and if psychiatric training programs do not encourage development of the skills needed to provide such care, as well as the skills needed for other types of care. However, it is important to remember that the major impact of psychoanalysis on medical and psychiatric training has not been through training physicians for the practice of psychoanalysis. Instead, it has occurred through the wide dissemination and application of psychoanalytic theory and principles by psychoanalysts who have participated in the professional training of physicians, psychiatrists, social workers, psychologists, nurses, and other health-care personnel. The psychoanalytic approach to the understanding of human behavior, rather than a specific technique of treatment, has been the primary contribution of psychoanalysis to medicine and psychiatry, as well as to the behavioral sciences. This approach has, and rightly so in my opinion, become identified with excellence in psychiatric training.

If this assessment is correct, then I do not see the new developments as a threat, but agree with the commission's alternative view of them as a challenge. The greater availability of care under national health insurance can, indeed, result in even more patients benefiting from the contributions of psychoanalysis. The challenge to psychoanalysis is to remain in a position of influence in medical curricula, psychiatric training programs, and training programs for other health-care personnel, and thus assure a continued supply of competent professionals, and also well-motivated applicants for psychoanalytic training. If the contribution of psychoanalysis to health care is to be maintained and expanded, it must be done through the continued inclusion of psychoanalytic concepts in psychiatric and other mental health training programs. I use the phrase "inclusion in" rather than "integration with" here to avoid the dangers of reductionism to both psychoanalysis and psychiatry.

It may well be that the regional academic medical center will become the primary vehicle for enabling the medical profession to give effective expression to its concerns for excellence in patient care and training. If this is true, then association of psychoanalysts with these centers is essential. Since the commission's review indicates psychoanalysis' contribution and influence in both medical education and in psychiatric training is very significant, highly valued, and undiminished by the presentation of competing points of view, we should concern ourselves primarily with how the roles of psychoanalysts in such academic medical centers can become more institutionalized.

In connection with the concern that forces of socioeconomic change will isolate psychoanalysis and force it into a minimal role in the treatment spectrum, and ultimately in medical and psychiatric training, the commission is apprehensive that so-called prerogatives of traditional psychiatric approaches will be lost, as well as adequate recognition of the need for intensive treatment of individual psychopathology. If what is meant is the psychiatrist's prerogative to choose the most appropriate treatment method available and to provide the indicated treatment irrespective of the patient's economic or social circumstances, then the commission's position can be supported wholeheartedly. This is not the case, however, if what is meant is the psychiatrist's prerogative to apply his preferred method of treatment to the patients he prefers, with too little regard for over-all health-care needs. It is the arrogation by physicians of such prerogatives to themselves that has led to increasing demand for more equitable distribution of services. Failure to respond adequately to these needs may be one of the factors in the cutbacks in training program funding, and possibly also in the reduction of the time available for teaching. It is no more academic to expose residents mainly to psychoanalytic theories and to train them primarily for intensive treatment of individual psychopathology than to expose them almost exclusively to biological or behavior therapy. While at an earlier period it was essential to integrate psychoanalytic theory and psychodynamic treatment methods with general psychiatric training in this country, the current inclusion of teaching about the social and community factors in mental health and mental illness and its treatment provides a needed balance in many academic teaching centers.

When the commission predicts that the use of third-party payments with professional-standards-review systems will emphasize short-term crisis-intervention approaches at the expense of long-term psychotherapy, which is indeed the situation today, I assume that they include in their concern the possible need for long-term psychotherapy for the chronically or recurrently psychotic patient, in conjunction with whatever chemotherapy or social intervention is indicated in a total treatment program. For many years, the academic psychiatric training for long-term care of such patients has not been a credit to the field of psychiatry. To the extent that psychoanalytic influence on these training programs may have contributed to this neglect, there is some justice in the recent shift of emphasis in residency training programs.

Now we come to events within the health sciences themselves, and their current and anticipated impact on psychoanalysis. Here the stimulus is clearly a challenge, since as members of the health-care and scientific community, we could scarcely view the explosion of knowledge in the health sciences as a threat. In its survey of medical education and residency training programs the commission found that the psychoanalysts associated with a department of psychiatry have played an important role and continue to exert a significant influence upon the medical school curriculum and upon what is taught within the department of psychiatry itself. In view of this, I believe it is particularly important for psychoanalysts involved in curriculum planning to recognize new knowledge, to accept soundly based innovation, and to join with other professionals seeking to use their scientific knowledge on behalf of patients in need of psychiatric care. The commission's recognition of the need for and welcoming of psychoanalytic influence with or without formal psychoanalytic institutional connections, and the reported absence of negative effects of behavioral-science teaching on the effectiveness of analytic teaching in psychiatry should reassure us of the value of our teaching in medicine and psychiatry, and eliminate the need for defensive efforts to downgrade or eliminate the influence of alternate or complementary points of view. Freud was convinced, as are many contemporary psychiatrists and psychoanalysts, that specific genetic and biological factors in the development of mental illness would eventually be discovered and such predictions, of course, are coming true. Let us not fall victim to our own narcissism by suggesting that psychoanalysis or even psychodynamics is all of psychiatry. If we fail to respect contributions from other areas of psychiatry, and if we function in such a way that medical students and residents feel forced to choose sides, then we shall, in fact, have no place in truly academic medical center programs.

Perhaps the most important issue raised by the commission is whether psychoanalysis is committed to medical teaching and psychiatric training, and if so what should be done to make this commitment more flexible and effective. The true threat to psychoanalysis lies here rather than with national health insurance. The commission has concluded that it is crucial for organized psychoanalysis, specifically the separate institutes and the Association, to play an active and ongoing role if the significant accomplishments of psychoanalysis in teaching medical students and psychiatric residents are to be maintained. I agree strongly with that recommendation and would underline the recommendation that the institutes prepare themselves most carefully for such a role. The experience of those psychoanalytic institutes that have already taken such a role should be studied to avoid unnecessary repetition of error and to cull the most successful approaches and methods.

SUMMARY OF CONFERENCE DISCUSSION

All the discussion groups surveyed not only current and anticipated changes in medical and psychiatric education but also in medicine itself. The recommendation of the commission that psychoanalysts and psychoanalytic institutes should seek to participate actively in medical and psychiatric education was generally supported. Many discussants pointed out that individual analysts in large numbers have long been active in these areas. Medical schools and psychiatric residencies have varied in their readiness to appoint psychoanalysts as teachers, but involvement has been widespread indeed. Reservations were expressed regarding the possible activity of institutes as such, in offering their teaching resources to medical schools and residencies. It was thought that such an arrangement might be feasible in certain locations, depending on the individuals involved, but that as always with such joint organizational efforts it would be an enterprise fraught with great potential difficulties. Over and over, the need for organizational care and sensitivity was stressed. While there is support for the institutes' exploring avenues of cooperation, it is evident that most reliance is placed on the continued effective participation of individual psychoanalytic teachers in medical and psychiatric teaching programs.

The commission's report was criticized in some of the discussion groups, as it was by its formal discussant, for its somewhat defensive and apprehensive tone and its view of current changes more as a threat than as a challenge for psychoanalysis.

While there was almost no question that psychoanalysis should endeavor to contribute whatever and however it can to medicine and medical and psychiatric education, the particular impact on psychoanalysis itself of changing health-education and health-care arrangements was not clarified even after extensive discussion. A variety of speculative views were offered, some wish-fulfillingly optimistic, others gloomily pessimistic, but none convincingly persuasive to most participants. Psychoanalysts, of course, are not alone in being unable at present to see clearly the impact of future developments in these areas.

In the discussion of this topic, the close relation of psychoanalysis to medicine was once again confronted. The traditional personal and organizational attachment to medicine is still powerful, and few analysts denied the great importance of the medical therapeutic application of psychoanalysis. However, all the discussions reveal a growing undercurrent of opinion that the tie may be too exclusive for the continued healthy growth of psychoanalysis. It was suggested more than once that the medical application of psychoanalysis should be considered as only one of several important applications rather than as the exclusive essence. The uncertainty about the economic implications of impending social changes contributed additional interest to the discussion of whether psychoanalysis, at least as represented by the Association membership, should stay with or move away from its exclusive relation to medicine.

Relationship of Psychoanalysis to Universities

Bernard Holland, M.D., Chairman
Richard S. Ward, M.D., Recorder
Ewald W. Busse, M.D.
Robert S. Daniels, M.D.
Maurice R. Friend, M.D.
Robert M. Gilliland, M.D.
Henriette R. Klein, M.D.
Lawrence C. Kolb, M.D.
L. Douglas Lenkoski, M.D.
Leo Madow, M.D.
James T. McLaughlin, M.D.
David Musto, M.D.
George A. Richardson, M.D.
Leonard L. Shengold, M.D.
Herman Stein, Ph.D.
Robert J. Stoller, M.D.
William C. Thompson, M.D.
Arthur F. Valenstein, M.D.

Relationship of Psychoanalysis to Universities

ORIGINAL CHARGE

How necessary is a formal relationship with the university? How should psychoanalysis be organized within the university? As a division in a department of psychiatry of the medical school, as with the present university-based institutes? Or as an autonomous institute, independent of, but related to the department of psychiatry of the medical school, the graduate school of social work, the graduate faculties in psychology, sociology, anthropology, political science, etc.? What are the possible advantages and the disadvantages of each proposed organizational arrangement?

PREPARATORY COMMISSION REPORT

The commission's goal was to examine the current patterns of collaboration and cooperation between psychoanalytic education and universities, review the history of such relations, draw conclusions, and make suggestions for the future. To accomplish this task, the commission drew upon the accumulated experience of its members, collected data from the various university-affiliated institutes, and reviewed past committees' reports on this topic.

All experience to date in the United States with analytic training in a university setting has actually been restricted to a single mode of relationship, namely, the analytic institute in a department of psychiatry of a university medical school. It would be clearer, therefore, to speak of medical-school-department-of-psychiatry-based institutes rather than university-based institutes.

Beginning with Freud, psychoanalysts have always believed that psychoanalysis has a place in the university. The values that psychoanalysts have sought in this association have included recognition of psychoanalysis as an important field of human knowledge, the opportunity for interchange with scholars in a university setting, and contact with university students, both to teach them about psychoanalysis and to attract some of them to psychoanalysis as a career. However, the prospect of psychoanalysis participating in the university must take into account the great complexity of the modern American university as an institution. There is usually a clear separation between general university programs and the professional schools; therefore, affiliation with the psychiatry department is almost as far removed from the rest of the university as an independent psychoanalytic institute. Frequently, a university medical school is even located in a different city. Thus, a medical-school-based institute does not, by itself, promise easy achievement of an ideally close relationship between psychoanalysis and the university.

Although the medical-school-based institute has been the only successful and viable form of university affiliation in the United States, this does not mean it is the only form possible, but rather that so far we have no experience to allow us to evaluate other forms of affiliation. Many psychoanalysts feel that psychoanalytic education may be tied much too closely to psychiatry and medicine, and that a psychoanalytic institute that related to the university as a whole could reach other disciplines more effectively. Several obstacles stand in the way of such a development. To date university affiliations of institutes have generally been supported by funds allocated for medical training. Even if funds became available from other sources, the university currently tends to be wary of additional independent structures. In many graduate schools, various departments have vigorously resisted the introduction of any educational program that seemed to encroach on their area. Finally, while it may be desirable to bring psychoanalysis closer to fields outside of medicine and psychiatry, given the noted separation between medical schools and the rest of the university, if the result is loss of contact with medicine and psychiatry, the loss to psychoanalysis might be greater than the gain.

The medical-school-based institutes, however, are not the only psychoanalytic institutes that presently have a relationship, however limited, with the university. Almost all institutes have some kind of contact with their local university. Thus, the distinction between the so-called university-based institutes and the independent institutes is not necessarily on an either/or basis with regard to their degree of participation in university life. Where the psychoanalytic institute is not administratively affiliated with a university, it may nevertheless have contact with one or more universities, in that members of its faculty may hold university positions and play significant roles in certain university programs. It should be clear, therefore, that the issue is not only whether analytic institutes should be formally related to the university, but also the possible modes of this relationship and their advantages and disadvantages.

The commission identified four major possible modes of relationship between psychoanalytic education and universities: (1) the medical-school-based psychoanalytic institute, (2) the independent psychoanalytic institute, (3) the university-based, interdisciplinary psychoanalytic institute, and (4) the psychoanalytic institute that strives to be a college or university in itself by providing its own courses in the appropriate basic sciences and in the related behavioral sciences and the humanities, in addition to the usual tripartite psychoanalytic curriculum. The commission attempted to estimate the advantages and disadvantages of each of these modes with regard to carrying on the tasks of analytic education. Unfortunately, the data for this examination are quite uneven with regard to these different modes; they are most adequate with regard to the independent institute, and obviously totally lacking with regard to the hypothetical interdisciplinary university-based institute and the hypothetical institute as a college in itself. Almost all of the medical-school-based institutes were represented in the commission's membership, but representation of the independent institutes was limited. Moreover, the data collected by the commission relied primarily on the experience of the medical-school-based institute since, at the beginning, the commission had not established the broader scope of its inquiry. A fuller and more adequate evaluation of the advantages and disadvantages of relationships between the independent institutes and universities would require further data gathering and larger representation of the independent institutes on the commission. Thus, in progressing through the modes from one to four the data grow weaker, and the conclusions and suggestions increasingly tentative, as they are based on estimate and extrapolations from present-day experience. These limitations should be made clear at the start.

The commission listed several objectives of analytic education that go beyond training students for professional competence in psychoanalysis. We believe these objectives are fundamental to the survival and development of psychoanalysis and are, in largest part, the institutes' responsibility. Evaluating the way in which the particular relationship between an institute and a university facilitates or interferes with them may clarify the advantages or disadvantages of the various modes.

The medical-school-based institute seems to have an obvious advantage in recruitment of students from the group of psychiatric residents available in the psychiatry department. This is certainly true with regard to the particular psychiatry department with which the analytic institute is directly affiliated, although less true with regard to other universities. This recruitment advantage obviously develops from the visibility of analytic faculty to residents who have an opportunity to know analysts either as teachers or clinicians and are motivated to gain some of the competence demonstrated. However, when faculty members of independent institutes are teachers or clinical preceptors in psychiatry departments, they achieve the same visibility and, incidentally, the independent institute in certain areas may even relate to several medical schools. Thus, it does not seem to be the administrative affiliation that is critical in this regard, but rather the visibility of analytic teachers in the university setting. It was pointed out that sometimes the independent institute cannot control the kind of impression it makes upon potential students because the teachers who are most visible are not necessarily the ones the institute would choose to be its representatives. In this respect, perhaps, the medical-school-based institute has some advantage, and full-time analysts in the medical school provide important role models for medical students and residents. The independent institute may, on the other hand, find it easier to be visible to potential nonmedical students, if the acceptance of nonmedical students becomes a trend of importance. The university-based cross-disciplinary institute would presumably also be visible to nonmedical students, through undergraduate and graduate courses, cross-disciplinary research collaborations, and extension programs.

Most graduates from psychoanalytic institutes have gone into the private practice of psychoanalysis. There is little question that the cost of psychoanalytic training has been an important determining factor in this decision. Most of the cost of training is borne by the student, who must earn the money, usually through private clinical work, to pay the training analyst, tuition for courses, and clinical supervisors. To the extent that the student's financial burden is lightened in university programs, there is at least the increased opportunity for some students to make a career choice other than that of private clinical practice. However, training subsidies have not been extensive in the past and probably will be even less so in the near future. The medical-school-based institutes have come under more and more financial pressure as a result of loss of support for their parent departments.

A widely held view within the Association has been that the full-time clinical practitioner is the only fully competent analyst. Certainly it is true that continuing practice of analysis is essential for a graduate to retain clinical competence; however, it is unclear just how much practice is actually necessary. In the 1950's and 1960's a large percentage of the newly appointed department of psychiatry chairmen in this country were analysts, and the influence psychoanalysis enjoyed depended to a significant degree upon the important role of psychoanalysts in medical school and residency teaching programs. If analysts ceased to be offered department chairmanships, or if they regularly refused these posts, this influence would be lost to psychiatrists untrained in analysis or hostile to it. The factors leading analytic graduates to seek or avoid academic positions are clearly more than economic ones. Certainly a significant factor is the identification with respected teachers. Some analytic institutes have an excellent record in graduating analysts who go into academic positions. This is probably a result of self-selective recruitment, i.e., those students interested in an academic career tend to apply to that institute. The commission feels that this area deserves more study, both by individual institutes and the Association. Although there is no existing example of the university-based institute, whether interdisciplinary or not, one can speculate that there would be more stimulation toward an academic career than there is within the independent institute.

The commission saw little evidence that the mode of relationship with a university has had much effect upon the freedom of psychoanalytic teachers to engage in research and the advancement of psychoanalytic knowledge. Although full-time university professors are presumably freer to pursue research and writing than are private practitioners who donate their extra time for teaching in an independent institute, in practice we don't know that the medical-school-based analysts have actually been more productive. In this respect, analysis and psychiatry are perhaps different from some of the other medical disciplines where practitioners are usually much less productive in scholarly work and research than their academic counterparts. There does not seem to be any evidence that one kind of institute is doing better at promoting research careers than another. Nowhere is there adequate funding for research. Again, it is difficult to assess how the hypothetical university-based institute might perform in this area, except to say that if such an institute were adequately funded it could support more productivity than institutes narrowly dependent on fees for teaching and clinical service.

One consideration offered by some psychoanalysts is that university affiliation would confirm a social recognition of psychoanalysis as an important field of knowledge and promote its understanding in the university community. The commission feels that experience over the past twenty years has shown that entrance into the university, at least in the form that has been achieved by the medical-school-based institutes, has not been a golden road to acceptance of psychoanalysis. Communication with other disciplines is something that requires much time, effort, and good fortune in finding a receptive audience. Some of the medical-school-based institutes have indeed achieved a measure of success in this regard and they are to be applauded. However, it is clear that for a psychoanalytic institute to be a part of a department of psychiatry in a medical school does not necessarily confer upon it great visibility with regard to the rest of the university or even the medical school. There are other ways of achieving dissemination of psychoanalytic knowledge in the university—for example, by offering extension courses in the university-at-large. The university-based institute would probably have an easier time in communicating with the nonmedical undergraduate and graduate school departments, though it should not be overlooked that these departments often have difficulty in communicating with each other. Furthermore this increased communication with the nonmedical unversity might be offset by an increased difficulty in communication with the medical school.

Experience has shown that being based in the medical school does not necessarily make it easier to collaborate with other disciplines. Modern universities are organized by departments and cooperation between departments is often more wished for than achieved in real life. The gulf between the medical school and the rest of the university is even wider, and this is especially true when there is some geographic separation. Collaboration has been achieved, but only because of considerable time and effort devoted toward that end. While there may be some advantage in belonging to the university family, it is likely that the same results could be secured, regardless of the mode of administrative relationship between the analytic institute and the university, if sufficient efforts were made. The university-based cross-disciplinary institute would seem to have a clear advantage here, in that some of these disciplines would be included in its own structure, probably with joint appointments in the respective related university departments. The institute functioning as an independent psychoanalytic university would, by deliberate composition and organization, aim at collaborative efforts.

Most medical-school-based psychoanalytic programs have become a part of the clinical resources of the medical school and their clinical work is visible in the psychiatry department. The medical-school-based programs have also been able to provide some low-fee analysis for colleagues and students in allied disciplines, but there have been sharp limits to available financing. The independent institutes have, in fact, carried on the same function to an equivalent extent through their low-fee clinics. A program within a university has the previously noted advantage of visibility to the university community. Presumably this same advantage would be enjoyed by the hypothetical university-based institute. The equally hypothetical institute organized as a university would function like the independent institute.

The pattern that continuing medical education will take is not yet clear. There is pressure from various health legislation developments for recertification and relicensure programs, with emphasis upon continuing education and retesting for competence. It is hoped that the greater emphasis will be on continuing education since this aims at raising standards of practice rather than simply monitoring the profession. It seems logical that the primary responsibility for accreditation of training institutions, certification of students, and approval of local continuing education programs in psychoanalysis should rest with the Association. In the university-based institute, the broader university connection might have less meaning, since the certifying authority of the university medical school would be crucial.

There also is a need for continuing medical education programs for nonanalytic psychiatrists, and nonpsychiatric physicians, to which a psychoanalytic institute can appropriately contribute. This may be equally well done by the medical-school-based institute or the independent institute.

The commission attempted to appraise the advantages and disadvantages of university affiliation through an exploration of the specific experience of existing medical-school-based institutes, and a questionnaire was circulated to these institutes. The results of the questionnaire can be summarized as follows: All of the medical-school-based institutes have experienced, in varying degrees, considerable advantage from financial and material subsidy by the universities to which they are attached. Not the least important has been space and secretarial help. Along with this support, however, there has been a certain restriction of program planning, policy, and fund raising, which comes from belonging to a larger unit with its own policies and procedures. To date there has been negligible interference with the actual educational program of the analytic institutes. However, one university-affiliated institute recently indicated that this freedom had been endangered by medical school/university authorities who wished to assert their right to choose the institute director, whether or not the institute faculty concurred in the choice. Furthermore, the department chairman wished to recruit for the post a researcher-psychoanalyst who would aim to produce new generations of research psychoanalysts, and have the authority to revamp the psychoanalytic curriculum as needed to effect this goal. The advantage of being located inside the university in terms of recruitment of students, access to patients, collaboration with other disciplines, and so forth, has been considered significant by most of the medical-school-based institutes, but in no instance has it been a dramatic advantage. Similarly, few of the institutes have felt any crucial drain upon the analytic program from the demands of the encompassing structure, the department of psychiatry or the medical school, although there is some complaint about committee work and occasional hostility from medical school faculty members who do not understand or favor the analytic teaching program and feel that the analysts are not contributing enough to the general medical school program. The most difficult problem occurs when, because of funding shortages or through change of leadership in the medical school or the department of psychiatry, a lower priority is put upon analytic training. Such a change toward indifference or even opposition can create a distressing situation for the psychoanalytic institute.

The commission discussed this problem at some length. Clearly university leaders have the right and authority to change priorities in their programs and this includes downgrading or completely eliminating analytic training from the university. It is equally clear that the psychoanalytic institute has a legitimate concern for the continuance of its activities and for the right of its students to receive an uninterrupted education. Obviously, the more the psychoanalytic institute is financially dependent upon the university, the more crucial the issue becomes. A previous committee on this topic recommended that at the time of organization of a medical-school-based institute, there should be discussions with the dean of the medical school and, as far as possible, a clear understanding of the university, medical school, and department of psychiatry commitment to the support of psychoanalytic training. Such a commitment, of course, cannot completely preclude a future change in priorities, as with the advent of a new dean or department chairman. There should be explicit contingency plans, preferably written, for the safeguarding of analytic training in the event that the university ceases its support or makes it difficult for good training to continue. There is a current trend in universities toward the formal adoption of bylaws governing the operation of departments, which would provide a basis for some increased security for an analytic training program in a university department against arbitrary actions of a department chairman or dean.

Bylaws for the internal operation of the analytic institute itself are also of great importance. Such bylaws not only establish orderly procedures to carry the institute through a difficult period of change of leadership, but can also serve as a means of educating the rest of the medical school to the goals and responsibilities of an analytic institute. Their existence further defines the institute as an entity within the medical school and establishes its relative autonomy. The institute bylaws should take account of the possibility that the psychoanalytic institute might some day have to function independently of the university. The bylaws should certainly recognize the right of institute faculty to choose the administrative leadership of the institute, the central role of the education committee in determining educational policy, and the nature of the institute as being constituted by the group of training analysts and accredited by the Association.

It is obviously important to have an understanding and acceptance by the university of the institute's relation to the Association and the various committees of its Board on Professional Standards, as well as an understanding by the Association of the traditional prerogatives and jurisdictions of universities. Medical schools, of course, are used to working with accrediting bodies, such as the AMA, the specialty board, the AAMC, etc.

The commission feels that it is desirable that independent institutes be as much involved with universities in their area as is practicable without, however, being distracted from their central analytic objective. The favorable climate that analysis has experienced in the past 30 years in the United States has depended in large part upon the influence psychoanalysts have exerted through their participation in universities, medical schools, the NIMH, and similar agencies. Independent institutes can reach out to universities through extension programs and through encouragement of their members to seek or continue contributing roles in university programs. This should not, however, lead to a dilution of commitment to psychoanalysis. While no analytic institute is yet funded by a university as a cross-disciplinary institute, an independent institute could possibly achieve the same result by informally building its contacts with different departments in the university, providing circumstances are favorable and it has no great need for financial support from the university.

To date no psychoanalytic institute has yet been established in an American university as an independent university department or institute. The idea is attractive because it would recognize psychoanalysis as an independent area of scholarship and scientific knowledge as well as a form of professional training. From such a base the psychoanalytic institute might find it easier to get input from university scientists and scholars, and might be able, with the greater financial support, to experiment more freely with recruitment of nonmedical students for training. Unfortunately, in the opinion of some observers these are not times in which it will be easy for a financially hard-pressed university to consider sponsoring a new institute. The experience of some existing institutes (not psychoanalytic) in universities suggests that they often have severe problems in communication with the rest of the university, not too different from the problems of the department of psychiatry in the medical school.

Obviously, the psychoanalytic institute as a university in itself requires an independent and dependable source of funds. It is unclear what kind of acceptance such a psychoanalytic university would receive from the established universities and accrediting bodies.

The commission finds no clear recommendation to make about university affiliation for new or developing analytic institute programs. In the past, decisions of this sort have been made almost entirely in terms of the local situation and the opportunities available to the group of analysts trying to start an institute program. There are obvious areas of mutual interest between a department of psychiatry and the psychoanalytic institute. This is especially true when the local department of psychiatry recognizes psychoanalysis as a basic theory and discipline of psychiatry, and psychoanalytic training as one of the important forms of specialty training in psychiatry. Under favorable circumstances, a psychoanalytic training program strengthens a department of psychiatry, and affiliation with a department of psychiatry gives support and opportunities for broader function to a psychoanalytic training program. To what extent the circumstances are favorable will differ from area to area and will even depend on the personalities involved. Finances have clearly played a most important role in the decision in years past, and will probably continue to do so.

THE RELATIONSHIP OF PSYCHOANALYSIS TO UNIVERSITIES THROUGH THE MEDICAL-SCHOOL-BASED INSTITUTE: AN INDIVIDUAL VIEW—LAWRENCE C. KOLB, M.D.

I am offering the following comments after working for two decades with the oldest university-based psychoanalytic institute, an institute that is highly visible and effective on both the medical and general university campuses. The Lewin and Ross (1960) report on psychoanalytic education should be updated to indicate the influence of psychoanalysis on the university as a whole as well as on the schools of medicine. There is also a need to note the influence of the university environment upon the psychoanalytic institutes, to record and assess successes as well as failures, and to acknowledge the influence of the Association's Board on Professional Standards in the nurturing of psychoanalytic education within and related to the university setting.

The Columbia Psychoanalytic Clinic had a number of strong, imaginative, forward-looking analysts on its early faculty. As a young chairman, I had, as almost my first responsibility, the duty of advising the first director of his imminent retirement in accordance with university statutes. This may well have been the first instance in which a group of psychoanalysts, working to establish an institute within the university framework, were directly confronted with the university's rules of governance. We managed to work out our problems within our own departmental family and have found it possible to handle successfully the special issues of authority and the transfer of authority within the university-based institute.

At the time of my first experience with the Columbia Institute—it was then almost ten years of age—there also existed within the framework of the Association the university-based institute at the Downstate campus of the State University of New York. There was an offshoot of that institute developing at the School of Medicine in Rochester, New York. Training centers were just getting under way at Western Reserve in Cleveland and at the University of Pittsburgh. There was some hope of a possible facility at the University of Cincinnati. Later, full institute status was conferred on both the Cleveland and Pittsburgh university-based institutes. A new university-based institute evolved in Denver and another has been growing in Atlanta. There is now a university-related but not university-based institute in North Carolina, which came about through the active interest and support of the chairmen of the departments at Duke and the University of North Carolina.

Thus, in the past two decades under the aegis of the Association, there has been a significant spread of psychoanaltyic institutes within the university setting. One conclusion seems evident to me: the diffusion of psychoanalytic education in the United States during the past two decades has occurred more through the active personal interest of chairmen and faculties of university departments of psychiatry than from any other source.

By their continuing life and vigor some of the university-based psychoanalytic institutes have demonstrated a stability that perhaps has surprised their early critics. Others failed to evolve within the university framework and finally elected to move outside. The problems encountered, however, are similar to those in non-university-based institutes. It should be possible to identify from this very considerable experience those factors that have made for success and failure in the attempts to evolve psychoanalytic education within a modern university.

What indeed are the advantages to psychoanalysis in general and psychoanalysts in particular of the university-based institute? The placement of the psychoanalytic institutes within universities provides a major mode of contact with the intellectual forces of the country. The universities have provided the majority of society's leaders in the arts, the sciences, the professions, and politics. The immediate availability of a psychoanalytic faculty in the universities offers an early opportunity to help educate these individuals.

Even though the present psychoanalytic institutes exist within the framework of the medical school, the record shows an extensive penetration of some of the university-based psychoanalytic faculties into all portions of the universities. This is particularly so in those institutes that have been active in the university for a considerable period of time. In short, in addition to the professional training offered to psychoanalytic students, an important task is already being done by the university institutes through their varied teaching activities with the general student body. The university faculties also have a large number of highly talented scholars available for psychoanalytic educational and research collaboration.

The range and quantity of patient material within the university community for the study of healthy or pathological functioning may be more readily available to university-based institutes than to independent institutes. Persons from all socio-economic and ethnic groups enroll and teach and may present themselves in clinics and hospitals related to the universities. Therapeutic help for them, even analysis, may be subsidized in part by funds available through the university.

The university-based institutes have access to enormous bibliographic and technical resources, including the computer and videotaping facilities for the recording of human behavior. Most of the technologies have indeed been used extensively by faculty members of the university-based institutes for both teaching and research purposes.

The university-based institutes have received financial support in the form of salaries for faculty, maintenance of institute office space, and support of certain research projects. Furthermore, university-based institutes today may have easier access to government fund-granting agencies or private foundations.

For the faculty, the university-based institutes have provided the satisfaction of academic status.

One might question whether there has been enough time for adequate evaluation of the contributions of the university-based institutes to the theoretical and practical knowledge of psychoanalysis. However, one can cite the definite contribution of these institutes to improved methods of faculty governance, curriculum development, and free interchange of ideas — all matters of the greatest importance to the educational process. The university-based institutes were the first to establish psychoanalytic education in the context of day education and to establish laws of governance modeled on the operations of other university departments. They were also the first to recognize the importance of the orderly retirement of teachers to protect the students.

The vicissitudes of the development of psycho-analytic education within the university framework reflect the presence of certain strengths in those universities where the process has gone forward and possible weaknesses in those where the process has faltered. Indeed, in the university settings where the process has moved forward well, the soil was tilled long before the establishment of the institute by the interest of psychiatric and medical faculty members in working with psycho-analytic colleagues who were initially individually related to the university. With regard to the failures, in one instance, psychoanalysts who had long practiced independently abroad were brought into a university-based institute as senior faculty members and were not fully committed to the university setting. They were confronted with the policies and procedures of the university before they had clearly formulated their own status within the university. In another instance, the conflict that led to the separation of a strongly supported and financed university psychoanalytic institute from the university was aggravated because the institute faculty had not achieved sufficient security through explicit agreements protecting its integrity within the university framework. The separation occurred shortly after appointment of a new department chairman whose attitude was non-supportive of psychoanalytic education. Indeed, it is understandable that the primary focus of a department of psychiatry must be the education of medical students and psychiatrists; the education of psychoanalysts is necessarily a secondary consideration.

The potential dangers to the present university-based psychoanalytic institutes will be met with varying success depending upon the organizational strength of the institute. They will be well met where the psycho-analytic members of the faculty can meet the multiple demands of the university environment. In the establishment of the university-based institute the university often has been quite generous in appointing psychoanalysts unknown to the academic world and whose credentials did not clearly identify them as scholars or investigators. Appointments have been granted on the urging of the psychiatric faculty. In the future, however, the psychoanalyst on the university faculty may be required to supply credentials comparable to those of the faculties in other departments.

Under increased financial strain, the universities will certainly tend to effect economies in the areas they conceive as less central; therefore, the continuance of the university-based institute within the university will depend on evidence of effective teaching activity, the continuing enrollment of adequate numbers of students, and the development of some self-supportive income.

PLENARY DISCUSSION—JOSE BARCHILON, M.D.

Science is the product of a special attitude that generates its own unique atmosphere; wherever that attitude prevails, psychoanalysts should try to participate. It is important to note that there have always been psychoanalysts, including Freud, who have been interested and active in promoting more participation in and interchange with universities.

The ideas we have been discussing here are certainly not new to us. The Onchiota Conferences, sponsored by the National Institute of Mental Health and the Department of Psychiatry at Einstein Medical School, were concerned with several closely related topics. There were four annual conferences altogether: 1961, "Integration of Psychoanalysis with Universities and/or Medical Schools"; 1962, "Psychoanalytic Content in Residency Training Programs"; 1963, "The Role of the Psychoanalyst in Teaching Psychotherapy in Residency Training Programs"; and 1964, "The Role of the Psychoanalyst in Supervising Psychotherapy." This historical reminder illustrates the fact that even excellent, ultimately desirable ideas may require considerable time and thought before they can be brought to fruition. Let us hope that the ten or twelve intervening years have indeed brought us closer to their realization. The late Bertram Lewin, one of the Onchiota Conference participants, described the main problem as the limited number of analysts available to accomplish all the tasks that needed to be done. That limitation is still true today.

There are now very few universities in which psychoanalytic ideas are not used or presented by one professor or another in teaching or research in the humanities, anthropology, or psychology. The fact is that we do have something positive and unique to offer human knowledge and science. We have an understanding as general psychologists and specialists in unconscious mental functions that the other scientific disciplines need, even if they do not always recognize it. As long as we continue to illuminate human motivation and persist in our efforts to communicate our insights meaningfully, we need not fear for our future in the world of science and art.

Psychoanalysis may now be in the position that psychiatry was in the thirties when it existed within various departments of medicine or neurology. The Commonwealth Foundation offered to endow separate departments of psychiatry and was firmly refused by various medical schools, including Hopkins and Harvard. The University of Colorado Medical School welcomed the aid, and many at this conference received their training from Franklin Ebaugh, who was one of Adolf Meyer's students.

Are we ready for a similar development? Let us consider the proposal that a foundation, perhaps of our own Association, seek out a suitable college or university and endow a Chair of Psychoanalysis. Should we be concerned that they might only teach Psychoanalysis 101? Perhaps the students who took Psychoanalysis 101 or 201 would turn out to be more humanistic business men or professors of surgery, or they might even eventually decide upon a career in psychoanalysis, after traversing a circuitous path through psychology, medicine, or some other allied profession.

As for the institutes already affiliated with medical schools at Columbia, Downstate-New York, Pittsburgh, Cleveland, or the Department of Psychiatry in Denver, their problems and advantages are discussed elsewhere and are well known. We have accumulated a valuable body of experience within that structural arrangement.

We may even have learned how to avoid certain pitfalls. For example, we now know the importance of formulating clear, workable ground rules, aims, and limits as a basis for working cooperatively with others. That knowledge will help us greatly when and if institutes are organized differently within a university. I therefore believe we are better prepared than some may think to experiment with new models.

However, it is much more likely that in the immediate future universities will be interested in only certain limited areas of mutual interest. We should be quite gratified and encouraged by such beginnings. When I speak as a psychoanalyst at university departments of Literature or Humanities on the origins of esthetic feelings, the development of artistic stylizations, or literary symbols, my views are received by most students with interest and curiosity, even if they are rejected by some. If it is true that we are experts on the unconscious roots of dreams and psychopathology, those manifestations of the primary process that are private, and we have a theory explaining those mental activities, it is equally true that the professional students of art and literature are experts on the public and expressive aspects of the selfsame processes. As scientists we are concerned with psychological explanations as they relate to the creation and appreciation of art and literature, and our contributions are basic and relevant for the critics and teachers of art and literature.

Finally, to illustrate what Freud meant when he apologized for the fact that his case histories read more like short stories, and declared that the analysts couldn't afford to leave the creative writer alone, nor the writer the analyst, let me quote from *The*

Scarlet Letter, written in 1850 by Nathaniel Haw-thorne.

Thus Roger Chillingworth scrutinized his patient care-fully, both as he saw him in his ordinary life, keeping an accustomed pathway in the range of thoughts familiar to him, and as he appeared when thrown amidst other moral scenery, the novelty of which might call out something new to the surface of his character. He deemed it essential, it would seem, to know the man, before at-tempting to do him good. Wherever there is a heart and an intellect, the diseases of the physical frame are tinged with the peculiarities of these. In Arthur Dimmesdale, thought and imagination were so active, and sensibility so intense, that the bodily infirmity would be likely to have its ground-work there. So Roger Chillingworth—the man of skill, the kind and friendly physician—strove to go deep into his patient's bosom, delving among his princi-ples, prying into his recollections, and probing everything with a cautious touch, like a treasure-seeker in a dark cav-ern. Few secrets can escape an investigator, who has op-portunity and license to undertake such a quest, and skill to follow it up. A man burdened with a secret should especially avoid the intimacy of his physician. If the latter possess native sagacity, and a nameless something more,—let us call it intuition; if he show no intrusive ego-tism, nor disagreeably prominent characteristics of his own; if he have the power, which must be born with him, to bring his mind into such affinity with his patient's [I can almost hear Hawthorne say 50 years later, if he be analyzed and capable of empathy], that this last shall un-awares have spoken what he imagines himself only to have thought [i.e., if he free associates and thinks aloud]; if such revelations be received without tumult, and acknow-ledged not so often by an uttered sympathy, as by silence, an inarticulate breath [now you can surely hear him say-ing, ah hum!], and here and there a word, to indicate that all is understood; if to these qualifications of a confidant be joined the advantages afforded by his recognized character as a physician; — then, at some inevitable moment, will the soul of the sufferer [read here unconscious of the patient] be dissolved, and flow forth in a dark, but transparent stream, bringing all its mysteries into the daylight [pp. 157-158].

This quotation aptly illustrates what analysts mean when they suggest that the creative artist expresses esthetically what the scientist must laboriously extract from clinical data and explain by theoretical concepts.

We must continue to improve the effectiveness of our contributions in medical schools, but also extend as much as possible our efforts to teach elsewhere in universities and colleges. Nothing of course prevents any institute from including these activities in their current framework. In fact, I believe that such efforts would only improve training for the practice of psychoanalysis. Many psychoanalysts are already teaching in psychology, law, anthropology, the social sciences, mythology, esthetics, or the arts at their own institutes or in various universities. Such work deserves our full support and is vitally important as an opportunity to share and to increase knowledge about the inner man and his motives.

SUMMARY OF CONFERENCE DISCUSSION

In addressing this general topic the discussion groups achieved a remarkable unanimity of opinion. There were no categorical objections to the development of formal relationships between institutes and universities; indeed, there was considerable and enthusiastic support for the idea, tempered, of course, by the usual reminders regarding certain possible difficulties. It was pointed out, for

example, that there might be special problems in arranging for adequate clinical training within a university
department outside of the medical school. The same
concern was voiced by several discussants who agreed that
university affiliation might enhance scholarly research in
psychoanalysis but wondered whether the effect on
clinical training would be entirely favorable.

As in other discussions on the organization and affiliation of psychoanalytic institutes, and even their relationship with the Association's Board on Professional
Standards, the issue of institute autonomy loomed large
as a possible problem in future formal participation in
university life. The past and existing relationships of institutes within medical school departments of psychiatry
were pointed to as demonstrating a wide spectrum of
possibilities, ranging from complete and mutually beneficial harmony to frustration. In approaching the university outside of the department of psychiatry, it was anticipated that the need to preserve essential independence
while actually becoming a part of the university would
require careful planning and monitoring.

Everyone seemed to recognize that they were not discussing some simple negotiation between an institute and
the university, but rather a hypothetical development
with several conceivable evolutionary paths and forms,
dependent on many factors related to time, place, and
personnel. All discussants supported the view that local
circumstances should and would best determine the optimal structure of psychoanalytic education and the form
of its relationship with the local university. It was
therefore understood that in certain situations the institute might be incorporated within the university as a
separate department; in other situations it might func-

tion as an interdisciplinary institute; in still others it might exist, as some already do, as an institute within the department of psychiatry. There might even be a form that combined several of these models in some practical way. Finally, it might remain an independent institute that maintained an active but altogether informal relationship with the local university.

The discussion primarily revealed a widespread readiness to consider the possibilities of closer structural ties with the university, and an inclination toward the view that such a development would be salutary in many ways. The extremely important economic benefit of direct university affiliation was certainly not overlooked. There was nevertheless an awareness of the distance between the ideal and the actual university. The frequency with which the conferees were warned not to idealize the university was probably some indication of the tendency to do just that.

Psychoanalytic Education and the Allied Disciplines

David Kairys, M.D., Chairman
R. Hugh Dickinson, M.D.
Rudolf Ekstein, Ph.D.
Joseph Goldstein, Ph.D.
Otto F. Kernberg, M.D.
Peter J. Loewenberg, Ph.D.
Jerome D. Oremland, M.D.
Arnold A. Rogow, Ph.D.
Ernst A. Ticho, Ph.D.
Emanuel Windholz, M.D.
Abraham Zaleznik, D.C.S.

Psychoanalytic Education and the Allied Disciplines

ORIGINAL CHARGE

How do various career lines, disciplinary backgrounds, and professional and educational goals affect analytic training? Should there be differing educational tracks with perhaps different prerequisites and qualifications for the training of psychoanalytic clinicians, researchers in psychoanalysis, or psychoanalytically competent researchers and scholars in related behavioral science fields? What should be the proper training for each background, each track, each goal? To what extent would those on special tracks have to be brought to the level of clinical psychoanalytic competence expected today of every student? For what purposes are abbreviated training sequences in order? Should graduation or qualification in a specialized aspect of a science be separated from certification as a competent independent professional?

PREPARATORY COMMISSION REPORT

From its earliest years psychoanalysis has attracted to its ranks individuals from disciplines other than that of medicine; indeed, some scholars whose original fields of interest were very far from psychoanalysis become important contributors.

The training standards established by the Association's Board on Professional Standards in 1938 allowed institutes to offer some partial form of training to students from fields other than that of psychiatry but did not permit these students to do the supervised clinical work necessary to make their training complete. In 1956 the Board created a Committee on Training for Research and charged it with the task of formalizing and regulating the conditions and safeguards under which qualified scholars in the behavioral sciences could obtain full psychoanalytic training as research students. This program had two stated goals: to enhance the ability of the student to conduct psychoanalytically informed research in his or her own primary field of scholarship and to enable the student to conduct research within psychoanalysis itself by way of the psychoanalytic process and using psychoanalytic data. In order for a nonphysician analytic student to conduct supervised clinical psychoanalytic work it was necessary for the institute to apply for a waiver of the usual training standards by the Board on Professional Standards. Action on the waiver was recommended after very thorough study by the Committee on Training for Research.

At the time this program was instituted, there was hope that it would strengthen the development of research in psychoanalysis. However, there was a certain apprehension among some Association members that the new program would open a back door for nonphysicians to obtain training and certification as psychoanalysts with a consequent weakening of the commitment of American psychoanalysis to medicine and psychiatry. Subsequent developments demonstrated that both the hope and the apprehensions were ill-founded. Instead of the flood of applications from nonphysicians predicted by some, the first ten years of the program produced only 28 waiver applications (of which 23 were ultimately approved), coming from only nine institutes, with five of the nine accounting for 24 of the applications. With approximately two students entering the research training program each year, it was clear that the program had fallen far short of its objective of increasing significantly the number of research workers in psychoanalysis or of analytically sophisticated investigators in allied fields. The impact on psychoanalytic research as a whole was minimal.

A careful study was undertaken by the Committee on Training for Research to discover why the program did not achieve its goals. The Committee met with research students, with spokesmen for a number of the institutes in which they were being trained, and with distinguished scholars in the behavioral sciences who were familiar with psychoanalysis. Among the reasons cited for the paucity of applicants for research training were: the view that psychoanalysis was relatively isolated from the rest of the scientific and intellectual community; the impression that psychoanalysts have only clinical professional interests; the fear that psychoanalytic training might interfere with individual research productivity; the obstacle of the enormous financial cost of analytic training, which for the academic individual is not offset by the anticipation of income from future clinical practice; the fact that the Board approved waivers for full training only for established and eminent researchers, who are less inclined to embark on an arduous new course of training that might interfere with their academic careers; and, finally, the observation that research applicants who had gone through complete training felt that their status was not fully equal to their medical colleagues, a feeling that was magnified since the research graduate was at the time ineligible for Association membership.

In the light of these findings the Committee on Training for Research made three recommendations to the Board in 1966:

1. Criteria of selection for training should be broadened so that applications could be accepted from younger individuals deemed to show promise as future researchers.

2. Psychoanalysts should make every effort to become more actively involved in teaching at the university level where they would come into more direct contact with graduate students in psychology or other behavioral sciences.

3. The Association should create an appropriate membership category for the graduates of the various research training programs in the institute.

Of these recommendations the first, the widening of the criteria for eligibility, was adopted soon after it was made. The second was a recommendation about which the Association itself could do nothing but express hope for positive individual responses. The third resulted in the appointment of a committee to study the question of membership for research graduates and it now appears that a Bylaw Amendment admitting research graduates to active membership is on its way toward a vote by the membership.[1]

In May, 1970 the chairman of the Committee on Training for Research reported that in the three years of operation of the more liberal admission and training guidelines only eight waiver applications had been approved, which was still less than three per year and not a particularly significant increase over the rate of the prior ten years. It was also noted that all but one of the eight were accomplished researchers who could equally well have been approved under the former, more rigorous criteria. By that time, a total of thirteen research students had been graduated throughout the country.

The trend toward broadening the eligibility for full psychoanalytic training of research students continued, and in May, 1971 the Board on Professional Standards approved a proposal from the Committee on Training for Research that the requirements be changed to include those persons whose primary commitment is in the area of scholarly endeavors, more broadly conceived. This would involve persons of promise or accomplishment as educators or administrators in the social sciences and humanities whose capabilities would be enhanced by full psychoanalytic training or whose activities in their particular professional role might significantly influence the career opportunities and choices of others. Responses to a questionnaire circulated in connection with the preparations for COPER indicated that in 1971 there were 774 students in institutes throughout the United States holding an M.D. degree and 34 non-M.D. students in the category of research training. The research students

[1] *Editor's note:* This was passed in May, 1974.

comprise 4.5 per cent of the total number of analytic students, whereas in 1958 they comprised 2.9 per cent; this cannot be considered a significant increase for the thirteen-year period. Of the 34 nonphysicians, twenty were psychologists.

The need for training colleagues from the allied disciplines rests on broader grounds than those indicated above, and we consider that this training may be critical to the growth of psychoanalysis as a science. Since the program of nonmedical training for research has not succeeded in its original objectives, a new approach is needed if we wish to increase the number of persons from related disciplines in our institutes.

An analytic institute may be described as having two functions: it trains clinical psychoanalysts, and it attempts to foster the growth of psychoanalysis as a science. There seems to be general agreement that the institutes have been relatively effective in the first of these functions but not in the second. The commission believes that the clinical-training function may tend to interfere with the function of scientific development in an analytic institute. The further development of psychoanalysis as a science requires a climate of scholarship, and despite our high standards, dedicated teachers, and excellent teaching, we may not sufficiently develop the motivation for scientific investigation among our students.

There must be a factor of self-selection in the applicants for psychoanalytic training that contributes significantly to the level of investigative interest in our students. If our institutes are primarily organized for the training of practitioners, by the same token those who apply will be chiefly persons whose central career goal is the clinical practice of psychoanalysis. Certainly, a change in one variable in this complex equation can have only a limited effect, but we see the increased recruitment of students from the allied disciplines as one possible means of enhancing an atmosphere of scholarship and research essential for the growth of any science.

Psychoanalytic institutes stand apart from the universities; and even where there is a university connection it is an affiliation to the medical school rather than to the university as a whole. Yet, the cross-fertilization and constant intellectual enrichment so essential to scientific progress must in some way be brought into our training centers. This stimulating interaction may be greatly enhanced if larger numbers of investigators and scholars from other fields can be brought into our institutes.

Research in applied psychoanalysis has for the most part been done by psychoanalysts, but the quality of these applied studies is often limited by the fact that the analyst is not sufficiently trained in the field of application such as history or biography. At the same time, when scholars in related fields undertake, without psychoanalytic training, to apply psychoanalysis to studies in their own disciplines, the results are often deplorable. One solution would be for medical psychoanalysts to obtain a thorough education in the discipline in which they wish to conduct research. Considering the age at which most psychoanalysts complete their psychoanalytic training, there clearly are sharp limitations to the number of people who would be able to pursue this path.

Another method of conducting investigations in applied psychoanalysis is by collaboration between a medical psychoanalyst and a scholar from another field. But again, the difficulties are often considerable. Optimally, this kind of research should be done by one person who has knowledge both of psychoanalysis and the field of investigation. This union of two bodies of knowledge in one investigator can be achieved through the psychoanalytic training of members of the allied disciplines. Psychoanalysis stands at the intersection of the biological, social, and humanistic disciplines. It seems inherently logical and strategically wise that members of these other disciplines who wish to learn psychoanalysis be encouraged to do so under the same roof as medical psychoanalysts.

We referred earlier to the desirability of having psychoanalysts engage in teaching at the university level, so that students, whether undergraduate or doctoral, might learn analytic concepts from fully qualified teachers. Analysts in large numbers are not likely to become active in university education in the near future. Should we, however, succeed in training significant numbers of colleagues from the allied disciplines, many of these individuals, who would have come to us from university faculties, would certainly take psychoanalysis back to the university campus.

Early in its work, the commission agreed that in training students from a variety of disciplines, who might enter psychoanalytic training at varying points in their own development and present a great diversity of aims and goals, it is essential that the institutes not attempt to fit all students into a single curriculum. Moreover, an increased number of training options might result in more applicants from the allied disciplines. We therefore propose that the analytic institute's curriculum be designed with two tracks plus one special program—the clinical track, the academic track, and a program of general studies in psychoanalysis.

The curriculum of the clinical track would be identical to the usual curriculum for clinical psychoanalytic training, which, in relation to nonmedical research students, has been referred to as complete training, to distinguish it from partial training not including clinical work. Applications for training would be invited from individuals in any of the allied disciplines. In view of the broadened criteria adopted by the Board on Professional Standards during recent years, this would not represent a departure from present practice. In assessing these applicants, the institute would evaluate motivation for training, and the accomplishment or potential for accomplishment in the individual's primary discipline. There would, of course, be an assessment of analyzability and of aptitude for conducting clinical analyses, a particularly difficult evaluation with applicants who would not have had any clinical experience.

The curriculum for nonmedical students admitted to the clinical track would be identical to that for medical analytic students, and both groups would attend the same seminars. It is assumed that students entering this track would be enabled to conduct clinical analyses after graduation in conjunction with the development of their career interests. For some nonmedical graduates of this program, the conducting of analyses would be essential to their research. For others, it might be necessary in order to maintain the analytic understanding gained during training.

The commission does not intend that this position be considered as a stand one way or another on the complex issue of lay analysis. The purpose of the clinical track is not to train nonphysicians for a career devoted primarily to the clinical practice of psychoanalysis. At the same time we feel it would be inconsistent, after providing appropriate clinical training, to restrain nonmedical graduates from conducting analyses. We are aware, however, of the considerable social responsibility borne by every institute with regard to the competence of those it certifies as psychoanalysts.

Many commission members felt that the training institute has the responsibility to provide adequate supervised clinical experience in psychotherapy for the nonpsychiatrically trained student, before supervised analytic work is undertaken. This may be done through the institute's treatment center or in a nearby mental health facility. Others believed that the institute should decide on an individual basis the desirability of such experience.

The commission strongly favors arrangements by which nonphysician graduates of the clinical track will be eligible for membership in both local and national psychoanalytic organizations; there should be no implication that the nonphysician graduate is a second-class member.

The academic track is proposed for those students from the allied disciplines who do not wish to enter the clinical track or do not have the necessary qualifications for that track. This program would emphasize psychoanalytic theory, and although it would include some experience in clinical seminars, the academic students would not undertake supervised analytic work. The commission agreed that although the students in this program should be encouraged to undertake a personal analysis, the analysis should not be required and that the certificate offered upon completion of training should distinguish between those who have had an analysis and those who have not. We are fully aware that this recommendation represents a sharp departure from a central principle of psychoanalytic training and that some explanation is warranted.

It has long been assumed that it is impossible to learn psychoanalysis in any meaningful way without having had the experience of a personal analysis. We certainly do not minimize the great importance of the personal analysis, but simply suggest that selected academic students might still profit from a program not including a personal analysis. Some members of the academic community who have an interest in applying psychoanalytic knowledge to their own fields might wish not to have an analysis. This choice, up to the present, has not been available, that is, the student must enter personal analysis or be disqualified from further training in an institute. We are suggesting that it is time to reconsider this policy. The commission feels further, that yet another option should be made available in selected instances, namely the possibility that an academic student be encouraged, although not required, to enter psychotherapy.

The academic track might include a number of required courses, but beyond this the student would, in consultation with a faculty advisor, design an individually appropriate program very much as is done by university candidates for a doctoral degree. At the same time, we feel that the students in this track, as in the clinical track, should be included in the regular institute seminars. Exceptions to this practice might arise if an institute lacked a seminar specially needed by the academic students and it was possible to organize such a special seminar just for that group. It would be most desirable to seek collaboration with university departments in those instances where the student is a university graduate student below the Ph.D. level. The university might be persuaded to recognize and credit work in the institute courses. There are already precedents for such arrangements. At Harvard, students are permitted to take a reading course at the Boston Psychoanalytic Institute and the course is supervised by a member of the Harvard University faculty. At the Yale Law School, credit may be authorized for work in departments outside the Law School, including psychology and psychiatry. The Southern California Psychoanalytic Institute has an interdisciplinary seminar in psychohistory for which institute students receive institute credit, and UCLA graduate students receive credit from the history department.

With regard to the two proposed tracks, we also favor the possibility of transfer between tracks. It should be possible, for example, for a student who begins training in the clinical track to switch to the academic track if this proves to be desirable. By the same token an individual who begins his training in the academic track might be permitted to switch to the clinical track if that seems appropriate.

The program of general studies has been so named to set it apart from the two tracks just described. The clinical and academic tracks represent programs of continuous training with progression to a point of completion, and the awarding of some form of certificate in the specific competence achieved. In the program of general studies work would not necessarily be continuous, matriculation would not be required, and no certificate would be awarded.

While the teaching activities connected with general studies already exist in the extension divisions of various institutes or societies, the commission feels the change in designation is useful. Extension programs, by their very name, indicate activities outside or beyond the central institute function. Their role should be upgraded and the new title reflects that intent.

The general studies program would provide information or education in special and clearly defined areas of psychoanalysis to both the community-at-large and to a variety of professional groups, including psychiatrists, physicians in other specialities, social workers, teachers, nurses, lawyers, ministers, probation officers, judges and parents. A fully developed program of general studies might encompass a variety of teaching activities, such as:

1. *Workshops.* Ongoing workshops attended by the members of one selected profession, for example school teachers, have proved quite successful in some institutes. Such workshops are chaired by a psychoanalyst, and present special aspects of psychoanalytic theory relevant to the particular group, or stimulate a discussion of problems that the participants themselves bring in from their own professional work.

2. *Interdisciplinary colloquia.* Interdisciplinary colloquia have been very successful at national meetings of the Association, and the format can be and has been utilized in local general-studies programs. For example, a psychoanalyst and a historian might chair a weekly seminar open to both historians and psychoanalysts.

3. *Lectureships.* Lectures by outstanding psychoanalysts, open to members of the community, can supply a valuable community service and bring psychoanalysis into closer contact with the community.

4. *Co-sponsored programs*. Under this arrangement a symposium on a given topic is organized as a joint venture between the psychoanalytic institute or society and another appropriate educational institution in the community. Successful experiences with this format have demonstrated that it is an excellent way of bringing a variety of educational audiences into contact with analytic teachers.

Adequate funding is crucial to the development of a successful training program for the allied disciplines. No matter how attractive we make our training programs, we will not succeed in recruiting any significant numbers of students from related disciplines unless we are able to cope with the high cost of psychiatric training. According to the figures arrived at by the recent COPER survey, the cost of complete psychoanalytic training is approximately $30,000 or more. This figure is based on an estimate of $24,000 for the personal analysis, $5,000 for supervision, and $2,000 for tuition fees. Analytic students from an allied discipline who intend to use psychoanalysis in research do not have the prospect of a large future income from private practice, nor can they depend on a high present or future income to pay for training costs or loans. In every institute offering training for research students there have been instances in which promising applicants withdrew when there seemed no possibility of paying for the expenses of training. Discussions of this problem always lead to the recommendation that institutes should seek outside sources of funds for the support of students. It is true that a small number of research students have been helped in the past through NIMH career-investigator grants. However, with the future of all funding for mental health purposes gravely in doubt, this is clearly not a solution to be counted on in the forseeable future. The support of various private foundations is also regularly suggested, and this avenue should be explored. Foundation funding would require a very large amount of money to support a significant increase in the number of students from allied disciplines.

The commission considered carefully various ways in which training funds might be developed within the individual institute. It was noted that certain institutes have already established research training fellowships to aid nonmedical students in financing their training. Probably many institutes could afford the expense of such loans or fellowship plans if their members were sufficiently eager to foster this type of training. There are some possible problems entailed in loan funds — problems in the transference reactions within the student's analysis, in the student's relation to the institute to which he or she becomes financially indebted, etc. — but the potential difficulties are probably not as great as is often supposed.

It has been suggested that the burden of the largest item in the total expense of training — the training analysis — might be diminished by a pooling arrangement. Under this arrangement the student would pay a fee determined by his or her financial situation. All of the analytic fees would then be pooled in such a way that each training analyst would be paid at the same rate, regardless of the financial ability of the particular students who were with that training analyst. This arrangement would clearly require the training analyst to accept a much lower average fee for training analyses than in the past.

During this discussion of training costs, it was noted that the nonmedical graduates of the clinical track would be able to pay for their training from future earnings

provided they engaged in private practice after graduation; thus, the nonphysician graduate would then be in
the same financial position as physician colleagues. In
opposition, various commission members pointed out
that planning financing on such a consideration would
only increase the likelihood that those who had undertaken training in order to do research would tend to
become primarily engaged in private clinical practice.
After considerable discussion the commission was unable
to reach a consensus on the problem of financing the
training of students from the allied disciplines.

In summary, the commission has reviewed the
history of research training, considered anew its
importance to psychoanalysis, and proposed an approach
to suitable training programs for members of the allied
disciplines. We have endeavored to retain the values and
standards of our usual clinical training, while at the same
time encouraging a greater climate of scholarship in our
institutes. We have suggested offering a larger range of
options for prospective students through a multiple-track
system. We have proposed, for certain specially considered students, a departure from the rule that every
student must have a personal analysis. These proposals
could make analytic training more attractive to persons
in related disciplines. At the same time it is necessary to
stress the crucial importance of the financial problem
confronting these potential applicants and the institutes.

PLENARY DISCUSSION — KENNETH T. CALDER, M.D.

The commission noted that only 4.5 per cent of our total
student body are nonphysicians, that only thirteen re-

search students had been graduated from our component institutes by 1970, and that we have averaged only three applications for research training per year. The commission provided a succinct recommendation for this problem: Psychoanalysis should act vigorously to promote the recruiting and training of students from the allied disciplines, as this may be critical to the future development of analysis as a science.

Before exploring the commission's recommendations, we should consider two questions. Do we want the allied disciplines? And are we willing to work in order to enable them to join us? It is much easier to want the allied disciplines in Hot Springs, Virginia than in New York City, Chicago, Boston, or Los Angeles. Away from the time, energy, and economic considerations of our profession, and surrounded by colleagues who by their willingness to attend this conference have attested to their interest in a long-range overview of our field, we can easily champion the invitation to the allied disciplines. The support in our local societies, however, may be much weaker, prompted by several considerations, one of which is the economic threat.

I have reached two conclusions that further encourage my own support for our assisting the training of students from allied disciplines. First, we need them at least as much as they need us. Although it is difficult for them to master our field after approaching it through extraordinary channels, it probably is even more difficult for us to master their fields, which are as complex and demanding as ours—we don't start early enough and we aren't able to give enough of ourselves to the effort. Second, while it is almost always true that students from the allied disciplines need financial support, they risk losing something professionally by joining us, that is, in developing and advancing their careers in their primary field.

There are several reasons why one might oppose efforts to facilitate training in psychoanalysis for students in related disciplines. Teaching them demands our time, energy, and money. They often challenge our narcissism with their doubts, sometimes sophisticated doubts, about us. Should they use their analytic training for private practice or to train others for private practice, they would become our economic competitors.

The commission report implies that many traditions in psychoanalytic education do not match the needs of students from related disciplines and, further, that these traditions may be determined by wishes or fears rather than by objective data. Accordingly they recommend that we experiment with new methods of teaching them psychoanalysis.

I will list five important and debatable questions stated or implied in the commission's report.

1. Should students from related disciplines have a larger role in the design of their individual curricula at psychoanalytic institutes than has been the custom?

2. Should we consider the experiment in which some students may have extensive training without a personal analysis?

3. Should we consider experiments in which some students would receive a modified psychoanalytic training in that they would have psychotherapy rather than a personal analysis?

4. Should there be a pooling of funds at psychoanalytic institutes in order to support the analysis of students from related disciplines?

5. Should we establish multiple-track systems and programs of general studies in psychoanalysis in our institutes?

I find these formulations direct and at least arguable. The statistics cited by the commission demonstrate that we have not yet been sufficiently successful in encouraging individuals from allied disciplines to seek analytic training; however, the value of their training, for them and for us, seems quite clear. I therefore conclude that we have more to lose if we don't attempt certain of these experiments than if we do. Furthermore, we may reap an additional benefit in that some of our traditional concepts may be significantly modified and much improved. Our immediate task, however, should be a continuing discussion on all these issues here at the conference, in our local institutes, and in our national association.

SUMMARY OF CONFERENCE DISCUSSION

All the discussions reflected a general readiness to institute a variety of systematic training programs for students whose primary academic background was in one of the so-called allied disciplines. Contrary to the wish of the commission, most discussants still referred to the usual tripartite analytic education as full training and programs omitting one or another of the usual three elements as partial training. It was noted that past experience with institute academic programs that omitted the personal analysis and supervised clinical work did not seem particularly fruitful for either the institute or the student involved. A number of conferees felt that the omission of the personal analysis as a systematic requirement in most instances would probably hamper adequate mastery of psychoanalytic thought. It was generally held that students in the so-called academic track would also need the personal analytic experience for full comprehension and meaningful scholarly application of psychoanalysis.

Along with the general conference enthusiasm for welcoming both junior and senior members of the allied disciplines to obtain what they wished and needed from psychoanalysis and offer what they could from their own backgrounds, there were also several expressions of cautious concern over the possible dilution of psychoanalytic concepts. Others acknowledged that such a danger existed, particularly if overambitious programs strained available teaching resources or lowered educational or professional standards; nevertheless, they suggested that the possibility of such excesses or miscarriages of intention should not prevent prudent experimentation and careful follow-up of the results.

The economic problems were confronted again in the context of this topic but a definitive solution or clear-cut plan of action toward possible solutions continued to elude the conference.

Contained within the discussion of the greater inclusion of students from the allied disciplines was the pervasive theme of the predominant medical affiliation of psychoanalysis and its implications. In spite of repeated statements to the contrary, there was some evidence of a tendency toward idealization of the nonmedical academic as the messenger of science, often with relatively little distinction between the very young graduate student of promise but little actual experience or accomplishment and the senior academician who has made research contributions of acknowledged substance to a primary field of inquiry. The balancing idealization of the medical professional, whose training was thought to provide a unique sense of ethical responsibility, was also observable. However, throughout all the discussions, the strong emphasis on individual evaluation rather than group generalization possibly minimized the pitfalls of both extreme views.

Caveats and concerns notwithstanding, the prevailing opinion was in favor of developing programs, within the practical limits of local institute resources, for the training of nonmedical as well as medical analytic students with a variety of clinical as well as academic career objectives and with a degree of flexibility informed by careful individual assessments.

Relationship of Psychoanalysis to Social and Community Issues

Reginald S. Lourie, M.D., Chairman
Gene Gordon, M.D., Recorder
Bernard Bandler, M.D.
Viola W. Bernard, M.D.
Donald L. Burnham, M.D.
Jules V. Coleman, M.D.
Elizabeth B. Davis, M.D.
Robert M. Dorn, M.D.
Aaron H. Esman, M.D.
Willard M. Gaylin, M.D.
Robert M. Gibson, M.D.
Alex H. Kaplan, M.D.
Edward H. Knight, M.D.
John E. Mack, M.D.
Charles A. Malone, M.D.
Charles A. Pinderhughes, M.D.
Howard H. Schlossman, M.D.
Norman E. Zinberg, M.D.

Relationship of Psychoanalysis to Social and Community Issues

ORIGINAL CHARGE

How may psychoanalysis achieve an optimal relatedness to the social problems and concerns of our time? What is the contribution of psychoanalysis to such mental-health-related social issues as crime and delinquency, drug abuse, the "hippie" phenomenon, current youth unrest? What is the possible contribution of the psychoanalytic perspective (in concert with the other behavioral science approaches) to such complex and compelling problems as war and peace, racism, poverty, overpopulation, and pollution? On the most direct and immediate level, what is the proper contribution of psychoanalysis to the community mental health movement, dedicated to making mental health services available, both therapeutically and preventively, to all in need of them?

PREPARATORY COMMISSION REPORT

In terms of its stated goals, organized psychoanalysis has an obligation to extend its activity beyond the training of practitioners, who in their lifetimes will be able to treat only a limited number of patients from a relatively narrow social segment of our population. Not only do public health needs demand such extension but the theory and practice of psychoanalysis would be deficient insofar as it failed to account for such factors as social-class differences in personality development and organization, the cultural relativity of symptoms and adaptive patterns, and variations in external reality.

Society faces many problems requiring the attention of all scientific and professional disciplines that can contribute to their alleviation. Not only has psychoanalysis much to offer, but it would benefit from a continuing explicit awareness and study of social issues. The history of the interaction between psychoanalysis and society amply demonstrates the substantial mutual benefit of such interaction.

Psychoanalysts moved into the mainstream of American psychiatry and medical education for the first time during and after World War II. During the war, many analysts found themselves confronted with the psychiatric problems of large populations, particularly with the problems of military personnel from rural communities, small towns, and deprived social status, who would otherwise never have come to an analyst's attention. The adaptability of military personnel was often impressive, even under the most trying circumstances, and often regardless of the presence of severe psychiatric symptoms or a previous history of psychiatric disorder. This adaptability was directly related to the well-functioning social support systems provided by military units with good morale. It was observed that in military units with effective leadership psychiatric breakdown could often be prevented, and when it occurred the support system could contribute to its rapid resolution.

But the period before the war does not lack for brilliant examples of how psychoanalysis and socio-cultural research could prove mutually enriching. During the 1920's and 1930's the Vienna psychoanalytic societies sponsored a child-guidance clinic for young children (Edith Sterba), a child-guidance clinic for adolescents (August Aichhorn), discussion groups for teachers with problem students (Willi Hoffer), an experimental day nursery for infants (Edith Jackson, Dorothy Burlingham, and Anna Freud), and a three-year postgraduate training course for teachers. In Berlin, Simmel, Staub, and Alexander contributed as hospital psychiatrists, advisors to the legal profession, to educators, etc. Other analysts involved in such activity were Pfister in Switzerland (education and religion), Vera Schmidt in Moscow (nursery school observation), and Flugel in Great Britain (psychology and study of the family).

Some analysts grappled with political and social issues. Federn was interested in trade unionism and Zionism. Bernfeld's (1925) observation of war orphans in special schools was an early manifestation of a lifelong commitment to youth and education. His ideas on psychoanalytic education were partly a consequence of his knowledge of both youth and educational processes in general.

More recently, during the London blitz, Dorothy Burlingham and Anna Freud (1943) were involved with the care and teaching of children who had been evacuated from London. This led them to important observations on the mother-child relationship and the effect on the child's personality of premature separation from the mother. René Spitz's landmark contributions (1957, 1959, 1965) were derived from observations he made in foundling homes and orphanages. Many others have observed the Kibbutz movement in Israel to study the effects of a form of child rearing quite different from the traditional nuclear-family system.

Other studies, although stimulated and informed by psychoanalytic thought, have not yet been integrated into the main body of psychoanalysis. One example is a comparison of mother-child relationships in Japan and in the United States. Another is a study comparing the value systems of families from four different ethnic sub-cultures in the Boston area. Important, but not yet sufficiently discussed, investigations of the dynamics of prejudice and of ethnic-related symptomatology have been conducted by psychoanalysts and by psychoanalytically informed researchers. The same may be said of a number of studies of historical movements, social unrest, revolution, ideologies, and religions.

The psychoanalytic movement in the United States seems to have evolved two points of view reflecting important differences of interest and commitment. One is represented by those analysts who are occupied primarily with the practice of clinical psychoanalysis and the study and teaching of psychoanalysis, and the other by those who are interested in analytically oriented practice, but devote substantial professional time to psychiatric education and consultation, social issues, community psychiatry, and interdisciplinary research.

Many analysts maintain that psychoanalysis as a distinctive method of investigation and treatment is continually endangered by possible dilution or abandonment of its traditional methods, which focus on the

individual, and in particular on the intrapsychic unconscious forces that determine not only individual behavior,
but also contribute to the behavior of social organizations. This orientation differs from that which emphasizes external reality and interpersonal factors as behavioral determinants. The psychoanalytic method requires
that the analyst be neutral and receptive; certainly he or
she should not manipulate, reform, or educate the
patient. In contrast, the role of a social activist or re-
former requires precisely the opposite qualities, particularly if the goals include sweeping institutional changes
and so-called social management. This may be why many
analysts avoid active involvement in social issues and
community problems, and it may also explain why many
analysts are critical of those colleagues who are heavily
involved professionally in activities other than analysis.

It may be that we have overdrawn the lines of this
argument. Surely, many questions can be raised, and the
two positions cited are not necessarily incompatible. Most
psychoanalysts in the United States today do not fit an
ivory-tower image of isolation and insulation from social
issues. In the first place, while psychoanalytic patients
come for treatment of pressing, even crippling, personality difficulties, it is well understood they do not leave
current social problems and pressures behind them. It
may even be noted that the effective analysis of an
individual patient is in itself a social contribution, be that
patient a housewife, nursery school teacher, superinten-
dent of schools, psychoanalytic student, or physician in
private practice. However, it is difficult to assess whether
the analyst would make a larger contribution by direct
participation in the solution of social institutional problems, rather than by specifically professional work in

analyzing patients who may then be better able to use their special talent and training for more effective activity in the sociopolitical sphere. Beyond this is the actuality that the professional activities of most analysts do extend beyond strictly psychoanalytic practice. They devote professional time to a remarkable diversity of activities, including consultation at a variety of social agencies and teaching in many different educational settings.

It would be desirable for the institute to include, much more systematically than they have to date, the available information on social issues and opportunity for discussion of the psychoanalytic bearing on those issues in the student's curriculum.

PSYCHOANALYTIC EDUCATION AND SOCIAL ISSUES

If sociocultural data are to be included in the psycho-analytic curriculum, they should be genuinely integrated with our theory, practice, and research. Courses on personality development should consider more fully sociological and anthropological studies on social-class and cultural differences in family structure and child-rearing practice. Our theory of personality structure should become more precise on the influence of social history and value systems on ego, ego-ideal, and superego formation. The study of aggression should consider the social and cultural forces contributing to action-prone-ness, intolerance of delay, and violence. Comprehension of phenomena of drive control and discharge requires both an understanding of inner processes and structures and an awareness of the alternative channels and patterns of control and release provided in various cultural settings.

We do not lack examples of the possible, mutually enriching integration of psychoanalytic principles and sociocultural data. The problem is how to accomplish this integration so that it attains a more central position in the institute curriculum.

RECOMMENDATIONS

1. *Candidate selection.* We recommend the acceptance into training of more persons from minority groups and from all disciplines concerned with human behavior. This should include anthropologists, sociologists, political scientists, historians, psychologists, teachers, lawyers, and others. The high cost of psychoanalytic training has severely limited the professional and social range of persons able to afford it. Some means of remedying this problem must be found, so that a scholar on an academic salary, for instance, will not be excluded from training purely on economic grounds.

2. *Teacher selection.* It is important to select enough faculty members whose interest and knowledge encompass both basic psychoanalytic theory and practice and sociocultural studies, and who have been able to integrate the knowledge from these different sources. It has been suggested that the best setting for cross-disciplinary collaboration is in the same head.

3. *Course design.* A potentially effective course would be a continuous case seminar in which a patient was presented from a sociocultural background other than white middle class. Another possibility would be a clinical seminar in which two patients of differing sociocultural backgrounds would be compared. The success of these proposals would of course depend on how well the

previous recommendations on student and teacher selection had been implemented.

Another possibility would be a seminar in which each of the participants would be engaged in field work with a social agency. The seminar would focus on the relevance of psychoanalytic principles and techniques to the problems encountered in the agency and attempt to identify the general principles the various social-agency situations may have in common, rather than focusing only on the clinical problems specific to each situation. Another approach would be to cut across traditional course lines by organizing a course to look at a specific social problem from a variety of psychoanalytic perspectives. For instance, violence could be looked at from the perspectives of child development, drive theory, fantasy and dream function, superego formation, capacity for sublimation, and forms of symbolic expression. A seminar on the psychoanalyst as a consultant to social agencies could provide knowledge about a professional role that is usually omitted from formal instruction.

Participation in such seminars need not be limited to students, but could include graduates as well. Indeed, such seminars might be particularly useful for programs of continuing education for graduate analysts.

The introduction of new courses into already full curricula always stimulates some concern about possible dilution and diffusion of effort or even greater difficulties in integration of the knowledge the student is expected to master. It seems more likely, however, that in the long run the student's psychoanalytic grasp would be firmer if the relevance to social problems were made explicit and given full discussion in the curriculum.

It is unlikely that such sweeping changes of psycho-analytic curricula would be accomplished quickly. Socio-cultural studies are not the primary interest of most Association members, and we know that exhortation has little effectiveness in altering attitudes. A slow process of change is more probable, activated by broadened student selection and encouragement of the integration of professional skills, psychoanalytic knowledge, and con-cern with social problems. As the value of sociocultural perspectives to psychoanalysis is recognized and shared with students, those analysts who already have such an orientation will be joined by greater numbers in the next analytic generation. Continuing significant new research and teaching contributions in this area will help to prevent the isolation of psychoanalysis from social reality.

PSYCHOANALYTIC RESEARCH ON SOCIAL AND COMMUNITY ISSUES

The Association has begun to contribute to community mental health programs through its Committee on Community Psychiatry, which has stimulated the development of similar committees in most affiliated societies. For example, the Association's committee is developing a method for evaluating the function of com-munity mental health centers and for identifying their strengths and weaknesses. Most of the societies are still doubtful about the relevance of community psychiatry to their own area of responsibility; however, those members involved in local community-psychiatry committees are quite enthusiastic about the work.

The usefulness of combined social and psychoana-lytic research in adding fundamental information to both fields is demonstrated by the research analysis of young black children from ghetto environments. Through this research program, co-sponsored by the Baltimore-D.C. Society and the Children's Hospital of D.C., new dimensions have been added to the understanding of the impact of social influences on early ego development. This, in turn, has had important implications for planning preventive measures in the social-welfare programs for inner-city children.

Institutes and societies related to medical schools and other university departments would be in an excellent position to sponsor and collaborate in research on social problems to which psychoanalytic thinking might contribute. One example is the insights analytically oriented studies have provided on the origins of racial prejudice in the early years of life. Obviously we hope that it may become possible to offer new and useful data to the effort to counter the development of racism.

We will presume to repeat the cliché that we live in an era of social upheaval. The changing value systems that apply to the status of women, sexual mores, family mobility, group child care and communal living patterns all have an effect on individual psychosexual and ego development, and commission members recommend that psychoanalytic societies sponsor further research on these matters.

The climate of mistrust between the neurosciences, social sciences, and psychoanalysis is presumably beginning to dissipate with current efforts by a number of institutes to train more research students from the basic and social sciences. The development of the Psychoanalytic Institute for Psychosocial Studies in Chicago is one bridge being built between fields that have much to learn from each other. Together, they can do much toward the understanding and amelioration of mankind's problems. Exposure to and involvement of students in such joint research ventures will influence future psychoanalysts toward still further facilitating communication with the allied disciplines in the behavioral sciences.

PSYCHOANALYTIC PRACTICE AND SOCIAL AND COMMUNITY ISSUES

The commission identified more than 60 social issues in twenty broad areas of interest to which psychoanalysis could make a meaningful contribution. One of the commission's subcommittees subsequently reduced the general categories of issues to six: (1) Racial, class, and ethnic differences; (2) male-female differences; (3) social problems relating to patient care; (4) values, beliefs, moral systems, and ethics; (5) the environment, including urbanization, cultural atmosphere, educational atmosphere, and familial atmosphere; (6) child development and developmental issues. The sixth, child development, is influenced by all social issues. Indeed, in certain respects, each of the categories listed overlaps the others.

RACIAL, CLASS, AND ETHNIC DIFFERENCES

We considered the attitudes and patterns of practice necessary for psychoanalysis to make substantial contributions to these social issues, and we call attention to the insularity of analysis impeding more effective involvement.

The composition of the Association is highly skewed compared to the composition of our national population.

Whites, males, Jews, Protestants, persons of Northern European origin, and those of middle-class orientation constitute a high proportion of all analysts and their patients. There are plausible and reasonable explanations for this situation, but its perpetuation, in the light of current social pressures toward integration, raises the possibility of a bias stemming from unconscious motivations. Racial prejudice has received relatively little direct attention in the analytic literature.

If psychoanalysts are to contribute to the psychological problems of race, social class, ethnic background, and sexual gender, we would do better to recruit students for training from a broader social spectrum. To increase the proportion of minority analysts will require active recruiting, which many analysts have been reluctant to undertake. Experience has shown that unless they are energetically sought and encouraged, most minority professionals have been hesitant to approach organizations that are overwhelmingly white and middle class. The statement by institutes that they wish to admit minority students but that relatively few apply may reflect more on the recruiting effort than on the actual or potential interest of minority professionals. Minority psychoanalysts and psychoanalytic students could contribute significantly to such institute recruiting programs.

It can be questioned whether it is appropriate for psychoanalytic societies to participate directly in planning programs for the relief of social ills. However, important contributions could be made indirectly through the active involvement of persons who have benefited from psychoanalytic treatment. Some modifications of technique may be needed to make the analytic process more effective in resolving the psychological problems of patients from hitherto rarely analyzed minority groups.

Where social distances between analyst and patient are greater than usual, the first phase of analysis would probably have to consider the special obstacles to a working alliance. Careful and specific attention to this question in the initial phase might at least decrease the conseqeunces of great social distance in the analytic situation. The problem of social distance may have cultural, sexual, or racial elements, and may also be manifested in the use of expressive language, which is significantly determined by a particular cultural background, but not always easily recognized or translated by the analyst.

Unrecognized racial bias in the analyst may take the form of "color blindness," with a denial that there are any special technical problems attributable to race. Such denial could lead to an essentially sterile analysis in which neither the white analyst nor the black patient (or vice versa) dealt with important conflicts relevant to the experience. On the other hand, unresolved racial bias could also lead to excessive focus on racial implications of the transference and be equally destructive to the progress of the analysis.

We recognize that the psychoanalytic societies and institutes lack adequate financial means to implement fully exploratory approaches to social and community issues. We therefore recommend that a committee of the Association be created to explore the feasibility of a National Foundation for Psychoanalytic Psychosocial Studies to provide support for such activities.

This discussion is influenced throughout by the clear awareness that we can contribute most by remaining

firmly based on our own particular science of psychoanalysis. Our suggestions and recommendations are
intended to help build further upon the foundation of
psychoanalytic theory and practice. Such building will
prepare us and our students to contribute professionally
as effectively to the solution of social problems as we have
so significantly contributed to the solution of individual
problems.

PLENARY DISCUSSION —
GEORGE H. POLLOCK, M.D.

Psychoanalysis, which originated and has mainly been
identified with the therapeutic situation, now faces new
problems as well as opportunities to apply its knowledge
and methods to areas beyond the clinical setting. The
work of the Robertsons (1967, 1968, 1969, 1971) in
England, and *Beyond the Best Interests of the Child*,
written by Joseph Goldstein, Anna Freud, and Albert
Solnit (1973), are already classics. Psychohistory, psychoanalytic anthropology, psychoanalytic aspects of education, studies of political leaders and their followers, and
investigations of creativity are additional new areas where
psychoanalysis has been making significant contributions. New groups started by psychoanalysts such as the
Hastings Institute of Society, Ethics and the Life Sciences
and the Chicago Center for Psychosocial Studies, are
promoting the examination by psychoanalysts and
experts in other disciplines of heretofore neglected topics.
Barriers that have hampered communication and
interdisciplinary study and research are being removed
and the results are exhilarating.

The commission has addressed itself to the relation of psychoanalysis to social and community issues. This involves consideration of how social, community, and political factors influence psychoanalysis and how psychoanalysis can contribute to the understanding and subsequent action requirements of social, community, and political phenomena. Obviously, governmental health legislation can influence psychoanalytic practice and therefore psychoanalytic education. Governmental planners have advocated a shift from office-based private practice to other modes of health care that will have a significant impact on the educational and professional experience of the physician in the next decade. The issues of relicensure and recertification, peer review, PSRO, confidentiality, and national health insurance reveal how social and economic factors can, and in some instances already have, influenced psychoanalysis. The executive and administrative officers of our Association are increasingly occupied with these issues.

We live in a world with changing values, ideals and objectives, and we must work to conserve a humanistic perspective of man. Our science and the therapeutic application of it must be maintained on the highest possible level if we are to remain significant to society. I quote from the prospectus of the Center for Psychosocial Studies:

> As the methods for the scientific analysis of society become more sophisticated through the use of computer simulation, multivariate analysis and other mathematical procedures, the "irrational" element in human behavior—its power to resist or advance social change and to defy attempts at prediction and control—becomes increasingly obvious. All of our major social problems, such

as urban decay and suburban flight, crime control and prison reform, the persistence of poverty and the plight of the poor, the disillusionment of the middle classes, and racism, have significant but poorly understood psychological dimensions at their core. These factors will be uncovered only by the development of new approaches that delve more deeply into those individual motives as they affect social behavior and public policy.

As practiced clinically, psychoanalysis provides the most intensive and revealing study of individual motives — their organization, origins, and expressions in social behavior — that has yet been developed. Psychoanalysis today is in a period of transition as its practitioners seek to define and expand further their roles in contemporary society.

More and more psychoanalysts are interested in making their unique method of access to inner experience work as a tool for understanding the problems of the black ghetto, social stress, political leadership, law and jurisprudence, child care and education. A growing pool of social scientists are combining psychoanalytic training with skills of quantitative social and behavioral analysis, cross-cultural experience, or historical research. These efforts, although important in illustrating the promise of psychoanalysis for understanding contemporary society, have been too often fragmentary, limited, or only suggestive of additional work that needs doing, and many of them have also been inadequately communicated among those who might carry that work forward.

There is growing recognition among leaders in the biomedical and social sciences of the need for an interdisciplinary approach to the study and solution of social problems. Institutional support for such efforts, however, has been virtually nonexistent. Psychosocial investigators at universities have often been discouraged in their attempts to go beyond the narrow bounds defined by disciplinary conventions; indeed, some of the most notable interdisciplinary experiments have had to be abandoned as a consequence. Although a number of professional associations have encouraged clinicians to take a greater interest in public problems, and their work has produced valuable results, they have lacked the resources and organization for a concentrated and cumulative effort.

The Chicago Center for Psychosocial Studies has recently been founded to give this field the support it must have to realize its full potential. The Center is an independent research institution, completely committed to the use of psychoanalysis in scholarly, investigative, and interdisciplinary educational exchange with researchers coming from other disciplines.

Can psychoanalysis shed light on the relation of intrapsychic processes to social behavior throughout the life cycle? Can psychoanalysis make constructive recommendations on these matters to legislators? When we speak of the relation of psychoanalysis to social and community issues, we must ask which aspects of psychoanalysis are applicable to the particular issues under study. Although Freud was one of the pioneers in group psychology, we do not specifically train psychoanalysts in group formation or group functioning and its importance to social and community organizations. Nor do we actively encourage psychoanalytic work with patients from different cultures; different racial, religious and ethnic groups; different socio-economic strata; and different ages, especially the older populations. Insofar as we do participate in such a variety of experiences, we gather new data to test existing theory and possibly generate new theory and further research.

Psychoanalysts have much information and understanding derived from clinical work that is indeed pertinent beyond the individual therapeutic context. In our search for knowledge to explain man, his behavior, his conflicts, his pleasures and sublimations, his relationships to his family and to society, we can make contributions not only by working individually, but also by participating in collaborative investigations and communicating with other scientists interested in similar studies.

Most psychoanalysts in the United States come from medical-psychiatric backgrounds and are primarily involved in therapeutic work. Some are involved in research, education, administration, and consultation, but their work is mainly connected with the therapeutic situation. I fully agree with the commission's recommendation that we should educate individuals "from all disciplines concerned with human behavior," e.g., anthropologists, sociologists, political scientists, historians, psychologists, teachers, lawyers, social workers, and many others. I believe that we also need to establish psychoanalysis as an independent science and profession, and that we should train students for whom psychoanalysis will be the primary profession from the start. These students must be carefully selected and their education should include, in addition to the core psychoanalytic curriculum, opportunities to work with specialists from the social, behavioral, and medical services that bear on their interest.

Can an institute involve itself directly with social and community issues? I will refer to a few examples of what has been done in the Chicago community by the Chicago Institute. The Chicago Institute has the largest low-fee clinic in Illinois in terms of patient therapeutic hours. The clinic receives state funding for this community service. The teacher education program has trained over 700 school teachers, many of them black and many from ghetto schools. The child-therapy training program has for more than a decade trained social workers, not for purposes of clinical practice, but for the trainees to return to their community social agencies and serve the community in consultative, therapeutic, and administrative roles. The institute has an ongoing regular consultation service with a Spanish-speaking community high school. The library makes psychoanalytic books, journals, films, and reports available to all Chicago and regional educational institutions. Courses for business executives, co-sponsored by the University of Chicago School of Businesss, have recently been inaugurated. Continuing-education courses for psychiatrists, social workers, teachers, and guidance counselors are continually oversubscribed. Only a few weeks ago the institute was asked about establishing a prevention-intervention service with an ongoing research component for which financial support was offered. For an analytic institute this would be another opportunity for community service and very worthwhile for analytic students and faculty alike.

What about research into social and community issues? I wish to quote again from the prospectus of the Chicago Center for Psychosocial Studies.

Psychoanalysis has long been recognized as an important instrument for the understanding of human behavior. Until recently few have extended its use beyond the clinical setting and into broad areas of public life where its impact can be equally, if not more, significant. The Center for Psychosocial Studies was established in 1972 to facilitate and encourage the wider application of psychoanalytic methods and experience to the study of contemporary society, with a view to understanding the psychological components of social, economic, and political life while proposing and evaluating approaches to the solution of contemporary social problems.

The Center provides a unique meeting ground for social scientists, psychoanalysts, educators, and others to share information and develop procedures for pursuing these goals. Basic and applied research, a fellowship program, and information exchange through conferences and publications are the primary elements of the Center's activities.

Psychoanalysis does have a responsibility to be involved with social, political, and community issues. Our depth of understanding can be utilized to great effect in the study of many areas of human concern in addition to individual psychological therapy. In summary, with regard to all the conference discussions, we can heed Freud's counsel given in "Beyond the Pleasure Principle."

> We must be patient and await fresh methods and occasions of research. We must be ready, too, to abandon a path that we have followed for a time, if it seems to be leading to no good end. Only believers, who demand that science shall be a substitute for the catechism they have given up, will blame an investigator for developing or even transforming his views. We may take comfort, too, for the slow advances of our scientific knowledge in the words of the poet.... 'What we cannot reach flying we must reach limping.... The Book tells us it is no sin to limp' [1920, p. 64].

SUMMARY OF CONFERENCE DISCUSSION

The commission's report stimulated a very active discussion of the fundamental issues involved in the relation of psychoanalysis to social issues. The conferees were quite receptive to the suggestion that a high social and scientific yield would accrue from the greater availability of psychoanalytic treatment to others in addition to members of the professional middle class. However, the practical implementation of the suggestion seemed difficult to formulate. Although individual private low-fee arrangements or institute low-fee psychoanalytic clinics already exist as modalities, they were considered inadequate for achieving any significant social impact.

There was general support for the recommendation that institutes should attempt to offer their students regular courses on the psychoanalytic understanding of group processes and social issues. However, certain responses suggested doubt that there was a sufficient body of uniquely psychoanalytic theory or data to justify such courses.

Strong opposition was aroused by the commission's recommendations insofar as they were understood to call for social activism by psychoanalysis or psychoanalysts representing psychoanalysis. One representative group discussion indicated that the usual view was that the scientific and professional statements of psychoanalysts should be carefully distinguished from the statements and activities of individual psychoanalysts as private citizens with personal value systems, and that without such a distinction serious overextension of knowledge, distortion of concepts, and discrediting would result. Several speakers remarked on the risks that would accompany a too hasty compliance with the demand to expand the social dimensions of psychoanalytic activity; namely, the danger of succumbing to grandiosity in our activities and aspirations, and the possible loss of a clear perspective on our legitimate area of expertise. The preponderant response to the commission's report was an affirmation of the need to learn and to contribute what we can as psychoanalysts to the knowledge of individual and social psychology and a rejection of any program of collective social activism.

Plenary Conference Summations

The Upward Spiral of Psychoanalytic Education

ALBERT J. SOLNIT, M.D.

Psychoanalytic education in the network of institutes of the Association has come of age and faces the future with concern, anticipation, and the need to take stock of itself. In this presentation I will try to describe a perspective that utilizes our inventory as preparation for the future. We have an obligation to be critical, imaginative, and to pass on a viable legacy.

Harvard's first commencement program articulated the longings of its founders ". . . to advance learning and perpetuate it to Posterity; dreading to leave an illiterate Ministry to the Churches when our present Ministers shall lie in the dust" (Bailey, 1974, p. 15). Although this is not our first commencement, we should accept periodic review, i.e., how to start anew from where we are as we accept the inevitability of rediscovery and try to shape the spiral in an upward direction. For a balanced perspective I hasten to add, as Kurt Eissler put it, "As long as psychoanalysis is practised, it will remain of use to man" (1969, p. 462). However, was Freud's fear that therapy would destroy the science of psychoanalysis a valid one?

Although the rate of change in our educational program may be slow, we do have the problem that changing social and economic situations require us to provide for adaptation. At the same time we must pursue a deliberate review of our institutes of higher learning in order to learn from the past and present, as a preparation for influencing developmental changes in the future. The movement toward third-party payment, peer-review organizations, and a process of relicensing or providing evidence for continuing competence is accelerating. The Association maintains committees to prepare us to influence and adapt to these trends of inevitable change. These activities place us at risk of changing our educational, clinical, and research activities under pressure, without first knowing where we are and how we can plan for desirable and necessary changes. However, it is consistent with the aims of the Association and its constituent institutes and societies that we deliberately review and analyze our present conditions to prepare us to plan and bring about changes that strengthen psychoanalytic theory, its practice, and its applications. The report of the Commission on the Relationship of Psychoanalysis to Current Changes in Medicine and Psychiatric Education had much to say about these trends. Perhaps we can view some of these socio-economic factors as the outside enemy or threat while considering other aspects as challenges and opportunities—just imagine if analytic treatment were subsidized significantly by a national health insurance plan without distorting or overburdening the psychoanalytic situation.

Why are we holding this review and inventory now? I can only speculate about our own historical imperatives.

1. There is a change in the psychopathology of those who now come to us for psychoanalytic treatment. We have not only accepted these patients for treatment as part of the widening scope of psychoanalytic treatment, but increasingly these are the patients who seek relief, understanding, and inner change.

2. The power of our theory has made it clear that we have a responsibility to be involved in planning how our educational, clinical, and scholarly resources can be transformed into improved learning and practice. I do not mean we have exclusive ownership, but that we know more about the method, the theory, and its applications than any other group. We thus have the opportunity and responsibility to help with the unfolding of psychoanalytic knowledge, even though we are not its sole custodians.

3. We have been successful in pooling many of our resources in education and in standard setting. At the same time we have not been successful in fostering psychoanalytic scholarship among young men and women who are imaginative, critical, and capable of independent psychoanalytic research.

In summary, my speculations about "why now?" are focused on: the substance of new clinical problems that we are facing, i.e., the widening scope of psychoanalysis; the continued power of our theory that deserves concerted thought about how we can sustain its productivity and avoid the obsolescence that all scientific fields risk if they do not change through critical review, innovative application, and thoughtful refinement; and our concern for creating and maintaining a clinical and scholarly learning environment in our institutes that will attract future psychoanalysts with the attitudes and motives associated with clinical competence, creative research, and scientific leadership.

THE WIDENING SCOPE OF PSYCHOANALYSIS

In the report of the Commission on Child Analysis in particular and in the discussions of its position paper as well as in several of the other discussion groups, the issue of the differences in the patients who are taken into psychoanalytic treatment received a good deal of attention. Although the psychoanalytic method has been considered a treatment and exploratory instrument for patients with psychoneurotic conflicts, over the years analysts have recognized that these neurotic pathologies are mixed with interrelated ego deficits and deviations, often with an unevenness of ego development and with preoedipal character distortions. Many of our colleagues have the strong conviction that patients differ in the ways I have noted. Others are convinced that our increased clinical experience and theoretical grasp have enabled us to understand more about our patients and that this is the major reason our patients appear different. These are questions for pooled research, for theory building, for our technique and its underlying theory that must be integrated into our psychoanalytic education.

Although there are conservatives among us who say that the psychoanalytic method is not designed to treat borderline patients or patients with mixed neurotic and ego-deviation difficulties, the fact is that most analysts have such patients in psychoanalytic treatment. These psychoanalysts are eager to help elaborate and refine our theory, to increase our capacities to explain and to make short-term predictions about such patients.

This will not be the first time we have applied our method to conditions for which it was not originally thought to be intended. These conditions, which have been investigated by psychoanalysts with psychoanalytic hypotheses, include psychosomatic conditions, deprivational states, and the dying process.

The psychoanalyst treating children, adolescents, young adults, and older adults has come to recognize that our understanding of ego deficits, conflict-free ego functions, and atypical development has provided us with a generation of researchable problems. These research questions are a challenge and an opportunity to increase our theoretical grasp and to refine our theory.

It is in this sense that the report of the Commission on Child Analysis provides us with the recommendation that developmental perspectives and concepts be integrated into our teaching and research activities. In fact, we know that the current curriculum and supervised clinical learning in our institutes already reflect these changes in our field. Genetic reconstructions enrich developmental formulations just as developmental observations and inferences refine and extend our capacities to understand genetic patterns. In dialogues between child and adult analysts we have significantly extended our skills in interpretatively reconstructing how the past lives on in the present and noting limitations of that reconstruction.

There are other examples of developmental data and perspectives, not limited to the psychoanalytic study and treatment of children and adolescents, that have had an impact on our curricula (e.g., infant observation).

What impact will these experiences in psychoanalytic treatment have on our research, theoretical assumptions, and technique? Will such pooled studies suggest applied research, especially in sharpening our ability to utilize direct observational studies to question, refine, and modify our theory about parenthood, family dynamics, and other vicissitudes of human development?

These are not new issues, but our need to approach them systematically is urgent. These issues can be shunted aside or they can provide pressure to consider desirable changes in our understanding, our teaching, and our determination to establish research climates that will influence candidate selection and assessment. For example, should a candidate take on as his or her second or third supervised case a borderline patient or one who has neurotic conflicts mixed with narcissistic disorders; or should he or she wait until a more suitable patient can be found? How long should we expect him or her to wait? Obviously, we need not accept an either/or constraint, but it is important to acknowledge our increasing awareness and to take advantage of the challenges and opportunities that such changes present.

Another implication of what appears to be changing psychopathology in those who seek psychoanalytic training is the need to better understand so-called healthy development and how it differs from neurotic, borderline, and atypical development. These formulations are not new but it is time to investigate them critically, to integrate them into our teaching, and to use them to refine our definition of the scope of psychoanalysis.

There are other potential benefits from this systematization of our studies. We can be more helpful to nonanalysts concerned with their studies, whether in psychiatry, pediatrics, psychology, or neuropharmacology. Conversely, we can be open to learning from social and biological scientists involved in studying psychosomatic disorders, psychotic states, and chronic illness. Achieving a fruitful balance of direct psychoanalytic studies, collaborative studies, and studies in which our theory is applied will offer us opportunities to refine and elaborate psychoanalytic theory and clinical knowledge. Such a dynamic balance provides another kind of insurance against stagnation.

This conference and the commission reports should be viewed as important catalytic agents to stimulate and assist institutes and societies, as well as our Association, in reviewing, assessing, and planning for the future. The conference and commission reports should not be considered as direct change agents.

ASSESSMENT, GROWTH, AND OBSOLESCENCE

Psychoanalysis is a theory, method, treatment, and field of knowledge that must, like all other clinical and non-clinical disciplines, contend simultaneously with changes that sustain its vitality and that increase the risk of its obsolescence. The commission reports and their discussion highlighted many of the forces involved in both growth and obsolescence.

The Association has been remarkably resilient in its multiple activities. It has taken leadership in standard setting, scientific stimulation, and in coping with the socio-economic and political threats to our future. The Association has also fostered a camaraderie in which peer review and scientific disagreements can be constructive. The Association is urgently needed to continue these activities of transforming risk into mastery, from outside and inside. This need is evident in most of the commission reports, which recommend that the Association assume an increased leadership in the problems of funding, supporting evaluation efforts, and maintaining and increasing our scientific vigor, resiliency, and pluralism.

The reports and discussions affirm that our first priority must continue to be the selection and development of competent clinical psychoanalysts with research attitudes and potential—without whom we will not survive. In fact, we may not survive if we do not go beyond that priority. We may also have less success and satisfaction if we are unable to move ahead in our quest for a diversity of male and female analytic students. These should include younger men and women, as well as those who come to us from nonmedical fields with a potential for research talent and creativity, and with interests in children and adolescents, as well as in adults of all ages and backgrounds.

The Association and our many institutes and societies must be both strong and confident enough to permit and encourage self-scrutiny, evaluation, interdisciplinary influences, and the growth-promoting tensions of constructive disagreement. Can we be that strong? I predict we will be. The commissions forecast a new balance of core training programs to develop competent clinical psychoanalysts and continuing-education programs to enable us to establish scholarly environments in our institutes and in some universities. The commissions encourage an increase of interdisciplinary collaborative studies with colleagues from medicine, the humanities, law, social sciences, and the arts.

There is room enough and work enough for all. Ernst Kris used to say that analysis was so fascinating and satisfying that it always seemed surprising that one was also allowed to earn one's living in that way. In the spirit of Ernst Kris, several of the commissions urge imaginative boldness in striving to create intellectual climates in which questioning and collaboration will enable us to sustain our contributions to psychoanalytic education and research.

ATTRACTING, ACCEPTING, AND PREPARING FUTURE PSYCHOANALYSTS

In most of the commission reports there are several recurrent themes that tend to indicate a pattern of issues and recommendations. This pattern constitutes an awareness that we make choices about whom we interest, whom we select, and how we teach or train them to become competent psychoanalysts with scholarly interests and capacities. As the Commission on Psychoanalytic Research clearly pointed out, there is a grave risk to the survival of psychoanalysis if those who become competent clinical analysts do not have a research attitude. Several commissions expressed the fear that we risk losing ground because of our relative isolation from the intellectual and scientific community.

In a sense the tripartite system of psychoanalytic education has parallel tripartite goals—the personal analysis as research on the self; the coursework as preparation for teaching and the development of a research attitude; and the supervised clinical work as the qualifying experience enabling the candidate to provide services through his or her psychoanalytic therapeutic work with patients. The tripartite system allows for different models of psychoanalytic education, ranging from the differing ways in which the training analyst relates to the education committee to a large variety of curricula and students from differing backgrounds.

All of the commission reports recommended a more scholarly atmosphere in which faculty and students could work together in challenging and learning to understand and extend the psychoanalytic method and psychoanalytic theory. Many of the reports also recommended closer collaboration or involvement with the universities, either in the medical school or as a university department. There was a persistent interest in systematic evaluation of the tripartite system, including the curriculum, selection process, supervision, and the training analysis itself. There was a tendency to look for one best model but a readiness to see the need for different models in different parts of the country with differing resources.

On the whole, the commissions tended to "play down" our emphasis on teaching and training. We were advised to emphasize the need for a graduate school climate in which self-starting and learning in an active way is, following analytic principles, the student's responsibility. There was a plea that any additions to the curriculum be associated with an equal amount of deletions. It was also urged that the gatekeepers become more self-searching about how they attract or discourage and select candidates. This exploration revealed a felt need to enable well-selected individuals to start their analytic training at a younger age. We were warned that there is no magic in numbers at either end of the age scale.

However, several commissions had the impression that we have failed to find and foster the development of psychoanalysts with the enthusiasm, curiosity, originality, versatility, and productivity of colleagues who were born and had all or most of their psychoanalytic education in Europe, especially Vienna. We have tended toward greater homogeneity in this phase of our history, perhaps because, as Kuhn (1962, p. 24) puts it, "Few people who are not actually practitioners of a mature science realize how much mop-up work of this sort a paradigm leaves to be done or quite how fascinating such work can prove in the execution." In a recent letter to the Editor, Eissler explicates his earlier (1969) paper by stating, "One idea in my paper was that since Freud's death, psychoanalysis has been chiefly engaged in such 'mop-up work'" (1973, pp. 374-375).

If Eissler is correct, how shall we anticipate the next twenty to thirty years of our learning from and practicing of psychoanalysis? There is considerable apprehension that we risk diluting our science, diffusing our energies, and losing the vigor and productivity of the psychoanalytic method as it is used in the treatment of adults with the so-called classic neuroses. The commission reports and their discussion mention this fear. There is also the implication of an equal or greater risk that if we limit ourselves by this fear we shall become, as Ernst Kris once warned (personal communication, 1954), specialists in treating only one kind of patient. He pointed out that the psychoanalyst, like the competent gardener who raises many kinds of plants, should be able to understand and treat many kinds of patients. He urged that we have confidence in our method and theory.

As several reports indicated, there are potential threats to psychoanalysis from the outside. These include future changes in licensing and relicensing for competence, and in funding of training and health-care

services. These changes could put psychoanalytic treatment, learning, and research at a severe disadvantage.
Our colleagues on several of the commissions have recommended that we encourage our Association and the local
institutes and societies to fight for our place in the sun
both by self-help devices and by joining other organizations with whom we have overlapping interests.

There are also potential threats from our own attitudes and conflicts. These include our imperfect ability
to evaluate our selection of future analysts, educational
activities, and scientific productivity in order to be more
prepared and effective in planning for and implementing
desirable changes in our institutes and societies and in
our Association. Is it good or bad for psychoanalysis to
view itself as an academy? Why are we so intrigued by
becoming part of a university? We may have forgotten
that until the Flexner Report, in the early part of this
century, most American medical schools were exclusively in the hospitals, clinics, and offices of physicians
and not in universities. Many still are. There seems to be
a trend toward wanting the involvement of nonmedical
students, not only for what we can give them, but just as
importantly for what they can give to psychoanalysis. In
this connection several reports are interested in the possibility of establishing multiple tracks for a larger variety of
students, e.g., the clinical track, nonclinical track, and a
course best described as general studies in psychoanalysis.

There are reservations about a full-time institute.
Although economic factors are prominent, it is crucial
that we become clearer about the risks of being too
narrow in our clinical work as well as doing too little
clinical work. Nor have we clearly distinguished the need
and capacity we have to support psychoanalysts who have

different patterns of productivity in their work—ranging from full-time practitioners who are among the best of our theoretical scholars, to colleagues who practice part time and who also may be among the best of our theoreticians, teachers, or researchers. Several of the commissions considered the establishment of a university department of psychoanalysis in order to provide the range of teaching and research activities desirable for the future development of psychoanalysis. This calls to mind Freud's recommendation that a professorial chair for psychoanalysis be established at the Hebrew University in Jerusalem.

The commission reports and discussion groups suggested we need diversity in our selection, in our tripartite system, in the role models we support, and in the interdisciplinary patterns in which we engage in teaching and research. This includes those psychoanalysts who have made and will continue to make valuable contributions to their own development as psychoanalysts by working together with nonanalysts in the community and in the analysis and shaping of social issues and policies. Other examples are found in the utilization of psychoanalytic theory to establish criteria for day-care programs and, at the other end of the life cycle, to understand the impact of losing one's job because of one's age.

From the commission reports and their discussion it appears that we are less at risk of lowering standards and losing the momentum of our scientific and clinical work if we view change as inevitable and desirable, than if we dig in our heels and feel we must preserve our legacy as we think it was passed on to us. If change is inevitable, how can we explore, evaluate and direct it? How shall we help ourselves to learn from our errors and our successes?

Psychoanalysis as a Profession and Psychoanalysis as a Science: A Stocktaking

ROBERT S. WALLERSTEIN, M.D.

It is a challenging, difficult, but rewarding undertaking, in the midstream of my own experiencing and learning process at this conference, to attempt to sort out my impressions in a reasonably orderly and meaningful way and to organize them into a distillation that can be presented within the alloted time and in a way that both does justice as a summary to the enormous complexity and richness of the thinking that has characterized this conference and at the same time highlights its salient issues so as to stimulate your participation in the fullest continuing dialogue about them in the ensuing discussion period.

The conference, at least from my perspective, has been enormously successful in more than fulfilling the hopes of those of us who were in on the initial conceptualization and have been party to the long and often tedious preparatory planning and arranging process. Our hopes

307

were for a vital and timely discussion, a deliberate and self-conscious stocktaking and consideration of where we are as a field, profession, discipline, and science; where we seem to be heading; where we would perhaps prefer to be heading; what forces are impinging on us from within and without to mold (or perhaps distort) that future; and what we can do to help chart that course more to our liking. It may be premature to judge the success of our collective undertaking here in fulfilling that mission, but I at least have a good feeling of satisfaction that at this point we are very much on the way.

First, I do want to say as an over-all observation that our originally chosen conference title, which gave us the easy acronym of COPER, is perhaps a misnomer. It seems to me now that the rubric of a Conference on Psychoanalytic *Education* and *Research* is too narrow to conceptualize what this conference has actually been about. We have, to be sure, been talking about psychoanalytic education every day at every meeting, even when discussing the commission report specifically concerned with psychoanalytic research. There have also been implications for research in much of what has transpired this week, though they have not necessarily been explicitly spelled out at each turn. But I think that we have been more preoccupied all week with a conference on psychoanalysis as a profession and psychoanalysis as a science and how these twin perspectives can best be fulfilled, in tandem and in harmony with one another, in fact interlocked and enriching and nourishing one another.

For that, I think, is what we have been all about — and that is, to me, the essential of the concern, the flux, and even the struggle of opposed viewpoints that have pervaded all of our deliberations. I have identified around this juxtaposition two main points of view. For exposition purposes I shall state this dichotomy, which I have previously (1972) characterized as one of the many fateful syncretistic dilemmas in which our field seems to abound, as the dichotomy between the interests and the requirements—at times, but not always, parallel and congruent—between psychoanalysis as a profession and psychoanalysis as a science. Let me, briefly at this point, characterize these perspectives in a perhaps overdrawn way. The concern with psychoanalysis as a profession sees us as the proud carriers of a legacy bequeathed to us by Freud, concerned with our practice and the melioration of neurotic suffering as our central activity and claim upon the conscience and support of society. To maintain and perpetuate that practice we have developed our institutes to be basically independent of other organized entities in function and structure, and have developed them in their familiar "tripartite" educational form. We have come with justification to regard them as adequate vehicles through which to give the training for our profession and to protect its standards from erosion and its central truths from dilution. The institute, as we know it, has had a history marked by expanding theoretical and technical knowledge garnered for the most part through the classical clinical case study method, by widening the scope of our applications to psychopathological categories beyond the so-called classical psychoneuroses around which our theory was originally built, and by the seriousness of educational investment to which all of us associated with institute teaching and operation can testify out of many overtime hours—someone has even characterized us as schools run by the overtime energies of tired men and women.

Those most committed to this view of our essential functions for the most part also feel proud that we are doing reasonably well by this way of organization and activity, that we of course can and should try to do better in all respects, and that some of this conference's recommendations are indeed efforts to do just that, to do it better—even much better— within this framework. But they feel that the framework itself and its continued maintenance is our best way to maintain our standards, and to guard against an assimilating and leveling process that would ultimately destroy the uniqueness of our achievement and our contribution.

The other perspective, the concern with psychoanalysis as a science, sees us as the custodians of a stewardship also bequeathed to us by Freud—the stewardship of a science, of which practice is but one, albeit an important application. If we are to produce research and researchers, if we are to continue to advance our scientific frontiers in concert and imbricated with other related bodies of knowledge, with all the hoped-for consequences for psychoanalysis in its therapeutic application, as a growing science, and as an integral part of the fabric of the wider intellectual-scientific-academic world, then we are declared, in our present organization to be grossly deficient. We live in relative isolation from the world of the university, the best repository yet devised for the world's knowledge and wisdom and its propagation into new generations. And in that isolation we are declared to have suffered grievously; it has been an isolation that has been to our detriment and—*pari passu*—to the detriment of the entire scientific-intellectual community as well. Further, it is an isolation that, though enforced upon Freud, has been maintained by us long past its historical necessity or helpfulness.

To the holders of the first position, who look to the maintenance of our integrity as a profession, see positive values in this isolation, and point to the uniqueness of our subject matter—the subjectivistic world of unconscious mental forces—and to the special institutional arrangements we require to teach access to that world through the play of transference and countertransference forces; to them the holders of the second position in effect say: "We are now at a different position in our growth and maturity as a science and in a differently evolving social-political-economic surround as well as intellectual surround than existed in Freud's day, so that going on as we have been, even if we do it better, will no longer suffice to maintain even what we have accomplished and professionally cherish the most." They tell us that we must change, that the life we save may be our own.

Herein lies the tension and the dialectic that I think has characterized both the preparatory period and the undercurrent of this conference. Let me turn now to how this dialectic has been addressed by the various commissions. A major example of addressing issues from within the framework of the first perspective was the lead-off report and discussion of the work of the Commission on the Tripartite System of Psychoanalytic Education—not that those on the commission are necessarily at odds with the counterposed view, or would not, at least some of them, go along with it to some extent. What I mean rather is that this commission accepted our present organizational structure and functioning as a given, in the sense that it is the best that we have to build upon at present, and then sought out ways to improve this existing model within the framework in which it functions.

The report was a long one and it gave us many

thoughtful recommendations, of which I can only outline what I consider to be the major highlights. Basically the report conveyed a ringing reaffirmation of the tripartite educational structure as the best way devised so far to carry out our psychoanalytic educational enterprise. This basic premise incidentally was not directly questioned by any of the other commissions, no matter how many changes in structure and function they otherwise advocated. As the commission reminded us, this system involves not only a tripartite sequencing, but also an intermingling of the experiential learning of the training analysis, the cognitive learning of the formal didactic curriculum, and the instrumental learning of the clinical supervision.

What is the main thrust of the recommendations made to improve our functioning in this framework? Several key words stand out. The first is *integration,* integration of the different kinds of learning, of theory and practice, of the didactic and the clinical, of the educational and the therapeutic aspects within the training analysis. Second are *assessment* and *evaluation,* which take place at each step of the developmental progression. Assessment and evaluation must of course be linked to well-defined teaching and learning objectives for each educational step against which progress and accomplishment can be weighed. What is meant is monitored progression (at one step it is a formal matriculation) with a clear specification of the criteria for each step; the commission is squarely against the concept of automatic time progression. A monitored progression would provide an active pedagogic as well as analytic study of each step in the process and include self-evaluation and full student participation in the evaluation process.

Another key concept is that this kind of evaluation does not have to be *judgmental*. It is what one does with it, how one uses it, that keeps the fact and the consequences of evaluation neutral, objective, nonjudgmental, or not. *Reporting* is another key word—a highly loaded one. The distinction is drawn between the inappropriateness of reporting personal information, which of course should be confidential within the privacy of the training analysis, and the propriety of reporting "derivative information," judgments arrived at concerning the stage of development and release from neurotic conflict and inhibition of those ego functions necessary for the conduct of analytic work. Here the commission's philosophy can best be put as "the obligation to assess and the prerogative to report."

Yet another key concept is that of the *seriousness* with which the formal didactic component of the curriculum is taken. The commission put it most strongly, "It alone is the difference between psychoanalytic training and psychoanalytic education." Here of course are all the issues the commission takes with our training school atmosphere, our lock-step educational progression, our part-time night school, our clinging to often outdated 30- to 70-year-old basic textbook insufficiently supplemented by more modern developments, the deficiencies of our historical rather than systematic model for fashioning our curriculum. And lastly there is the emphasis on the *phase* of training as a critical variable with a more important place in our educational scheme than we usually explicitly accord it. For instance, in our supervision work we do not stress the unfolding general pattern of sequential development (where a student is compared to where he might or should be) as much as we stress the particular influence of the student's idiosyncratic psychology (at times psychopathology).

In the small group discussions of this report two major issues were focused upon as areas of controversy. The first was that of assessment, and more than that, of reporting of any kind by the training analyst. The crux of this argument can be condensed in the statement that the opposite of integration in the sense advanced by the commission is not necessarily isolation, but rather insulation, and that if the decision-makers in the progression and education committees are not allowed to be privy to anything learned from the couch, then inevitably they will be forced to do better pedagogical assessments upon the data coming from other sources of knowledge of the candidate. The second major controversial area was that of the proper "therapeutic" as against "didactic" tasks of the analytic supervisor. What are the proper reach of and proper limitations upon the "intervening supervisor"?

As one might expect, no consensus was arrived at in regard to these controversial questions. Some thought that in such discussions the issues get overdichotomized and driven to untenable extremes that few of us would willingly espouse as our own. Others insisted, to paraphrase one discussant, who was paraphrasing *Ecclesiastes,* that there is a time for integration and a time for differentiation. I think all will agree that it is indeed easier to take certain principled stances when dealing with normal-neurotic, average-expectable candidates, and more difficult in the more extreme cases.

So much for our view from within the current tripartite psychoanalytic training model. Assuming that it is functioning at its best, improved in all the ways we can collectively decide upon out of all the recommendations brought before us, however we may modify them —

are we then doing well enough? Or as well as we can? Here is where our central differences emerge, not only in this conference but I am sure equally so in the larger psychoanalytic body. Five of the nine commission reports have essentially been devoted to various aspects of this over-all question. I will therefore discuss the arguments and the recommendations of these five commissions — The Ideal Institute, Age and the Psychoanalytic Career, The Relationship of Psychoanalysis to the Universities, Psychoanalysis and the Allied Disciplines, and Psychoanalytic Research — as a group, in a way that of course will necessarily simplify and focus on their commonalities, but in a way that I hope they each feel recognizes the main emphasis of their own special area of contribution.

The basic argument here was most succinctly stated in the closely reasoned formal discussion by Philip Holzman in the plenary session devoted to the work and the recommendations of the Commission on Psychoanalytic Research. I have already presented much of that argument in my earlier statement of how I saw the main themes of the conference develop and how I would place the various commission reports in relation to those themes. It is again the syncretistic dilemma between our concern with training for a profession and educating for a science. Here I want to outline briefly the range of proposals made by those represented in the five commission reports I am now drawing upon, who essentially advocate the second position that we are not doing well enough and that in fact we are in increasing danger as a science, and thus ultimately as a profession, and who therefore answer in the negative the question — are we doing well enough, or as well as we can?

Although these advocates share a concern to protect what we have that is special and precious in our psycho-

analytic functioning—our practice and our training—
they nevertheless articulate with varying degrees of
urgency the changes they feel we must make to ensure our
own continued future viability and growth both as a
science and profession. These are changes in the direction
of increased academic scholarship in our ranks, cross-
disciplinary fertilization and study and research, and the
attraction of diverse cohorts, not only as future practitioners but as scholarly and academic contributors to
our discipline who are trained or educated in analysis
from within and can work collaboratively with it from
without for our collective over-all scientific growth.

What are their recommendations? Again, I will only
cite the highlights of the proposals made by these several
commissions and will put them roughly into some ascend-
ing order of far-reachingness with those easiest (and
quickest) of possible implementation first.

The first proposal is for a broadening of the mix of
our student body beyond the usual essentially medical
pool, beyond even what we usually understand when we
talk of nonmedical candidates. Actually this was called
for, with some individual variation, by six of the commissions. What is meant is a planned mix of candidates from
all of the helping professions, as well as the admission of
people from the variety of related academic disciplines in
the social and behavioral sciences, and even of administrative and legal practitioners. In addition, the Commission on Social Issues calls for a greater diversity in social
class and ethnic background of our students. The intent
is a broad one—to enhance the base for our growth in
science and scholarship. There are, of course, an inci-
dental obligation and consequence here. The obligation
is the institute's different responsibility in adequately

preparing the student from a nonpatient-oriented or nonmedical background for the assumption of clinical responsibility for patient care. The consequence, a future consequence, of a different mix in the student body is ultimately a different mix in the analytic faculty. This will bring to our faculty ranks the diversity of interests, background, and branches of scholarship, the absence of which we have long deplored as contributing to our at times excessively parochial outlook.

A second, usually linked, proposal is a real commitment within our institutes to a track system that would transcend our usual lock-step curriculum (a holdover from our medical school models and training school heritage), provide varieties of full and partial training, and ultimately lead to individually tailored programs similar to a graduate school model. Let me here state for example the broad three-track system proposed by the Commission on Psychoanalysis and the Allied Disciplines. The first is the clinical track, our familiar and current "full training," to be offered to both those medical and nonmedical candidates who qualify for it through interest, adequate preparation, and adjudged capability, i.e., analyzability and teachability in relation to the demands of analytic work. The second is an academic track with appropriate, individually tailored, selected curriculum—it being an open question as to whether personal analysis or perhaps analytic psychotherapy is required or recommended for all or for selected students in this track. And third is a general-studies curriculum upgraded from our present extension division programs but brought more centrally into the institute for students for whom work with us is more ancillary to other interests than it is for those on the other two tracks.

A somewhat harder over-all proposal to implement is that of a significantly earlier, perhaps even a whole decade earlier start of training for at least a fair number of candidates in our field. This proposal was argued not just by the Commission on Age and the Psychoanalytic Career to whom it was so central but by two other commissions as well. The idea involves all the potentials for the future analytic career, with its increased length and also its probably increased productivity, if we go by all the data on the peaking of creativity in fields as diverse as mathematics and physics on the one hand and lyric poetry on the other, not to mention that the average age of our country's Founding Fathers during their constitutional deliberations was no higher than the current average age of our candidate body. Those who advocate the drastic extension downward of the age of candidate admission are fully aware of the many consequent problems related to the selection process, judgments of analyzability, funding, enforced early career choices and career immobilizations, etc. I will refer to the funding problem later on. In regard to the mobility issue the Commission on Age and the Psychoanalytic Career suggested that institutes might perhaps consider enhancing mobility by giving up one aspect of their individual autonomy so as to make admission interchangeably valid and transfer of those in good standing more automatic.

Perhaps all of the proposals cited thus far lead inevitably to the most sweeping, the grandest, some would say the most grandiose—that of the true university institute, considered in most detail by the Commission on the Ideal Institute. The university institute in this sense does not mean the medical-school-based institute as we now know it (the problems of which were one of the central charges of the Commission on the Relationship of Psychoanalysis to Current Changes in Medical and Psychiatric Education). Rather, it embodies a new concept, one also advanced by knowledgeable people from outside our organizational ranks—that of a full and autonomous university department or even school of psychoanalysis, separate from but with links and traffic with all other related domains: the medical school, the school of social welfare, graduate departments in other behavioral and social sciences, etc. In this school of psychoanalysis there would be a professional school, graduate and undergraduate academic divisions, and psychoanalytic residencies. If successful, such a model might even replace at some point our present "transitional form," the psychoanalytic institute within the medical school department of psychiatry.

Last in this graded catalogue of proposals and propositions are the central concerns of the Commission on Psychoanalytic Research. The obstacles to proper development of research have been recounted many times, as they are in this commission's report. If one, or better, if most of the proposals here advanced were implemented, would we not then have the kind of ambience, role models, open academic climate, commerce with the other sciences concerned with man's behavior, and, very importantly, the kinds of supporting institutional structures in which all the research needs and directions charted for us by this commission could truly flourish? These latter include research studies into psychoanalysis itself, its outcomes, effects, processes, and nature, as well as interface or collaborative study in all the realms of interdisciplinary research vital to us, ranging from child development to psychosomatics, psychoanalytic experimental psychology, and neuro-physiologically linked sleep-dream research.

This is truly an imposing and ambitious array of undertakings. Is any or all of it really within our potential grasp? In this regard, one of the discussants reminded us of the transformation of psychiatry during the fifties into the beginnings of an academic and research-oriented discipline. Of course, then there was the help of a funding climate at NIMH favorable to precisely that development. We do know that movement in these directions would create new problems for us even as it helped solve some of our oldest, most vexing, and most important ones. If we moved (or some of us moved) all the way toward the true university institute, in the sense represented here, there would be the issues of institute autonomy in relation to the university regulatory system; control over admission policy, standard setting, and the training function; internal governance; and the relationship to the Association and its educational regulatory functions as vested in the Board on Professional Standards. But given that these problems seem to have been resolved through some kind of working accommodation in at least some of our present medical-school-based institutes, the members of the five commissions whose reports I am at this point drawing upon are convinced that the advantages to be gained significantly outweigh the dangers, and that further there are very real risks to our science if at least some of us do not take this path in order to create this kind of enterprise for all of us.

There is of course the very major practical problem to which I have already referred, the problem of funding the special high costs of psychoanalytic training both for much younger medical school candidates not yet earning their living and their analytic expenses in their professional practices and for nonpractitioner candidates for whom the estimate average $35,000 cost of completed psychoanalytic training will not be recoverable. The solutions to this problem may have to come from within psychoanalysis itself—arrangements such as local or national loan funds subsidized by psychoanalysts or pooling arrangements for training-analyst fees that keep the burden of special low-fee training analyses from being inequitably borne by those training analysts with nonpractitioner candidates. Perhaps the National Psychoanalytic Research Foundation called for by the Commission on Psychoanalytic Research for fund-raising and disbursing purposes could even have its purview broadened to support not just research but also training for research.

The funding problem aside, why try to embark at all on this uncertain path? Why not be content to stick as long as we can with what we know well and have tested thoroughly? Let me put the question in reverse, as it was brought up at one of the small discussion groups. If the university is truly man's best-devised repository for learning and scholarship in all the areas of human knowledge, and if psychoanalysis is truly a science as we wish and declare it to be, then isn't the burden of proof on the one who says that this branch of science has such a special uniqueness that it alone, of all of them, can flourish best outside the university?

As an addendum to this whole discussion perhaps two caveats should be noted. The first is that analytic concepts may after all not be so fragile, may not need so much special protection for their nurture, but may be sturdy enough to hold their own comfortably in the marketplace of ideas. The second is that with our present organizational scheme of things we have to try to make quite *special* arrangements to nourish our *scientific* enterprise; let us be willing if we are in universities to forge whatever special arrangements we require to maintain the *clinical* enterprise.

So far I have covered the major concerns of only six of the nine preparatory commissions. Fortunately, my fellow panelist, Albert Solnit, undertook in our not very precise division of labor to devote a significant portion of his remarks to the most important report of the Commission on Child Analysis. I want only to include here the statement that that report far transcends the special concerns of child analysis, that it came from a commission composed not just of child analysts but of interested adult analysts as well, and that it has put before us the most far-ranging proposals for a fundamental reconceptualization of our entire formal curriculum as well to a lesser extent of our whole training system—a happy contrast with the otherwise relative lesser interest in curriculum problems and curriculum reform in our ranks. Incidentally, its proposals, like those of the Commission on the Tripartite System of Psychoanalytic Education, were conceptualized within the framework of our current educational structure, seeking within that framework to do it better—much better.

Which leaves me with two commission reports to encompass. This is not meant to downgrade the vital importance of the concerns of the Commission on the Relationship of Psychoanalysis to Current Changes in Medical and Psychiatric Education and the Commission on Social and Community Issues. It is rather that the areas and the reports of these two commissions have not fitted so neatly into my own organizing framework for this presentation. I only wish I could devote at least comparable amounts of time to their vital reports.

Briefly, the commission studying our relationship to changes in medical and psychiatric education took into its purview much more than its original charge, and encompassed not only changes in medical and psychiatric *education* but also in professional *practice,* the conditions of practice, and the whole evolving social-economic-political scene as well as professional scene in relation to what have come to be called health-care delivery systems. This includes the whole world of third-party payers, national health insurance, PSRO's, auditing and peer-review mechanisms, certification, licensure, and recertification procedures; the new world of medical school tracks including behavioral-science tracks, widened electives, and earlier specialization; and also the widening world of psychiatry with its multiplying areas of equally honorable alternative career choices — unlike when most of us here came to psychiatry, when psychoanalysis appealed unchallenged to the best and the brightest.

The answer of the commission and the formal discussants to these pressing issues was, in a word, a call for more *involvement* in *all* these areas, not just of analysts individually but of organized analysis, which has been notoriously reluctant and ambivalent. The fear of "dilution" was discounted because the fear for survival seemed more impressive — that is, the maintenance of analysis as a viable therapeutic and educational activity in a rapidly altering social, professional-practice, and higher-education scene. The discussant told us that otherwise we risk psychoanalysis' becoming an increasingly marginal activity and are in danger of total extrusion from the organized health-care field.

All of this would necessarily link psychoanalysis more closely to the medical and psychiatric mold and raises the logical next question. What then of our distinctness as a profession and a science, not to mention my emphasis in this presentation on the call for our reaching into the university-academic-intellectual world? The answer arrived at in the two small discussion groups in which I heard this question debated was the not facetious one of having it both ways — our typical syncretistic solution. We need to preserve psychoanalysis as a thing in itself, as an independent science and profession, and at the same time to see it as one of the basic sciences of psychiatry, as an applied healing effort, in concert with knowledge from the biological and social realms as well.

And last, but certainly not least, is the message from the Commission on the Relationship of Psychoanalysis to Social and Community Issues. The premise is briefly that analysts and analysis have a responsibility that goes beyond the clinical and therapeutic — to social and community affairs. As *individuals* we discharge it varyingly, perhaps in an even more widespread way than is usually acknowledged. *Institutionally,* however, we are deficient both in our social-directed activities and in our related teaching endeavors. The commission report and the accompanying discussions have specified some of these deficiencies as follows: (1) We are often inept in our understanding of our own social structure and operations and how these hinder knowledgeable articulation with social issues outside that impinge upon us and to which we should contribute; (2) we are often inept in our relation at the individual therapeutic level to persons from a different social class or ethnic background than our own; and (3) we are insufficient in our recruitment, in the enlargement of our own ranks with the diversities that make up our societal structure, the various minority groups.

The recommendations offered are geared to overcoming these deficiencies. They range from a different kind of recruitment net designed to broaden our standards without lowering them (and this report specifically calls for the broadening of the candidate mix to include those from minorities and from other than middle-class backgrounds), to wholly new institutional arrangements either within or alongside our training centers, such as the already existing Chicago Center for Psychosocial Studies mentioned by the discussant or the National Foundation for Psychoanalytic Psychosocial Studies called for by the commission report. The involvement with social and community issues in ways that truly deploy our expertise can range from low-fee clinics, through teacher education programs, child-care worker programs, child-therapy and psychotherapy training programs, to extension courses reaching into the whole array of health, education, and welfare agencies and disciplines.

And lastly, as one of the discussion groups pointed out, a warning about the limits of our knowledge in this easily seductive area. Our social applications are best and easiest in the child-development, child-care, and child-rearing area. They are much more difficult—that is, our own established knowledge base is much much less—in such areas as drug addiction and criminal behavior, not to speak on the global level of poverty and war/peace issues. But perhaps as consultants in varieties of arenas we are equipped (better equipped than others?) to be psychologically sophisticated learners who can work in concert with others with related areas of expertise. And maybe we will be willing to bring what we learn back into our institute teaching structure.

So much for a kaleidoscopic and nonetheless quite incomplete survey of some of the exciting thinking that COPER, both in the hard work of the various preparatory commissions and in the conference itself, has brought forth. It is an accomplishment of which I think we can all be proud. These are not laurels, however, on which we can rest. Rather, we are at the point at which we need to look ahead to the even more arduous tasks of carefully weighing all these recommendations, shaping them in terms of urgency of priorities and feasibility of timetables, and working to implement them insofar as we can in our own professional lives through our various institutional forms, our institutes and our societies locally, the Association nationally, as well as in the wider world in which we move and have influence—medical schools, universities, the over-all intellectual and sociopolitical scenes. I trust that the willing excitement with which we have all come thus far down the road bespeaks an equal willingness to work into that future.

A Survey of Psychoanalytic Education in 1971: A Report for the Ad Hoc Committee on Planning for National Conference on Psychoanalytic Education and Research of the American Psychoanalytic Association

Philip S. Holzman, Ph.D., Chairman
Ernest A. Haggard, Ph.D.
George H. Pollock, M.D.
Kenneth R. Cecil, Research Assistant

A Survey of Psychoanalytic Education in 1971: A Report for the Ad Hoc Committee on Planning for National Conference on Psychoanalytic Education and Research of the American Psychoanalytic Association

In 1972 the Committee on Psychoanalytic Education and Research appointed a subcommittee to update, as quickly as possible, much of the information contained in the Lewin and Ross study of psychoanalytic education, which was completed in 1960, but which contained data for the year 1958. The committee began its work in the spring of 1972. Three questionnaires were sent out to local institutes. These forms requested information similar to that contained in a large segment of the Lewin and Ross study in order to allow COPER to scrutinize psychoanalytic education with some recent data in hand. The questionnaires were sent in June, 1972 to the twenty psychoanalytic institutes and one training center. The first questionnaire was to be completed by each matriculated student. The second questionnaire was to be completed by the institutes' training and supervising analysts. The third questionnaire, to be completed by the institute secretary, requested information about applications for training and their disposition from 1958 to 1971. It is well known that getting 100 per cent return is an extremely difficult task in any survey, unless there are site visits to obtain the data, as in the Lewin and Ross study. It took more than one year to receive a sufficient number of returns to comprise a representative sample of institutes, analysts, and students. The data are as complete as we could manage, and are probably sufficient for arriving at reasonable answers to the questions posed. Since the figures in the present study, unlike those in the Lewin and Ross study, do not represent a complete population, percentages rather than absolute numbers will enable the reader to obtain a more representative picture of the 1971 data.

THE PSYCHOANALYTIC INSTITUTE

INSTITUTES APPROVED BY THE ASSOCIATION IN 1971

The American Psychoanalytic Association in 1971 officially approved twenty psychoanalytic institutes and societies and one training center. Those approved since 1958 are indicated by an asterisk. No comparisons of course can be made between 1958 and 1971 for them.

INSTITUTES

Baltimore-District of Columbia Institute for Psychoanalysis
Boston Psychoanalytic Society and Institute

Chicago Institute for Psychoanalysis
Cleveland Psychoanalytic Institute*
Columbia University Psychoanalytic Clinic for Training
and Research
Denver Institute for Psychoanalysis*
Division of Psychoanalytic Education, State University of
New York
Institute of the Philadelphia Association for Psychoanalysis
Los Angeles Psychoanalytic Society and Institute
Michigan Psychoanalytic Institute
New Orleans Psychoanalytic Institute*
New York Psychoanalytic Institute
Philadelphia Psychoanalytic Institute
Pittsburgh Psychoanalytic Institute*
San Francisco Psychoanalytic Institute
Seattle Psychoanalytic Institute*
Southern California Psychoanalytic Institute
Topeka Institute for Psychoanalysis
Washington Psychoanalytic Institute
Western New England Institute for Psychoanalysis

TRAINING CENTER

University of North Carolina-Duke University Psychoanalytic Training Program

NUMBER OF APPLICATIONS REQUESTED AND PERCENTAGE APPLYING

The number of applications requested yearly and the percentage applying were relatively consistent for the fourteen-year period within each particular institute, although there were a few variations from this. All the students who requested applications from Denver, Philadelphia Psychoanalytic, and UNC-Duke applied, while approximately 25 per cent did so at Washington. The percentage of those who actually apply to institutes tends to remain stable within institutes, but it varies considerably between institutes.

APPLICATIONS AND THEIR DISPOSITION

Once an application is received by the institute, it can be: (1) accepted—the applicant is allowed to train at the institute; (2) rejected—the applicant has not met certain standards required for admittance by the institute; (3) deferred—the applicant will be reconsidered at some later date; (4) withdrawn—the applicant has changed his or her mind and wishes to remove the application from consideration. The number of applications has remained relatively constant since 1959. The number of acceptances, however, after fluctuating only minimally around the 50 per cent point, increased to 60 per cent in 1971-1972. The number of deferrals and withdrawals is so small that any generalizations concerning trends within these groups would not be valid.

The comparison of the disposition of applications by institute presents certain striking features: (1) the large number of applications by Boston, Chicago, New York, and Washington; (2) the relatively low acceptance rate at New York and Michigan, and high acceptance rate at Baltimore-D.C., Philadelphia Psychoanalytic, and UNC-Duke.

Some institutes such as Baltimore-D.C., New York, Philadelphia Psychoanalytic, and San Francisco do not defer applications, while others such as Pittsburgh,

Seattle, and UNC-Duke do so infrequently. Only Chicago and Washington held over applications with any degree of regularity. The number of withdrawn applications is small, with the percentage withdrawn exceeding five per cent only at Michigan. Thus, once an applicant decides to apply, there are rarely changes in that decision. The differences among institutes in number of accepted applicants probably reflects the size of the institute and the size of the pool of potential students; the larger the urban-academic center, the larger the number of applicants.

In general, the number of admissions to the individual institutes has not increased from 1958 to 1971, but rather the observation of Lewin and Ross for the period from 1944 to 1957 is probably also valid for 1958-1971 — that a good part of the increase in the number of students has been due to the establishment of new institutes. It should also be pointed out that the number of admissions varies from year to year within each institute. This is a reflection of changes in the personnel and philosophy of the evaluative selection process during the year.

Although there is considerable variation from year to year and among institutes, the trend is for more students to be graduated in recent years. From 1958 to 1964 the mean total number of annual graduates for all institutes was 63, compared with 76 for the years 1965 to 1971.

TRAINING AND SUPERVISING ANALYSTS

NUMBER

Of twelve institutes for which data allow comparison all except Baltimore had more analysts in these categories in

1971 than in 1958. Cleveland and San Francisco show an increase of 100 per cent, Southern California 130 per cent, Los Angeles 176 per cent, and Seattle 300 per cent.

AFFILIATION WITH TWO OR MORE INSTITUTES

Thirty-one analysts have joint appointments at two institutes and two have appointments at three institutes. The Chicago and Denver Institutes have seven analysts with appointments at both, while the Washington Institute and UNC-Duke Training Program have five analysts involved with both.

AGE

The mean age of all training and supervising analysts in 1958 was 54.7 and in 1971, 56.8. This difference in the analysts' ages represents a statistically significant increase ($p < .01$). (The median age was 54 years of age in 1958 and 55.25 years in 1971, a difference of 1.25 years.) There were five analysts over 79 years of age in 1958. The presence of five octogenarians in 1971 and a general trend toward fewer analysts under the age of 50 account for the increase in training and supervising analysts' ages from 1958 to 1971.

Training and supervising analysts were being appointed at a somewhat later age in 1971 than they were in 1958. In only three institutes was the mean age of training and supervising analysts lower in 1971 than it was in 1958: Cleveland, Columbia, and Topeka. However, the small number of training and supervising analysts in Cleveland and Topeka would suggest that this trend has only chance significance.

Age at Graduation from Psychoanalytic Institute

The mean age at which training and supervising analysts surveyed in 1971 graduated from a psychoanalytic institute was 37.7. There is little variation over the country in the age at which future training and supervising analysts complete their psychoanalytic training. It is interesting to note, however, that the age at graduation of future training and supervising analysts is, on the average, about two years younger than the age of the aggregate of students.

Age on Appointment to Psychoanalytic Institutes

The national mean age on appointment was 44.5 in 1958 and 46.0 in 1971. Lewin and Ross suggested that there might be a tendency for the age on appointment of training and supervising analyst to become older since students were graduating from the psychoanalytic institute at an older age. The data, however, suggest that there is no systematic trend toward an older age at graduation. Institutes are appointing somewhat older training and supervising analysts in 1971 than they were in 1958.

In comparing the ages on appointment in 1958 and 1971, the mean age seems to have remained relatively stable within institutes. Exceptions to this were an increase from 40.5 to 45.8 at Cleveland, a decrease from 43.4 to 40.1 at Southern California, and an increase from 40.3 to 47.3 at Western New England.

The average number of years between graduation from a psychoanalytic institute and appointment as a training and supervising analyst is 8.3.

THE TRAINING ANALYST:
TIME SPENT AS DIDACTIC ANALYST

The training analysts at the larger institutes (e.g., Chicago, New York, Washington) work as such fewer hours per week than those at the smaller institutes. This reflects faculty-student ratios: the larger the faculty, the fewer hours each training and supervising analyst is required to devote to didactic work. Interestingly, 114 training and supervising analysts record themselves as giving no hours per week to training analysis and almost all institutes have at least one such analyst.

In 1971 more training analysts worked fewer hours per week and fewer worked at the largest number of hours per week than in 1958. This trend might be a reflection of the increased number of training and supervising analysts in 1971.

Both the mean number of hours worked per week and the mean number of students per analyst were significantly less in 1971 than in 1958. The national mean number of hours per week spent conducting training analyses was 10.0 hours in 1958 and 6.9 hours in 1971. The mean number of students in analysis with each training analyst was 2.4 in 1958 and 1.5 in 1971. In addition, there was much variation among institutes in work loads, the analysts at the larger institutes usually having lighter loads. The one exception is Baltimore, where work loads seem to have almost doubled since 1958.

SUPERVISION

Of the time the psychoanalytic student spends in training about 35 per cent is spent with a supervisor.

HOURS PER WEEK SUPERVISING

Of the supervising analysts 24.5 per cent supervise one to four hours per month, 26.9 per cent five to eight hours per month, 19.4 per cent nine to twelve hours per month, 12.8 per cent thirteen to sixteen hours per month, and 8.1 per cent work more than twenty hours per month. Over 50 per cent of the active training and supervising analysts spend no more than eight hours per month in supervising students. Only about eight per cent devote more than twenty hours per month (or about five hours per week) to supervision.

A comparison was made between the supervision work loads of training analysts in 1958 and 1971. As was the case with the training analysis, there was a larger percentage of analysts supervising at lower rates in 1971 than there was in 1958. This may reflect more favorable faculty-student ratios, which would spread the supervisory load over more supervisors. Indeed, the faculty-student ratio changed from 6.9 in 1958 to 4.1 in 1971.

The average number of hours worked per month as a supervisor was 13.4 in 1958 and 8.6 in 1971. All of the institutes from 1958 to 1971 show a decrease in hours supervising analysts worked per month, except for Baltimore. Again, this reflects the increased number of supervisors available.

The average number of students assigned to each analyst was 2.7 in 1971. The supervisors at the smaller institutes generally supervised more students: Cleveland 4.0, Pittsburgh 5.6, Western New England, 4.2, and UNC-Duke 5.4. Comparable figures for 1958 are not available.

AGE OF SUPERVISING ANALYSTS WORKING
AT DIFFERENT RATES

No significant correlations were found between the number of hours supervising and the analyst's age in either 1958 or 1971. Older and younger supervisors work at supervision the same number of hours per month.

OTHER RESPONSIBILITIES

Besides being involved in the training and supervision of psychoanalytic students the analyst often teaches formal courses at the psychoanalytic institute, has an established private practice, or is involved in other activities such as committee work, private consulting, research, or university teaching.

TRAINING ANALYSTS WHO TEACH AND THEIR TEACHING LOAD

In 1971, 80 per cent of the analysts taught on the average of 5.2 hours per month. Generally a higher percentage of the available analysts taught more hours at the smaller institutes. No data for 1958 were available.

TIME SPENT IN PRIVATE PRACTICE AND OTHER ACTIVITIES

The average number of hours the working and supervising analyst spent in private practice was 30.5 hours per week. Many training analysts included in their private-practice hours time spent in training analysis. If the mean number of of hours in private practice did not include institute activities, the mean would probably be about 24 hours per week. The mean number of hours per week spent on other activities was 6.4. This did not vary much among institutes.

THE STUDENT

NUMBER

Unlike the training and supervising analyst population, there is no uniform trend over the institutes for an increase in the number of students enrolled in 1971. There were substantial changes in the number enrolled in some institutes: Baltimore ($+69$ per cent), Philadelphia Society (-51 per cent), and Southern California ($+633$ per cent). These changes reflect a significant ($p < .01$) shift in the number of students enrolled at these institutes from 1958 to 1971. But the increase in the total number of psychoanalytic students in training principally reflects the opening of new institutes; already established institutes tended to remain relatively constant in their enrollment.

Also noteworthy is the reduction of the analyst-student ratio in all instances (where sufficient data were available) except at Baltimore and Southern California. The mean ratio changed from 1:3.55 in 1958 to 1:1.49 in 1971.

SEX

According to the survey 86 per cent of the students sampled in 1971 were male and fourteen per cent female. This reflects the fact that there were five per cent more females enrolled in the institutes in 1971 than in 1958. Although women still make up a small percentage of the total number of psychoanalytic students, the number of women enrolled in psychoanalytic institutes is quite high compared to the number of women in some selected medical specialties. For example, on December 30, 1971 women physicians accounted for 7.1 per cent of all active M.D.s. Only pediatrics (nineteen per cent) and general medical specialties (25 per cent) claimed more women physicians than psychiatry (fourteen per cent including child psychiatry). Psychoanalysis thus attracts more women than most other medical specialties.

RACE AND RELIGIOUS AFFILIATION

The racial distribution is: 97.7 per cent Caucasian, 1.4 per cent Negro, and .9 per cent Oriental. The distribution of religious affiliation is: 40.7 per cent Jewish; 20.8 per cent Protestant; 5.9 per cent Catholic; 2.0 per cent other; 30.5 per cent none. We could not determine a comparison with other medical specialties since information about race and religion was not available.

AGE ON ADMISSION TO INSTITUTE

The national mean age on admission to the psychoanalytic institute for 136 students enrolled in 1958 was 32.1. This group was compared with the 855 students in our survey whose mean age on admission was 32.8. The difference between the two years was not statistically significant, nor was there a significant difference among the institutes.

AGE ON GRADUATION FROM INSTITUTE

No apparent trends are evidenced in examination of the data for this fourteen-year span of time. The mean age on graduation ranges from 39.8 in 1964 to 41.6 in 1970.

Medical School Education

M.D. degrees were received from 102 American and Canadian schools and 40 universities in Europe, Asia, Africa, New Zealand, and Latin America. As in 1958, Harvard graduated the most students (6.1 per cent).

Previous Training

In 1958, 97.1 per cent and in 1971, 95.5 per cent of all analytic students had M.D.s. In 1971 as in 1958 the largest number of students without M.D.s had Ph.D.s in psychology. In 1971, there were twenty from psychology; two each from history and education; one each from anthropology, sociology, social work, speech pathology, English literature, divinity, and law; three students had less than the Ph.D. degree.

Previous Applications

The majority of students applied only once to the institute at which they are enrolled. However, 11.2 per cent of all applicants were admitted after having been refused once, and 20.7 per cent had applied to other institutes.

Activities at and After Time of Admission

Upon entering the institute the student is ordinarily either a resident in psychiatric training or is further along professionally and holds a staff position at either a hospital or university. There is also the probability that the student has established a private practice and devotes at least part of his or her time to it.

BOARD CERTIFICATION

Approximately one half of the students (46 per cent) were certified by the American Board of Psychiatry or an equivalent board. New Orleans has the most students certified (100 per cent) and Columbia the fewest (28 per cent).

WAITING PERIODS FOR BEGINNING ANALYSIS

Approximately one half (56.9 per cent) of all students surveyed had begun training analysis three months after they were accepted; 18.2 per cent, however, waited four to six months, 10 per cent waited seven to nine months, 6 per cent waited ten to twelve months, and 8.9 per cent waited over twelve months. The unavailability of the analyst was the reason for the delay 49.4 per cent of the time, the unavailability of the student 38.2 per cent of the time, administrative reasons 9.2 per cent of the time, and a combination of personal reasons with the unavailability of the analyst 3.2 per cent of the time.

LENGTH AND COST OF TRAINING ANALYSIS

The national mean for number of hours to complete analysis was 772.6 (48.2 months). The didactic analysis took the most hours to complete at the Cleveland Institute (mean: 1386 hours) and was most quickly completed at the UNC-Duke Training Center (mean: 506.6 hours). The average number of hours per week spent in training analysis per active student was 4.2 in 1958 and 4.4 in 1971.

The mean fee per hour of analysis was $19.51 in 1958 and $29.48 in 1971. The fee paid in 1971 was significantly higher ($p < .01$) at all institutes and training centers in 1971. In 1958 Cleveland's average fee per hour was the lowest ($15.00) and Western New England's fee was the highest ($25.00). In 1971, Los Angeles had the highest mean fee ($36.13) and Topeka the lowest ($19.52).

PREVIOUS ANALYTIC TREATMENT

The student entering the institute is likely to have experienced some form of psychotherapy. Of those surveyed 42 per cent had been psychoanalyzed, 56 per cent of that total by a training analyst, 42.3 per cent by a nontraining analyst, and 1.7 per cent by both training and nontraining analysts. Of the 845 surveyed 34.3 per cent had also been in psychotherapy other than psychoanalysis. Thus, two out of five students had sought analytic treatment and over 75 per cent had been in some kind of psychotherapy prior to applying to the institute.

SUPERVISED ANALYSES

SELECTION OF PATIENTS

The majority (62 per cent) of the total number of students enrolled in institutes in 1971 had their patients for supervised analysis selected by either their supervisor or the institute. However, at Baltimore, Boston, Chicago, Columbia, Denver, Michigan, and New York students determined the selection of patients most of the time. Much of the selection process is done by the student in consultation with either a supervisor or an institute committee.

ASSIGNMENT OF SUPERVISORS

The majority (53.1 per cent) of students chose their own supervisors. The institutes allowing students to choose their own supervisors were: Baltimore, Boston, Los Angeles, Philadelphia Psychoanalytic, Philadelphia Society, Pittsburgh, San Francisco, Southern California, Washington, and UNC-Duke.

FREQUENCY OF SUPERVISION

The national mean in 1958 was 6.1 hours per month and in 1971 was 6.3 hours per month, but some institutes showed a considerable difference between the mean number of hours of supervision per student in these two years (Columbia, New Orleans, Philadelphia Psychoanalytic, Philadelphia Society, and San Francisco). The comparative figures are: Columbia, from 5.0 to 7.3 hours per month; New Orleans, from 10.5 to 4.1 hours per month; Philadelphia Psychoanalytic, from 8.8 to 6.4 hours per month; Philadelphia Society, from 12.7 to 8.1 hours per month; San Francisco, from 5.6 to 8.1 hours per month.

COST OF SUPERVISION

The national mean fee per hour of supervision in 1971 was $23.13. The comparatively low fees at some of the institutes can be explained by the fact that the cost of a student's supervision is partially covered by the tuition fee at these schools. The national mean would be significantly higher if the supervision covered by tuition were excluded.

COST TO PATIENTS

The distribution of fees paid by patients in supervised analysis for the years 1958 and 1971 shows a significant difference ($p < .01$) between the fees paid for the two years. In 1958, 76 per cent of the patients paid less than $20.00, while in 1971 only 60 per cent paid less than $20.00. In 1958, 41 per cent of patients paid less than $15.00, while in 1971, 48 per cent paid less than $15.00. In 1958, 27 per cent of patients paid less than $10.00, while in 1971, 33 per cent paid less than $10.00.

DISPOSITION OF FEES

Each institute has its own policy concerning the distribution of the fees received from patients in supervised analysis. The national totals were 64.5 per cent kept by the student, 33.3 per cent kept by the institute, and 2.2 per cent divided between the student and the institute. There is no information on whether these figures represent distribution of fees for the first, second, third, or fourth supervised case.

INCOMES OF PATIENTS

The common belief is that only the rich receive the benefits of psychoanalysis. In supervised analysis this does not seem to be the case. Approximately 62 per cent of the students' supervised patients surveyed in 1971 earned less than $15,000 per year. The distribution of patients' income levels for 1958 and 1971 was very similar. Income refers to the income of the person who paid for the treatment, not necessarily the patient's personal income. One hundred thirteen persons (7.56 per cent of the total number) seen in supervised analysis in 1971 were patients whose parents paid their fees. Health insurance often covered a patient's analytic fees.

Cost of Didactic Courses

Besides paying for training analysis and supervision the student pays for the seminar courses in the curriculum. For four years of courses the most expensive institute was Columbia (mean: $2,681 per year) and the least expensive Topeka (mean: $304 per year). The differences in the cost of tuition at the different institutes may be largely explained by the extent to which the cost of supervision and training analysis is covered in the tuition fee.

Sources of Funds for Education

The psychoanalytic student, generally speaking, pays for the analytic education from personal income and savings and only to a very small extent receives financial assistance from loans, family members, grants, and fellowships. The sources of support were similar for 1958 and 1971. The difference between the number entirely and partly supported by their own work is probably an artifact of the 1971 survey technique where students' responses often were not as specific as would have been desirable.

Child-Analysis Training and Research Students

In 1971 approximately 13 per cent of all students surveyed were training to work with children. The individual institutes' figures ranged from 41.9 per cent at Philadelphia Psychoanalytic to none at Cleveland and New

Orleans. In 1971, 35 students had been accepted for training as research students; twelve of those accepted were currently doing clinical psychoanalytic work as part of their research training.

SUMMARY OF TRENDS

Between 1958 and 1971 six institutes and one training center were approved by the Association. These new facilities accounted for the principal increase in the number of students in training. The number of training and supervising analysts, however, increased significantly in all institutes, except in the Baltimore Institute. This increase permitted a reduction in the time each training and supervising analyst devoted to both didactic psycho-analysis and to supervision. The ratio of training and supervising analyst to students changed significantly in a favorable direction as a result of the increase in training and supervising analysts. From 1958 to 1971 the mean ages of the training and supervising analysts increased, perhaps reflecting a tendency in 1971 for institutes to appoint training analysts at a somewhat later age.

The practice of psychoanalysis, at least as it is reflected in the didactic analysis, has not changed from 1958. Students enter analysis at about 32 years of age. Psychoanalysis lasts almost 800 hours and takes about four years. There is a barely perceptible increase in non-M.D. students in 1971. More women entered psycho-analysis in 1971 than in 1958. The cost of psychoan-alytic training is expensive: approximately $24,000 for the didactic analysis plus about $2,000 for formal course-work and another $5,000 for supervision, bringing the total amount to about $31,000.

Postconference Problems and Prospects

STANLEY GOODMAN, M.D.

This final chapter presents another individual response to the conference, in this instance written several months after the event, with special emphasis on certain underlying themes and their possible implications as subjects for further study and future action.

The conference was a success, not because it offered definitive solutions to the problems of psychoanalytic education and research, but because it contributed significantly to the better definition of those problems and clarified the relationship among them. Increased awareness of the way in which most conference topics were closely interdependent made the participants less susceptible to proposals that were unrealistic insofar as they focused on artificially isolated objectives. The crucial and primary issues requiring immediate attention were more clearly distinguished from the relevant but

distracting secondary issues. The conference also succeeded in providing definite indications and even specific
suggestions for the continuing intensive postconference
study of the many related aspects of psychoanalytic
education and research.

The convergence of most conference topics is well
demonstrated by even a very brief review of several
difficult problems deriving from the economics of psychoanalysis, an area of concern that obviously contributed importantly to the organizational motivation for
the conference. Although not an explicit assignment of
any preparatory commission, almost every one of them
gave considerable attention to the pervasive influence on
psychoanalysis of economic factors. It became quite clear
that the presence or absence of adequate and dependable
financial support for psychoanalytic institutes would
continue to have an important effect on the development
of psychoanalysis. The full-time institute was understood
to be quite impossible without funds for teachers and at
least partial support for full-time students. Analytic
students and teachers would not be freed from the necessity of devoting almost all of their time and energy to
private clinical practice unless alternative sources of
support for their educational and research activity could
be found. Even if for no other reason, students have been
drawn almost exclusively from among physicians planning to engage in private clinical practice because this
group has been practically alone in its ability to afford
the cost of training. The possible admission of qualified
younger or nonmedical students, as recommended by
several commissions, would depend crucially on the
question of financial support even after other aspects of
admission philosophy or policy were resolved. The

economics of psychoanalytic private practice is itself quite problematic at present. The usual private-fee structure markedly restricts the availability of appropriate psychoanalytic treatment for many potential patients and obviously is an important element in reducing the availability of analyzable patients, particularly for the younger analysts. The prospect of adequate coverage for psychoanalysis by health insurance plans seems quite doubtful, although not altogether impossible. The overall effect of these factors has been a regrettably diminished opportunity for an ample clinical practice of analysis by individual analysts.

The sharp delineation by the conference of several aspects of the relationship of psychoanalysis to other educational structures brought into focus many indications that the structure of the psychoanalytic institute is itself a relevant variable in the situation, affecting and affected by all the other factors. The several attempts to define the optimal relation of psychoanalysis and psychoanalytic education to medicine, psychiatry, and the university all raised the question, fortunately without encouraging an immediate facile answer, whether the institute's usual present form was the most suitable one for reaching the objectives collectively defined as desirable.

Why have so many psychoanalysts devoted so much time and effort to transmitting, as effectively as possible, what they have learned from their teachers and their own experience to new generations of colleagues? Everything reported from the conference—the intense concern with excellence in teaching, clinical competence, scientific as well as professional development, interdisciplinary studies, present and possible relationships with medicine, psychiatry, and the university—reflects the developmental position of psychoanalysis as a relatively young scientific enterprise, still in the process of achieving social definition and social acceptance. Of course, teachers in all areas of human knowledge have essentially the same general pedagogic intentions; however, the special and possibly unique developmental problems of psychoanalysis and psychoanalytic education have led psychoanalysts to express special concerns in their role as teachers.

Freud's discoveries stimulated a new approach to the systematic study of human behavior. Psychoanalysis was constituted by and remains a radical theory of mental life, subject to modification and elaboration by additional data, and a radical method of research in psychology, which is also applicable as a method of treatment. The psychoanalytic theory of the mind was not widely accepted when it was introduced by Freud, and acceptance of its basic concepts is still mixed and uncertain today. The undeniably profound cultural impact of psychoanalytic ideas probably is due more to the work of creative artistic interpreters than to direct efforts at popular education by psychoanalysts themselves. The negative and hostile response to the presentation of such a seemingly unflattering and even anxiety-provoking view of the human mind was generally, though not entirely, shared by the academic world and the medical profession, including psychiatrists. Physicians thus generally did not, and still do not, enthusiastically welcome psychoanalysis as a radical method of psychotherapy. In fact, they still seem to demonstrate strong reservations even toward nonanalytic psychiatry, except insofar as it may be called upon for diagnostic, custodial, or psychopharmacological expertise. Similarly, most psychologists in the universities have not welcomed or appreciated the investigative research potential of the psychoanalytic method, and they have rarely invited psychoanalysts to join them as scientific colleagues in the university. It is true, however, that even if they had sought to do so, they might not have found many analysts willing to join them there, except within the medical school.

The complex cultural and professional responses to psychoanalysis have, however, often included the un-acknowledged utilization or exploitation of fragmented and simplified aspects of psychoanalysis, including a multitude of psychological theories, the core of modern dynamic psychiatry, uncountable popular but transient systems of manipulative psychotherapy, and a variety of questionable psychological research strategems.

Freud was a physician, and in spite of the strong opposition within his profession and in the university, there was enough acceptance in the larger intellectual world for him and others who joined him to support themselves in private clinical practice by the therapeutic application of the psychoanalytic investigative method. Particularly in the United States, psychoanalysts have attempted to find their professional home within medi-cine and psychiatry, even though as a group they have not been enthusiastically invited or entirely comfortable there. It should be noted, however, that in the past 25 years a significant number, at times a majority, of departments of psychiatry have been chaired by psycho-analysts; that, however, does not invalidate the over-all view just expressed.

The medical and psychiatric orientation has been adopted for a variety of reasons, such as the more effec-tive organized control of individual entry into the pro-fession, the social prestige of medicine, and the advantageous economic factors. Nevertheless, there are now equally cogent reasons to study carefully the present effect and implications for the future of this self-definition as a primarily medical discipline.

These observations and speculations bear directly on why psychoanalysts are often particularly concerned about tendencies toward dilution, distortion, and neglect of the core of psychoanalytic theory, research, and therapy by new generations of psychoanalytic students as well as by psychiatrists, the medical profession, and the academic world. Since there has been so much interest in simplified or distorted elements of psychoanalysis, it has seemed extremely important to many psychoanalysts that the essential body of psychoanalytic knowledge should be clearly transmitted in all its complexity to serious and qualified students who would accept the responsibility not just to learn and apply the knowledge already gained, but to expand that knowledge through continuing study and painstaking research.

The understandable tendency toward protective concern for a scientific and professional discipline that has evoked a special social response does, however, create the need for a sustained vigilance against undue rigidity, excessive conservatism, and lack of adequate self-criticism. To the extent that overprotectiveness becomes an influential motivation, most criticism is apt to be too quickly dismissed as unreasonable hostility rather than accepted as valid reservation or relevant and appropriate questioning. In this way, open discourse with related fields of inquiry is not sought but rather avoided and is experienced as threatening rather than challenging. It must be apparent to all that such an attitude, whenever it exists, damages the development of a science much more decisively than would the action of any external opposition.

The conference discussion was, at almost every moment, struggling to balance the interplay of several tendencies: the wish for growth, the urge for constructive change, respect for the principle of flexibility, the wish to conserve the core, the need to achieve and preserve high scientific and professional standards, and the opposition to change for the sake of change. Most participants did not see loyalty to the pioneers in psychoanalysis in the rigid adherence to particular views, but rather in the continuing search for valid elaboration, necessary correction, and responsible application of psychoanalytic knowledge.

Assessment was, in a sense, the over-all theme of the conference and it was the explicit focus of attention in the discussion of the tripartite system of psychoanalytic education. Every aspect of the educational process—the integration of its major components, the inclusion of particular subject matter, proper methods of teaching, optimal conditions of learning, and the quality of educational results—was subject to close scrutiny for any deficiencies due to lack of precise assessment or to incomplete integration.

There was certainly no difference of opinion as to the obvious desirability of careful assessment and thorough tripartite educational integration; the discussion centered entirely on the appropriate and available methods for accomplishing this more effectively. The already much discussed but as yet insufficiently resolved question of the training analyst's evaluative reports to the institute's education committee received considerable further attention. The pros and cons of reporting and nonreporting by the training analyst were ably presented and argued at the conference, as they have been in the literature in recent years. It has been generally acknowledged that there are relevant and valid analytic and educational considerations on both sides of this discussion. Perhaps it would be more conducive to the resolution of the issue if the discussion now moved from a confrontation between the principle of confidentiality and that of assessment to a more detailed investigation of what is essential and specifically germane to appropriate respect for both principles in the actual context of analytic training. It should be possible to define much more clearly than has been done so far the requirements and the limits, if any, of confidentiality in the training analysis. It should also be possible to specify the particular kind of data or assessment that could come from the training analyst, and demonstrate convincingly its value and necessity for important educational decisions about the student. Only then will it be possible to achieve a more meaningful and useful appraisal of the consequences of reporting and nonreporting to essential confidentiality, the analytic therapeutic goal, and the educational process. It would also be desirable, in the interest of attaining precision of communication while protecting confidentiality, to evolve a relatively standard language of reporting that is both concise and adequately descriptive. Reports in such a language would be much more helpful to evaluative decisions than impressionistic comments that may say too little that is useful while coming close to revealing too much that should remain private.

The continued study and clarification of the analytic as well as educational implications of reporting by the training analyst should prove extremely valuable; it is clearly one of the topics that deserves, and will undoubtedly receive, serious and extended postconference attention. Every training analyst is well aware that the issue of reporting is only one of several special problems that arise in the analysis of those persons who have a professional as well as therapeutic objective. It is a reasonable expectation that such problems would occur whether or not the analysis were conducted by a designated training analyst in an organized educational context that included evaluative reports by the analyst. Whatever the optimal administrative arrangements that can be effected, it is the systematic exploration and resolution of these issues by analytic means within the analysis that is the crucial and, indeed, the most practical solution.

Another postconference project of obvious merit involves the development of an appropriate language and assessment guidelines for the reports of supervising analysts and seminar instructors. Although work has already been done in this area, much still remains to be done.

The discussion of the preparatory commission report on child analysis provided the stimulation for postconference study of at least three topics: the useful integration of the concepts and data designated as a developmental approach and orientation; the construction of an optimal common core curriculum for the education of future adult and child analysts; and the proper relation of special training for child analysis to the so-called regular program of psychoanalytic education.

The preparatory commission proposed that accumulating observational and clinical data require a newly defined approach to the psychoanalytic study of the mind. This is a most important suggestion because of both its theoretical and clinical implications. Confirmed knowledge of early or late development, based on sound observations, has always been valued and eventually incorporated into psychoanalytic theory and practice; however, the necessity for introducing what was referred to as a new approach demands a much more detailed substantiation of its conceptual necessity and advantage than was offered in the commission's presentation. The much needed further discussion of the issue requires that both the advocates and the critics review the body of existing analytic theory with extreme critical rigor. At this point, the clarification of what is new in the developmental approach and orientation constitutes an interesting challenge for many analysts. Whether the suggested approach will prove to be a valid and valuable contribution to psychoanalytic theory can be determined only after much further consideration. The clinical importance of the approach as a new clarifying perspective in the psychoanalytic treatment of a variety of psychological problems also remains to be demonstrated. It must be emphasized that the recognition of the unquestioned value to psychoanalysis of developmental data and the potential value of certain developmental concepts are quite independent of an eventual judgment of the value of the developmental approach as a new organizing concept distinguished from the genetic point of view.

The project of constructing an integrated core curriculum incorporating recent developmental data will certainly continue to occupy the institutes' attention. A national workshop on the topic is already at work under the sponsorship of the Child Analysis Committee of the Board on Professional Standards.

How much should the training of future child and

adult analysts differ after they have completed the shared core curriculum? Should separate tracks, if there are to be such, start early or late in their studies? It would be well to keep in mind that premature specialization in psychoanalytic education could prove limiting to future competence in the field of specialization, whether in adult analysis, child analysis, research, or application to related areas of inquiry. There are of course practical limits to the length and comprehensiveness of training, just as there are individual variations in talent or interest for one or another aspect of analysis. Nevertheless, it would be difficult to defend the rationale of a system of professional psychoanalytic education in which at least some level of experience or basic competence had not also been attained in fields other than the one of primary interest. It would be just as regrettable if a child analyst had never analyzed an adult, as it is that many present adult analysts have had no experience analyzing a child. Similarly, many analysts seriously doubt that significant research using psychoanalytic theory can be accomplished without adequate clinical experience and competence. These observations are offered with due regard for the actual and possible exceptions to all such generalizations. There have been a number of notably competent and creative analysts whose training and experience was one-sided or limited by the usual criteria. However, as in any organized effort, while it is desirable to allow for the exceptional it is necessary to plan for the probable. The concept of educational tracks seems attractive and progressive, but should be implemented with caution as long as the avowed educational objective is the development of professionals rather than specialized technicians. The suggestion, for example, that child analysts might be considered specialists in development should be quite unacceptable as a guiding educational principle since every psychoanalyst must be a specialist in development, whatever his or her primary field of interest.

In most of the preparatory reports and throughout the conference itself, discussion returned repeatedly to the probable benefit to psychoanalysis of a greater heterogeneity in background and interests of analytic students and graduates. Yet, it is striking that the topic was addressed in largely categorical terms sufficient only for an initial approach rather than for a satisfactory understanding and resolution of the issues. Many of the statements on the advantage or disadvantage of a medical background, the value of previous research training, and the possible contribution to and from the university were general assumptions and untested preconceptions deserving further detailed study and documentation.

It now seems remarkable that the subjects of adequate preparation and appropriate selection for psychoanalytic professional education were not explicitly assigned and confronted as topics at the conference. In retrospect the omissions were unfortunate because the discussion was limited to the somewhat superficial pros and cons of medical versus nonmedical preparation and to the logically valid but quite unspecific view that a larger and more heterogeneous pool of applicants could result in the selection of a more optimal student population. Perhaps, however, the conferees had to experience the frustrating limitations imposed by the use of such overgeneralized, easily idealized, and just as easily depreciated concepts as Medicine, University, and Research to stimulate serious efforts to expand our useful understanding and move toward constructive action.

A full description of the tripartite system of psycho-analytic education would include by implication the necessary interests, skills, knowledge, and temperament required of the student. A major postconference project undoubtedly will attempt the explicit delineation of the essential preparation for that education in functional rather than largely professional-categorical terms. Even if its medical-therapeutic application were the only concern of psychoanalysis, the proper preparation for a professional life in psychoanalysis would deserve specification without complete reliance on the assumption that the usual medical (including standard premedical) preparation was both necessary and sufficient. To date, potential applicants for psychoanalytic training have, in a sense, been preselected or prerejected for the institutes by medical school admission committees. It has not yet been demonstrated adequately that the appropriate formal prerequisites and personal selection criteria for admission to medical schools and to psychoanalytic institutes are identical or even entirely compatible. Conceivably, however, when the range of desirable preparatory backgrounds is set forth after careful study, there may be a close resemblance to the usual formal premedical and medical training; but it is also possible that there may be significant, even crucial, differences. A committee on prerequisites for training has already embarked on its extremely important task in this area of study and clarification. After the completion of that task, the institutes may be in a much better position than at present to select students independently and to advise potential applicants on the probably multiple preparatory paths and essential prerequisites for professional analytic study. More than that, a clarification of the required preparation for the present tripartite institute program might indicate the advisability of institute responsibility for participation in certain aspects of that preparatory work. An obvious example would be the development of psychoanalytic residencies for both nonmedical and medically qualified analytic students.

The ideal institute would offer properly prepared students an optimal education for their continuing professional development as well as motivation to contribute to the common fund of scientific knowledge. The conference discussion was very attentive to the question of whether, in the light of that intention, psychoanalytic institutes should maintain their present almost exclusive concern with professional education for clinical competence. As previously reported, there was a clear consensus that whatever the field of professional application of psychoanalytic knowledge, clinical competence in the psychoanalytic therapeutic method was considered a *sine qua non*. It was generally agreed that the Association and institutes should be able to offer more stimulation, encouragement, and active support for research as well as for clinical practice; it now remains to be seen what can be accomplished in this direction with the teaching resources and funds available. The feasibility of a national psychoanalytic scholarship and research foundation, supported by psychoanalysts themselves, is already being studied intensively in the post-COPER period.

Anna Freud, in her (1966) discussion of the ideal psychoanalytic institute, carefully distinguished it from a utopian design impossible to achieve. Her potentially realizable ideal institute had many of the same features discussed and essentially supported at the conference. However, one characteristic that she stressed, the full-time structure, received relatively little attention. Perhaps this was due to preoccupation with the many real obstacles that preclude it at present and make it seem only a very remote possibility. The part-time organization of training, imposed by certain historical necessities, has become so imbedded in our analytic educational tradition that its uniqueness, shortcomings, and consequences are not appreciated sufficiently.

No other serious scientific or professional discipline considers part-time training a regularly acceptable or even tolerable arrangement for its students. While it is true that many graduate students seeking an advanced academic degree do have to work part time to support themselves, this outside work is usually secondary to a central focus and occupation with the academic work. In contrast, the analytic student is more usually primarily occupied with a full-time professional career, and training becomes an extra burden and more peripheral concern. Psychoanalysis has been described as a post-postgraduate subspecialty of a medical specialty. To the extent that such a characterization is assumed to be correct, there has been a tendency to consider psychoanalytic training as professionally supplemental, providing only an interesting additional approach and useful technique for the psychiatrist's therapeutic armamentarium. If psychoanalysts were more clearly self-defined as professionals primarily engaged in the study and application of psychoanalysis, then applicants, students, and future graduates alike would be much better prepared to make a full-time central commitment to psychoanalysis in both their training and later careers. Should such a perspective gain influence, as one hopes it will, psychoanalytic teaching would become actively dissatisfied with the many compromises and limitations in the present part-time educational arrangements. That dissatisfaction is an obvious prerequisite to more positive action in the intensive search for more optimal educational structures.

Beyond the recommendation to broaden the professional perspectives of analytic education, there was considerable expression of interest in institute programs that were not directed toward professional certification in psychoanalysis but offered courses of instruction to related professional groups, undergraduate and graduate students, and the general public. Many institutes already have very extensive programs of this kind and they have been widely judged to be useful and well worth the investment of effort. Expansion of these efforts in the direction of the so-called psychoanalytic university model has been restricted primarily by the local availability of teaching energy and, once again, adequate funding. It is true that the wish to respond to requests for so-called partial training has been tempered by some reservations about the adequacy of such training for a variety of intended purposes and by concern, perhaps overconcern, for the possible misapplication of limited knowledge. Educating for professional competence will undoubtedly remain the highest priority and central responsibility of independent institutes with marginal resource budgets.

Questions about the function of psychoanalytic institutes necessarily called for consideration of institute structure and organizational context or placement. As independent schools, institutes have been almost entirely supported by the graduate professional community through private practice. A small fraction of the necessary support has been provided by additional nonprofessional private philanthropy and NIMH training grants, the dependability of which has become increasingly uncertain in recent years. Many recommendations for a closer affiliation or even direct participation of psycho-analytic education in the university have included recognition that along with the probable intellectual and scientific benefits of such an association, psychoanalysis would also benefit from association with the usual agency through which society has provided financial support for professional training and scientific research.

The hope that psychoanalytic education and research might find a stimulating and supportive home in the university, not only in the medical school or within the medical profession, is very different, of course, from clearly describing and specifically planning for the establishment of such an arrangement. A recommendation to encourage or create a single national restructuralization would certainly not be advisable since the many factors in a particular institute, community, and university would properly determine the most effective local form. A variety of institute structures probably would be more desirable, just as a certain heterogeneity of students and teachers might also prove advantageous.

Organizational movement toward formal relationships with the university may occur in a manner analogous to the usual evolution of institute relationships with medical schools. Individual analytically trained psychiatrists first demonstrated their value as teachers to medical and psychiatric education; later, even though psychoanalytic professional education did not become an explicit component of the undergraduate medical curriculum or psychiatric residency program, psychoanalytic institutes received shelter and partial support from several medical schools. Only when a significant number of individual analysts remain in or return to the university, not only the medical school, and demonstrate the value of their training in their research and scholarship will the university have reason to offer support for a specific psychoanalytic educational structure, in several possible forms, within the university.

It is premature to be concerned with the logistical, administrative, or particular structural problems of such a possible eventuality. When a development in that direction evolves naturally, that is, as a result of patient and intelligent effort, it should be considered on the merits of the particular situation. It has been suggested that psychoanalysis has tended to overidealize its relation to medicine; it would do well to avoid a similar misguiding overidealization of its potential relation to the university and to academics in related fields of endeavor.

How do these considerations on the possible relation of psychoanalysis and psychoanalytic education to the university comment on the relation to medical and psychiatric education and medicine itself? Psychoanalysts could and should actively participate in medical and psychiatric education, whatever structural form is adopted by various psychoanalytic institutes or whatever shift occurs in the future away from an exclusively medical qualification for membership in the profession. The medical-therapeutic applicability of analytic theory, the psychoanalytic method, and psychotherapeutic modifications of it have been at least sufficiently confirmed for the medical profession to warrant sustained teaching efforts by psychoanalysts at medical schools and in psychiatric residencies. The central conference concern with the future of psychoanalytic research, psychoanalytic education, and psychoanalysis itself seemed to suggest the need for a careful balance and disposition of teaching effort. While isolation from medicine would be unfortunate, an excessive preoccupation of psychoanalysts with medical and psychiatric teaching might prove disabling as well. The actual value of psychoanalysts as teachers of psychiatric as well as psychoanalytic students depends very largely on their individual continued intensive involvement in the psychoanalytic situation, working with psychoanalytic data. Psychoanalysis should, therefore seek to offer psychoanalytically experienced teachers to medical and psychiatric education in preference to those who might better be described as psychoanalytically oriented, a category that may have been too much appreciated in the past, thus overextending and underserving both analysis and psychiatry.

It may be possible in certain localities to evolve combined or at least cooperatively related psychoanalytic and psychiatric residencies within medical schools, private hospitals, and clinics. The economic and possible administrative-jurisdictional difficulties involved are fully acknowledged but need not be so intimidating as to discourage serious efforts in that direction.

As indicated previously, economic considerations constitute a very important aspect of any discussion on the relation of psychoanalysis to medicine. Present individual and collective concerns range from the question of insurance coverage for psychoanalytic treatment to the feasibility of an active psychoanalytic private practice at the usual fee level under present economic circumstances. Particularly for younger psychoanalysts, professional activity has been greatly influenced by eligibility for remuneration by public and private health insurance plans for certain modes of practice. Another of the yet to be thoroughly scrutinized arguments for a close relationship and identification with medicine is that coverage for psychoanalytic treatment may be obtained for medical psychoanalysts only through the endorsement and support of medical colleagues and medical organizations. Medical psychoanalysts will continue to seek that support, but they must also continue to consider whether the retention of an exclusively medical orientation for their profession and professional organization is as justifiable on scientific grounds as it may currently seem to be for economically strategic reasons. Would medicine really not tolerate medical psychoanalysts as medical specialists if there were a somewhat higher proportion of nonmedically qualified psychoanalysts associated with them? This question is another of those evoking strong opposing opinions but not yet resolved by careful study and thoughtfully planned programs for action. I believe that medicine will probably continue to accept psychiatrists as medical specialists, even the relatively small number of psychiatrists who are psychoanalysts and are in formal association with well-qualified nonmedical colleagues. It has been assumed that there is some risk of the loss of eligibility for payment under a health insurance plan if psychoanalysts do not, as a group, retain their exclusively medical identity. In this regard, it is worth noting that both government and private insurers have increasingly considered nonmedical therapists with a variety of licenses or certifications as qualified to receive payment for provided services. More importantly, psychoanalysis will only gain increased acceptance by the medical profession as a valid therapeutic approach, just as it will only be accepted more fully by the broader scientific community, on the basis of its demonstrated practical and scientific value and not because of organizational arrangements or decisions of a political-tactical nature. Our primary collective concern must be for the substance and quality of our scientific and professional activities, which constitute the only legitimate and ultimate social validation and justification for the field and for the individual psychoanalyst.

The conference did not focus on particular research problems in psychoanalysis so much as on the general problem of research in psychoanalysis. To avoid unnecessary repetition of the many, by now familiar, observations on the topic, the reader's attention is here directed to the particularly close interdependence of this problem with the many pertinent professional, organizational, and economic issues noted previously in this chapter and set forth quite fully in the preparatory reports and discussions. It does seem probable, however, that the sound recommendations for better teaching of research methodology, for encouragement of research by modification of the institute or Association "ambience," for somehow increasing esteem within the profession for scholarly and research activities can by themselves effect only limited change. With full regard for the multiplicity of factors involved, it must be clear that more frequent serious commitment to careers with important involvement in systematic research, of the kind now urgently required for further significant advances in the science of psychoanalysis, will require strong long-term organizational support. Unless that support is obtained, whether from the profession itself, from society directly, or through the university, it may be of relatively little consequence to further increase the effort to teach or encourage research or esteem for research since only a very few analysts would have an adequate opportunity for active research careers. Even the nonmedical psychoanalysts, who it is hoped will provide research-activity stimulation and example for the profession, would inevitably be attracted, and indeed pushed, toward private clinical practice and away from research by economic pressures.

Furthermore, it may be seriously questioned whether psychoanalytic research or the choice of psychoanalytic research as a professional-career focus has been hampered by a supposed lack of esteem for research accomplishment. Original research and illuminating scholarship has, in fact, always elicited the highest respect and admiration within psychoanalysis, whatever the conflicting pressures that work against more extensive individual participation in such activity. The Committee on Scientific Activity of the Association has recently been established to encourage and support research studies, and the feasibility of a Psychoanalytic Scholarship and Research Foundation is now being explored.[1]

If, indeed, the primary consideration in selection for psychoanalytic education were an applicant's personal qualifications, including a formal academic background determined to be essential, then certain questions related to the problem of encouraging earlier training or the acceptance of students from other than the medical discipline might be viewed in more practical and realistic terms. As long as the recruitment of younger students or students from fields other than medicine did not become a disproportionately independent objective, the process of selecting qualified individuals rather than categorical representatives would inevitably result in a more heterogeneous mixture of students than at present. A program of selection based only on intellectual, emotional, and

---

[1] *Editor's note:* Psychoanalytic Research Foundation established December, 1975.

educational fitness rather than on a student's ability to pay for training is confronted immediately by the economic obstacle. Present efforts to solve this aspect of the problem, at least to the extent that initial scholarship programs may be instituted, will probably result in the formation of a national foundation to pool contributions initially from within the profession and later, it is hoped, from others. The contributions from training and supervising analysts could also include the provision of additional low-fee or even no-fee analytic or supervisory hours on some collectively shared and equitable basis.

To comment on the relation of psychoanalysis to social issues or state with any clarity the relevant postconference objectives in this area is difficult due to a number of considerations. The conviction is widespread that psychoanalysis still has much to learn about individual psychology before it will be able to speak authoritatively about social psychology and social issues. It is not necessary for a discipline to apologize for a responsibly perceived limitation to its present knowledge in a particular area, even though the wish to contribute may be understandably strong. Psychoanalysts are generally aware that the data of psychoanalysis do not permit easy extrapolation and direct application to most social issues; therefore, psychoanalytic caution and modesty has been appropriate on these matters and not primarily the result of personal disinclination or regrettable scientific neglect.

It should be recognized, of course, that it has already been possible for psychoanalysts, exercising both their scientific responsibility and their social concern, to communicate their psychoanalytic understanding of certain social issues to others in a meaningful and useful way. The broad social effect of such understanding has never occurred in direct response to a specific recommendation; the psychoanalytic view has usually been translated and transmitted through the work of writers, sociologists, legal scholars, economists, social planners, and others. Psychoanalytically sophisticated proposals on social problems and policy should continue to be expressed; it is hoped that same sophistication will determine a proper balance of knowledgeable assertion and appropriate restraint.

A close collaboration with other social scientists certainly holds promise for the future, particularly if dependable supportive structures for these efforts can be established. The Institute for Psychosocial Studies in Chicago has been mentioned as an already existing model of this type. The recommendation by the Commission on Social and Community Issues for a national foundation for social issues will be received quite favorably when there is further evidence that specific proposals for social research studies and programs are sufficiently promising and closely enough related to the central scientific and professional interests, capacities, and responsibilities of psychoanalysis.

Similarly, the recommendation that institutes include in their curricula courses on psychoanalytic social theory and its applicability to community psychiatry and other group and social problems requires more documentation and demonstration that a substantial body of teachable and applicable psychoanalytic knowledge is actually available. Although there is little doubt that a potential for such knowledge exists, there is considerable question whether enough special knowledge has already been acquired for its systematic and explicit inclusion in the already hard-pressed curriculum. If at all possible, it would be well to avoid a repetition of the excessive social promise, inevitable disappointment, and reactive devaluation that both psychiatry and psychoanalysis have already experienced. At present, most psychoanalysts would acknowledge that in social theory and social guidance they are still at the level of the interested amateur rather than the skilled professional. These remarks are clearly intended to emphasize the need for meticulous care in asserting claims of accomplishment while recommending enthusiastic support for relevant studies, thoughtful contributions, and effective teaching as knowledge expands in applied psychoanalysis.

The acceptance of well-motivated and personally qualified students for psychoanalytic training, without prejudicial social, economic, or professional discrimination, is such an obviously desirable objective in the context of the entire preceding discussion as not to require any further elaboration or recommendation.

It may be useful to conclude with a highly condensed summary of the principal organizational motivations for the conference, its major themes and issues, and its observed and anticipated consequences. The organizational motivations included educational, scientific, and economic considerations. One issue involved the clarification of the appropriate range of applicants' backgrounds in relation to a future optimal variety of graduate careers in clinical practice, research, teaching, and applications of psychoanalysis in related fields. Other issues related to achievement of a high teaching and learning standard for psychoanalytic education, the determination of its scope and specific contents, and the better integration of its several components. The educational issues were also reflected in various estimates of the scientific and professional outcome of the current and past training philosophy and organization. Economic concerns revolved around the many problems of financial support for possible full-time institutes or even the present part-time institutes, as well as for nonmedically qualified students, younger students, or others who might be financially handicapped, for teachers, for research and research careers, and for the broader provision of low-fee treatment.

Several major themes and issues were prominent throughout the conference discussion and received general endorsement by the conference participants. A firm consensus existed on the need for continued review, assessment, and integration of all aspects of psycho-analytic education. The relationship and mutual contri-butions of child and adult analytic theory and technique evoked particular interest for future exploration. There was unanimous affirmation of the crucial importance of developing psychoanalytic research and research careers. Although accompanied by caution and reservations about proceeding along any single path toward any single model of psychoanalytic education, there was broad approval of the long-term objective to enter more fully, in various ways, into the mainstream of scientific and humanistic knowledge in the university. A continuing over-all intention to maintain a close relationship with medicine and psychiatry as well as medical and psychi-atric education was asserted; however, there also seemed to be a growing body of opinion that the bond with medi-cine need not be an exclusive one in the interest of the op-timal development of psychoanalysis and even, perhaps, in the interest of its continuing contributions to medicine. Many recommendations throughout the conference thus urged exploration by individuals and institutes of the pos-sibilities for relating functionally to all fields of behavioral science to stimulate collaborative research and the practical application of acquired knowledge.

What have been the immediate consequences of the conference as well as those that must have a necessarily long term of development and are, therefore, not yet fully realized? The stimulation of intensive individual and organizational reconsideration and study of all the issues discussed is quite evident. Renewed studies are already under way or proposed in the following areas: the specifically appropriate formal educational prerequisites for psychoanalytic education; the personal, intellectual, temperamental, and developmental criteria for selection; the feasibility of psychoanalytic (as distinguished from psychoanalytically oriented psychiatric) residencies; the suitability of current and proposed psychoanalytic educational methods and approaches in assessment, reporting, seminar instruction, core and special-track curriculum design, supervisory techniques, progression evaluation, and graduation criteria; the adoption of necessary professional certification procedures; the increased encouragement of training for psychoanalytic research and professional analytic careers that regularly include systematic research activity.

A post-COPER committee has been charged with the responsibility for stimulating, collating, and reporting the results of continuing national and local studies and discussion of all COPER issues. It is hoped there will be continued exploration of participation in university and medical school programs. An intensive review has been initiated on the national level by the Association to discover dependable sources and modes of funding for educational and research programs that have been hindered, at least in part, by excessive economic dependence on private practice, part-time instruction and study, and the high cost of training. The search for funds has led to requests for even greater financial contributions from psychoanalysts themselves and a review of the availability of extraprofessional private philanthropy. There is a continuing quest for partial social support through increased government training grants and health insurance coverage for psychoanalytic treatment, and some hope for achievement of a most valuable long-term social support in the form of an evolved future affiliation with the university.

Much work has been done; much work remains to be done. With every conference topic, assertions and recommendations resulted in questions that deserve and must receive serious and intensive study. The conference discussion certainly highlighted the central questions but it could not have been expected to settle them. Whatever the issue — whether it be eligibility for training, the value of the training analyst's reports, the importance of medical or university affiliation, or the contribution of a new approach within psychoanalysis — it is now necessary to substantiate the validity and practicality of the various positions taken and suggestions offered. The many presently active study projects in psychoanalytic education attest strongly to the important impact of the conference and foster the reasonable expectation of good progress before the next conference on education and research is convened. The task of educators has been compared by Siegfried Bernfeld (1925) to that of Sisyphus, and he indicated the special difficulties and limits of education; however, the struggle toward those limits also includes both exciting challenges and gratifying rewards for teacher and student alike.

References

American Psychoanalytic Association (1950), Standards for the training of physicians in psychoanalysis. *Bull. Amer. Psychoanal. Assn.*, 6(2):1-5.

Arlow, J. (1972), Some dilemmas in psychoanalytic education. *J. Amer. Psychoanal. Assn.*, 20:556-566.

Bailey, S. K. (1974), Higher education American style. *Amer. Educ.*, 10(7):15-28.

Balint, M. (1948), On the psychoanalytic training system. *Internat. J. Psycho-Anal.*, 29:163-173.

———— (1954), Analytic training and training analysis. *Internat. J. Psycho-Anal.*, 35:157-162.

Becker, H. S. et al. (1961), *Boys in White: Student Cultures in Medical School*. Chicago: University of Chicago Press.

Benedek, T. (1969), Training analysis—past, present and future. *Internat. J. Psycho-Anal.*, 50:437-445.

Bergman, P. (1966), An experiment in filmed psychotherapy. In: *Methods of Research in Psychotherapy*, eds. L. A. Gottschalk & A. H. Auerbach. New York: Appleton-Century-Crofts, pp. 35-49.

Bernfeld, S. (1925), *Sisyphus; or, the Limits of Education*. Berkeley: University of California Press, 1973.

———— (1962), On psychoanalytic training. *Psychoanal. Quart.*, 31:453-482.

Bloom, S. W. (1973), *Power and Dissent in the Medical School*. New York: Free Press.

Breuer, J. & Freud, S. (1893), On the physical mechanism of hysterical phenomena: Preliminary communication. *Standard Edition*, 2:1-17. London: Hogarth Press, 1955.

Calder, K. T. (1972), Ten Years of COPE: Perspectives in psychoanalytic education: Introduction. *J. Amer. Psychoanal. Assn.,* 20:540-545.

Calef, V. & Weinshel, E. M. (1973), Reporting, nonreporting, and assessment in the training analysis. *J. Amer. Psychoanal. Assn.,* 21:714-726.

Coker, R. E. (1960), Study of choice of specialties in medicine. *N. Carolina Med. J.,* 21:96-101.

Dahl, H. (1972), A quantitative study of a psychoanalysis. *Psychoanalysis and Contemporary Science,* 1:237-257. New York: Macmillan.

Darwin, C. (1860), *Autobiography and Selected Letters,* ed. F. Darwin. New York: Dover, 1958.

Dewald, P. A. (1972), *The Psychoanalytic Process: A Case Illustration.* New York: Basic Books.

Eissler, K. (1969), Irreverent remarks about the present and the future of psycho-analysis. *Internat. J. Psycho-Anal.,* 50:461-471.

———— (1973), Letter to the editor. *Internat. J. Psycho-Anal.,* 54:373-377.

Eitingon, M. (1926), An address to the International Training Commission. *Internat. J. Psycho-Anal.,* 7:130-134.

Engel, G. L. (1968), Some obstacles to the development of research in psychoanalysis. *J. Amer. Psychoanal. Assn.,* 16:195-229.

Erikson, E. H. (1959), *Identity and the Life Cycle* [*Psychological Issues,* Monogr. No. 1]. New York: International Universities Press.

Feuer, L. S. (1963), *The Scientific Intellectual: The Psychological and Social Origins of Modern Science.* New York: Basic Books.

Fisher, C. (1965), Psychoanalytic implications of recent research on sleep and dreaming. *J. Amer. Psychoanal. Assn.,* 13:197-303.

Fleming, J. (1972), The birth of COPE as viewed in 1971. *J. Amer. Psychoanal. Assn.,* 20:546-555.

———— (1973), The training analyst as an educator. *The Annual of Psychoanalysis,* 1:280-295. New York: Quadrangle.

———— & Benedek, T. (1966), *Psychoanalytic Supervision.* New York: Grune & Stratton.

Freud, A. (1936), The ego and the mechanisms of defense. *The Writings of Anna Freud,* 2. New York: International Universities Press, 1966.

———— (1954), Problems of infantile neurosis: Contribution to the discussion. *The Writings of Anna Freud,* 4:327-355. New York: International Universities Press, 1968.

———— (1963), The concept of developmental lines. *The Psychoanalytic Study of the Child,* 18:245-265. New York: International Universities Press.

———— (1965), Normality and pathology in childhood: Assessments of development. *The Writings of Anna Freud,* 6. New York: International Universities Press.

———— (1966), The ideal psychoanalytic institute: A utopia. *The Writings of Anna Freud,* 7:73-93. New York: International Universities Press, 1971.

———— & Burlingham, D. (1943), *War and Children.* New York: International Universities Press, 1944.

Freud, S. (1900), The interpretation of dreams. *Standard Edition,* 4 & 5. London: Hogarth Press, 1953.

———— (1905a), Fragment of an analysis of a case of hysteria. *Standard Edition,* 7:3-122. London: Hogarth Press, 1953.

———— (1905b), Three essays on the theory of sexuality. *Standard Edition,* 7:125-245. London: Hogarth Press, 1953.

———— (1909), Analysis of a phobia in a five-year-old boy. *Standard Edition,* 10:3-149. London: Hogarth Press, 1955.

———— (1913), The claims of psycho-analysis to scientific interest. *Standard Edition,* 13:165-190. London: Hogarth Press, 1955.

———— (1920), Beyond the pleasure principle. *Standard Edition,* 18:3-64. London: Hogarth Press, 1955.

———— (1937), Analysis terminable and interminable. *Standard Edition,* 23:209-253. London: Hogarth Press, 1964.

Gill, M. M. (1972), Systematic research on the psychoanalytic situation. Presented at the Annual Meeting of the American Psychoanalytic Association, Dallas, Texas, May (unpublished).

Goldstein, J., Freud, A. & Solnit, A. (1973), *Beyond the Best Interests of the Child.* New York: Free Press.

Greenacre, P. (1971), *Emotional Growth,* Vols. I & II. New York: International Universities Press.

Greenspan, S. I. & Cullander, C. C. H. (1973), A systematic metapsychological assessment of the personality—its application to the problem of analyzability. *J. Amer. Psychoanal. Assn.,* 21:303-327.

Hamburg, D., Bibring, G., Fisher, C., Stanton, A., Wallerstein, R., Weinstock, H. & Haggard, E. (1967), Report of Ad Hoc Committee on Central Fact-Gathering Data of the American Psychoanalytic Association. *J. Amer. Psychoanal. Assn.,* 15:841-861.

Hartmann, H. (1950), Psychoanalysis and developmental psychology. *The Psychoanalytic Study of the Child,* 5:7-17. New York: International Universities Press.

——— & Kris, E. (1945), The genetic approach in psychoanalysis. *The Psychoanalytic Study of the Child,* 1:11-30. New York: International Universities Press.

Hawthorne, N. (1850), *The Scarlet Letter.* New York: Dell, 1960.

Hendrick, I. (1958), *Facts and Theories of Psychoanalysis.* New York: Knopf.

Jones, E. (1959), *Free Associations: Memoirs of a Psychoanalyst.* New York: Basic Books.

Jones, R. M. (1970), *The New Psychology of Dreaming.* New York: Grune & Stratton.

Kaufman, M. R. (1948), Required standards of the American Psychoanalytic Association for the training of physicians in psychoanalysis. Adopted December 17, 1948. *Bull. Amer. Psychoanal. Assn.,* 6(2):1-5.

Kernberg, O. F., Burstein, E. D., Coyne, L., Appelbaum, A., Horwitz, L. & Voth, H. (1972), Psychotherapy and psychoanalysis. Final report of Menninger Foundation's psychotherapy research project. *Bull. Menninger Clinic,* 36(1/2): 1-275.

Klein, G. S. (1954), Need and regulation. In: *Nebraska Symposium on Motivation, 1954,* ed. M. R. Jones. Lincoln, Neb.: University of Nebraska Press, pp. 224-274.

Klein, H. R. (1960), A study of changes occurring in patients during and after psychoanalytic treatment. *Current Approaches to Psychoanalysis.* New York: Grune & Stratton, pp. 151-175.

Knapp, P. H., Mushatt, C. & Nemetz, S. J. (1970), The context of reported asthma during psychoanalysis. *Psychosom. Med.,* 32:167-187.

Knight, R. P. (1953), The present status of organized psychoanalysis in the United States. *J. Amer. Psychoanal. Assn.,* 1:197-221.

Kohut, H. (1970), Scientific activities of the American Psychoanalytic Association: An inquiry. *J. Amer. Psychoanal. Assn.,* 18:462-484.

Kuhn, T. S. (1962), *The Structure of Scientific Revolutions.* Chicago: University of Chicago Press, 1970.

Lewin, B. D. & Ross, H. (1960), *Psychoanalytic Education in the United States.* New York: Norton.

Lipton, S. (1972), The requirement of a training analysis. Presented to the Chicago Psychoanalytic Society, October (unpublished).

Luborsky, L. (1967), Momentary forgetting during psychotherapy and psychoanalysis: A theory and research method. In: *Motives and Thoughts: Essays in Honor of David Rapaport* [*Psychological Issues,* Monogr. 18/19:177-217], ed. R. Holt. New York: International Universities Press.

———— & Spence, D. (1971), Quantitative research on psychoanalytic therapy. In: *Handbook of Psychotherapy and Behavior Change,* ed. A. E. Bergin & S. L. Garfield. New York: Wiley, pp. 408-437.

Lustman, S. L. (1967), The meaning and purpose of curriculum planning. *J. Amer. Psychoanal. Assn.,* 15:862-875.

Mahler, M. S. (1968), *On Human Symbiosis and the Vicissitudes of Individuation, Vol. I: Infantile Psychoses.* New York: International Universities Press.

———— (1972), On the first three subphases of the separation-individuation process. *Internat. J. Psycho-Anal.,* 53:333-338.

———— & McDevitt, J. (1968), Observations on adaptation and defense in *statu nascendi. Psychoanal. Quart.,* 37:1-21.

McLaughlin, J. T. (1973), The nonreporting training analyst, the analysis, and the institute. *J. Amer. Psychoanal. Assn.,* 21: 697-713.

Onchiota Conference (1961), *Integration of Psychoanalysis with Universities and Medical Schools.* (Unpublished.)

———— (1962), *Psychoanalytic Content in Residency Training Programs.* (Unpublished.)

———— (1963), *Role of the Psychoanalyst in Teaching Psychotherapy in Residency Programs.* New York: Yeshiva University Press.

———— (1964), *Role of the Psychoanalyst in Supervising Psychotherapy.* (Unpublished.)

Panel (1973), Committees of the Board on Professional Standards, J. T. McLaughlin, reporter. *J. Amer. Psychoanal. Assn.,* 21:576-602.

Panel (1975), National Conference on Psychoanalytic Education and Research, R. Emde, reporter. *J. Amer. Psychoanal. Assn.,* 23:569-586.

Pfeffer, A. Z. (1959), A procedure for evaluating the results of psychoanalysis: A preliminary report. *J. Amer. Psychoanal. Assn.*, 7:418-444.

Pollock, G. H. (1972), What do we face and where can we go? Questions about future directions. *J. Amer. Psychoanal. Assn.*, 20:574-590.

Potter, H. W., Klein, H. R. & Goodenough, D. R. (1957), Problems related to the personal costs of psychiatric and psychoanalytic training. *Amer. J. Psychiat.*, 113(11):1013-1019.

Rainbow Report (1955). American Psychoanalytic Association (unpublished).

Robertson, James & Robertson, Joyce (1967), Kate, 2 years 5 months, in foster care for 27 days. 16mm film, b/w, sound, 33 mins. Concord Films Council and New York University Film Library.

———— (1968), Jane, 17 months, in foster care for 10 days. 16mm film, b/w, sound, 37 mins. Concord Films Council and New York University Film Library.

———— (1969), John, 17 months, for 9 days in a residential nursery. 16mm film, b/w, sound, 43 mins. Concord Films Council and New York University Film Library.

———— (1971a), Young children in brief separation: A fresh look. *The Psychoanalytic Study of the Child,* 26:264-315. New York: Quadrangle.

———— (1971b), Thomas, 2 years 4 months, in foster care for 10 days. 16mm film, b/w, sound, 38 mins. Concord Films Council and New York University Film Library.

Sachs, H. (1947), Observations of a training analyst. *Psychoanal. Quart.*, 16:157-168.

Schwartz, F. & Rouse, R. O. (1961), *The Activation and Recovery of Associations* [*Psychological Issues,* Monogr. 9]. New York: International Universities Press.

Shapiro, D. (1973), The silver lining—facilitation of training analysis by the training situation. Reported to COPER Preparatory Commission on the Tripartite System of Psychoanalytic Education, American Psychoanalytic Association, January (unpublished).

Spence, D. P. (1970), Human and computer attempts to decode symptom language. *Psychosom. Med.*, 32:615-625.

Spitz, R. A. (1957), *No and Yes—On the Genesis of Human Communication*. New York: International Universities Press.

———— (1959), *A Genetic Field Theory of Ego Formation; Its Implications for Pathology*. New York: International Universities Press.

———— (1965), *The First Year of Life: A Psychoanalytic Study of Normal and Deviant Development of Object Relations.* New York: International Universities Press.

Wallerstein, R. S. (1968), The psychotherapy research project of the Menninger Foundation. In: *Research in Psychotherapy,* 3:584-605, ed. J. M. Shlien et al. Washington, D. C.: American Psychoanalytic Association.

———— (1972), The futures of psychoanalytic education. *J. Amer. Psychoanal. Assn.,* 20:591-606.

Weber, J. J., Elinson, J. & Moss, L. M. (1967), Psychoanalysis and change: A study of psychoanalytic clinic records utilizing electronic data-processing techniques. *Arch. Gen. Psychiat.,* 17:687-709.

Windholz, E. (1972), The consensual analysis. Presented at the Annual Meeting of the American Psychoanalytic Association, Dallas, Texas, May (unpublished).

Appendix

Albert J. Solnit, M.D.
Robert S. Wallerstein, M.D.
Edward M. Weinshel, M.D.

SUBCOMMITTEE ON SURVEY

Philip S. Holzman, Ph.D., Chairman
Ernest A. Haggard, Ph.D.
George H. Pollock, M.D.
Kenneth R. Cecil, Research Assistant

PARTICIPANTS IN PREPARATORY COMMISSIONS

COMMISSION I: THE TRIPARTITE SYSTEM OF PSYCHOANALYTIC EDUCATION

Joan Fleming, M.D., Chairman
Stanley S. Weiss, M.D., Recorder
Charlotte G. Babcock, M.D.
Victor Calef, M.D.
Jacob Christ, M.D.
Paul A. Dewald, M.D.
Alan J. Eisnitz, M.D.
Leon Ferber, M.D.
Sanford M. Izner, M.D.
Daniel S. Jaffe, M.D.
Aaron Karush, M.D.
John F. Kelly, M.D.
James Mann, M.D.
Paul H. Ornstein, M.D.
Arnold Z. Pfeffer, M.D.
Daniel Shapiro, M.D.
Troy Thompson, M.D.
Ralph W. Tyler, Ph.D.
Edward M. Weinshel, M.D.

COMMISSION II: THE IDEAL INSTITUTE

Stanley Goodman, M.D., Chairman
Herbert J. Schlesinger, Ph.D., Recorder
Norman B. Atkins, M.D.
Frances J. Bonner, M.D.
Homer C. Curtis, M.D.
Bernard D. Fine, M.D.
Heinz Kohut, M.D.
Maimon Leavitt, M.D.
Joseph M. Natterson, M.D.
Haskell F. Norman, M.D.
William R. O'Brien, M.D.
Ishak Ramzy, Ph.D.
Miss Helen Ross
Louis B. Shapiro, M.D.
Malvina Stock, M.D.
John J. Weber, M.D.

COMMISSION III: AGE AND THE PSYCHOANALYTIC CAREER

Samuel Ritvo, M.D., Chairman
Marshall Edelson, M.D., Recorder
Martin A. Berezin, M.D.
Daryl E. DeBell, M.D.
Ruth S. Eissler, M.D.
Frances Gitelson, M.D.
Janice Norton Kaufman, M.D.
Leo S. Loomis, M.D.
I. Floyd Mallott, M.D.
John B. McDevitt, M.D.
Arthur J. Ourieff, M.D.
M. Barrie Richmond, M.D.
Marshall D. Schechter, M.D.
Clarence G. Schulz, M.D.
Gertrude R. Ticho, M.D.

COMMISSION IV: RELATIONSHIP OF PSYCHOANALYSIS TO
UNIVERSITIES

Bernard Holland, M.D., Chairman
Richard S. Ward, M.D., Recorder
Ewald W. Busse, M.D.
Robert S. Daniels, M.D.
Maurice R. Friend, M.D.
Robert M. Gilliland, M.D.
Henriette R. Klein, M.D.
Lawrence C. Kolb, M.D.
L. Douglas Lenkoski, M.D.
Leo Madow, M.D.
James T. McLaughlin, M.D.
David Musto, M.D.
George A. Richardson, M.D.
Leonard L. Shengold, M.D.
Herman Stein, Ph.D.
Robert J. Stoller, M.D.
William C. Thompson, M.D.
Arthur F. Valenstein, M.D.

COMMISSION V: RELATIONSHIP OF PSYCHOANALYSIS TO
CURRENT CHANGES IN MEDICAL AND PSYCHIATRIC EDUCATION

Paul G. Myerson, M.D., Chairman
William W. Meissner, M.D., Recorder
Jose Barchilon, M.D.
O. Eugene Baum, M.D.
Samuel L. Feder, M.D.
Paul Jay Fink, M.D.
Theodore J. Jacobs, M.D.
Robert A. Nemiroff, M.D.
William S. Robbins, M.D.
Melvin Sabshin, M.D.
Joseph Sandler, M.D.

Elvin V. Semrad, M.D.
Roy M. Whitman, M.D.
Lyman C. Wynne, M.D.

COMMISSION VI: PSYCHOANALYTIC EDUCATION
AND THE ALLIED DISCIPLINES

David Kairys, M.D., Chairman
R. Hugh Dickinson, M.D.
Rudolf Ekstein, Ph.D.
Joseph Goldstein, Ph.D.
Otto F. Kernberg, M.D.
Lawrence S. Kubie, M.D.†
Peter J. Loewenberg, Ph.D.
Jerome D. Oremland, M.D.
Arnold A. Rogow, Ph.D.
Victor H. Rosen, M.D.†
Ernst A. Ticho, Ph.D.
Emanuel Windholz, M.D.
Abraham Zaleznik, D.C.S.

COMMISSION VII: PSYCHOANALYTIC RESEARCH

Morton F. Reiser, M.D., Chairman
Peter H. Knapp, M.D., Recorder
Samuel Abrams, M.D.
Elwyn James Anthony, M.D.
Jacob A. Arlow, M.D.
Charles Fisher, M.D.
Mrs. Selma Fraiberg
Merton M. Gill, M.D.
Leo Goldberger, Ph.D.
Mardi J. Horowitz, M.D.
Mark Kanzer, M.D.

† Deceased before 1974 Conference.

I. Charles Kaufman, M.D.
Lester Luborsky, Ph.D.
Peter B. Neubauer, M.D.
George H. Pollock, M.D.
Lewis L. Robbins, M.D.
Alfred H. Stanton, M.D.

COMMISSION VIII: RELATIONSHIP OF PSYCHOANALYSIS TO
SOCIAL AND COMMUNITY ISSUES

Reginald S. Lourie, M.D., Chairman
Gene Gordon, M.D., Recorder
Bernard Bandler, M.D.
Viola W. Bernard, M.D.
Donald L. Burnham, M.D.
Jules V. Coleman, M.D.
Elizabeth B. Davis, M.D.
Robert M. Dorn, M.D.
Aaron H. Esman, M.D.
Willard M. Gaylin, M.D.
Robert M. Gibson, M.D.
Alex H. Kaplan, M.D.
Edward H. Knight, M.D.
John E. Mack, M.D.
Charles A. Malone, M.D.
Charles A. Pinderhughes, M.D.
Howard H. Schlossman, M.D.
Norman E. Zinberg, M.D.

COMMISSION IX: CHILD ANALYSIS

Calvin F. Settlage, M.D., Chairman
Selma Kramer, M.D., Recorder
Herman S. Belmont, M.D.
Virginia L. Clower, M.D.

Robert N. Emde, M.D.
Phyllis Greenacre, M.D.
Marjorie Harley, Ph.D.
J. Cotter Hirschberg, M.D.
Marianne Kris, M.D.
Margaret S. Mahler, M.D.
Irwin M. Marcus, M.D.
Humberto Nagera, M.D.
Gerald B. Olch, M.D.
Fred P. Robbins, M.D.
Morton Shane, M.D.
M. Jeanne Spurlock, M.D.
Samuel Weiss, M.D.

Participants

Samuel Abrams, M.D.	Commission VII
Elwyn James Anthony, M.D.	VII
Jacob A. Arlow, M.D.	VII
Norman B. Atkins, M.D.	II
Charlotte G. Babcock, M.D.	I
Bernard Bandler, M.D.	VIII
Jose Barchilon, M.D.	V
O. Eugene Baum, M.D.	V
Herman S. Belmont, M.D.	IX
Martin A. Berezin, M.D.	III
Viola W. Bernard, M.D.	VIII
Harold Blum, M.D.	Conference Guest
Douglas D. Bond, M.D.	Conference Guest
Frances J. Bonner, M.D.	II
Donald L. Burnham, M.D.	VIII
Ewald W. Busse, M.D.	IV
Kenneth T. Calder, M.D.	COPER Committee
Victor Calef, M.D.	I
Jacob Christ, M.D.	I

Virginia L. Clower, M.D.	IX
Jules V. Coleman, M.D.	VIII
Homer C. Curtis, M.D.	II
Robert S. Daniels, M.D.	IV
Elizabeth B. Davis, M.D.	VIII
Daryl E. DeBell, M.D.	III
Paul A. Dewald, M.D.	I
R. Hugh Dickinson, M.D.	VI
Robert M. Dorn, M.D.	VIII
Marshall Edelson, M.D.	III
Alan J. Eisnitz, M.D.	I
Ruth S. Eissler, M.D.	III
Rudolf Ekstein, Ph.D.	VI
Robert N. Emde, M.D.	IX
Aaron H. Esman, M.D.	VIII
Samuel L. Feder, M.D.	V
Leon Ferber, M.D.	I
Bernard D. Fine, M.D.	II
Paul Jay Fink, M.D.	V
Charles Fisher, M.D.	VII
Joan Fleming, M.D.	I
Mrs. Selma Fraiberg	VII
Maurice R. Friend, M.D.	IV
Herbert S. Gaskill, M.D.	COPER Committee
Willard M. Gaylin, M.D.	VIII
Robert M. Gibson, M.D.	VIII
Merton M. Gill, M.D.	VII
Robert M. Gilliland, M.D.	IV
Frances Gitelson, M.D.	III
Leo Goldberger, Ph.D.	VII
Joseph Goldstein, Ph.D.	VI
Stanley Goodman, M.D.	II
Gene Gordon, M.D.	VIII
Phyllis Greenacre, M.D.	IX
Marjorie Harley, Ph.D.	IX
David R. Hawkins, M.D.	Conference Guest

J. Cotter Hirschberg, M.D.	IX
Bernard Holland, M.D.	IV
Philip S. Holzman, Ph.D.	Survey Subcommittee
Mardi J. Horowitz, M.D.	VII
Sanford M. Izner, M.D.	I
Theodore J. Jacobs, M.D.	V
Daniel S. Jaffe, M.D.	I
Edward D. Joseph, M.D.	COPER Committee
David Kairys, M.D.	VI
Mark Kanzer, M.D.	VII
Alex H. Kaplan, M.D.	VIII
Aaron Karush, M.D.	I
I. Charles Kaufman, M.D.	VII
Janice Norton Kaufman, M.D.	III
John F. Kelly, M.D.	I
Otto F. Kernberg, M.D.	VI
Mme. Evelyne Kestemberg	Conference Guest
Henriette R. Klein, M.D.	IV
Peter H. Knapp, M.D.	VII
Edward H. Knight, M.D.	VIII
Heinz Kohut, M.D.	II
Lawrence C. Kolb, M.D.	IV
Selma Kramer, M.D.	IX
Marianne Kris, M.D.	IX
Lawrence S. Kubie, M.D.†	VI
Maimon Leavitt, M.D.	II
L. Douglas Lenkoski, M.D.	IV
Peter J. Loewenberg, Ph.D.	VI
Leo S. Loomie, M.D.	III
Reginald S. Lourie, M.D.	VIII
Lester Luborsky, Ph.D.	VII
John E. Mack, M.D.	VIII
Leo Madow, M.D.	IV
Margaret S. Mahler, M.D.	IX

† Deceased before 1974 Conference.

I. Floyd Mallott, M.D.	III
Charles A. Malone, M.D.	VIII
James Mann, M.D.	I
Irwin M. Marcus, M.D.	IX
John B. McDevitt, M.D.	III
Francis McLaughlin, M.D.	COPER Committee
James McLaughlin, M.D.	IV
William W. Meissner, M.D.	V
Burness E. Moore, M.D.	COPER Committee
David Musto, M.D.	IV
Paul G. Myerson, M.D.	V
Humberto Nagera, M.D.	IX
Joseph M. Natterson, M.D.	II
Robert A. Nemiroff, M.D.	V
Peter B. Neubauer, M.D.	VII
Haskell F. Norman, M.D.	II
William R. O'Brien, M.D.	II
Gerald B. Olch, M.D.	IX
Jerome D. Oremland, M.D.	VI
Paul H. Ornstein, M.D.	I
Arthur J. Ourieff, M.D.	III
Arnold Z. Pfeffer, M.D.	I
Charles A. Pinderhughes, M.D.	VIII
George H. Pollock, M.D.	VII
Ishak Ramzy, Ph.D.	II
Morton F. Reiser, M.D.	VII
George A. Richardson, M.D.	IV
M. Barrie Richmond, M.D.	III
Samuel Ritvo, M.D.	III
Fred P. Robbins, M.D.	IX
Lewis L. Robbins, M.D.	VII
William S. Robbins, M.D.	V
Arnold A. Rogow, Ph.D.	VI
Victor H. Rosen, M.D.†	VI

† Deceased before 1974 Conference.

Miss Helen Ross	II
Melvin Sabshin, M.D.	V
Joseph Sandler, M.D.	V
Marshall D. Schechter, M.D.	III
Herbert J. Schlesinger, Ph.D.	II
Howard H. Schlossman, M.D.	VIII
Clarence G. Schulz, M.D.	III
Elvin V. Semrad, M.D.	V
Calvin F. Settlage, M.D.	IX
Morton Shane, M.D.	IX
Daniel Shapiro, M.D.	I
Louis B. Shapiro, M.D.	II
Leonard L. Shengold, M.D.	IV
Albert J. Solnit, M.D.	COPER Committee
M. Jeanne Spurlock, M.D.	IX
Alfred H. Stanton, M.D.	VII
Herman Stein, Ph.D.	IV
Marvin Stein, M.D.	Conference Guest
Malvina Stock, M.D.	II
Robert J. Stoller, M.D.	IV
Robert L. Stubblefield, M.D.	Conference Guest
Helen H. Tartakoff, M.D.	Conference Guest
Troy Thompson, M.D.	I
William C. Thompson, M.D.	IV
Ernst A. Ticho, Ph.D.	VI
Gertrude R. Ticho, M.D.	III
Ralph W. Tyler, Ph.D.	I
Arthur F. Valenstein, M.D.	IV
Robert S. Wallerstein, M.D.	COPER Committee
Richard S. Ward, M.D.	IV
John J. Weber, M.D.	II
Edward M. Weinshel, M.D.	I
Samuel Weiss, M.D.	IX
Stanley S. Weiss, M.D.	I
Roy M. Whitman, M.D.	V
Emanuel Windholz, M.D.	VI

Lyman C. Wynne, M.D.	V
Abraham Zaleznik, D.C.S.	VI
Norman E. Zinberg, M.D.	VIII

ADMINISTRATION

Helen Fischer, Administrative Director
Virginia Reminick, Assistant

Index